The Art of Clothing

UCL
PRESS

The Art of Clothing

A Pacific Experience

Edited by

Susanne Küchler

Reader in Anthropology, University College London

and

Graeme Were

Research Fellow in Anthropology,
The British Museum/Goldsmiths College London

UCL
PRESS

First published in Great Britain 2005 by UCL Press
An imprint of Cavendish Publishing Limited, The Glass House,
Wharton Street, London WC1X 9PX, United Kingdom
Telephone: + 44 (0)20 7278 8000 Facsimile: + 44 (0)20 7278 8080
Email: info@cavendishpublishing.com
Website: www.cavendishpublishing.com

Published in the United States by Cavendish Publishing
c/o International Specialized Book Services,
5824 NE Hassalo Street, Portland,
Oregon 97213-3644, USA

Published in Australia by Cavendish Publishing (Australia) Pty Ltd
45 Beach Street, Coogee, NSW 2034, Australia
Telephone: + 61 (2)9664 0909 Facsimile: + 61 (2)9664 5420
Email: info@cavendishpublishing.com.au
Website: www.cavendishpublishing.com.au

© UCL Press 2005

British Library Cataloguing in Publication Data

Were, Graeme
The art of clothing
1 Clothing and dress – Social aspects – Islands of the Pacific
2 Clothing and dress – Islands of the Pacific History
3 Islands of the Pacific – Social life and customs
I Title   II Küchler, Susanne

Library of Congress Cataloguing in Publication Data
Data available

ISBN 1-84472-015-2
ISBN 978-1-844-72015-6

3 5 7 9 10 8 6 4 2

Typeset by Phoenix Photosetting, Chatham, Kent
Printed and bound in Great Britain

Cover illustration: Wahgi dancers, 1980. Photograph © Michael O'Hanlon

Acknowledgments

We would like to thank all those people who have made the publication of this book possible; not least the other members of the 'Clothing the Pacific' project team. We are particularly indebted to the help and support of the staff in the Department of Ethnography at the British Museum who have accommodated us and provided us with excellent facilities, as well as the Anthropology Library staff who deserve our gratitude for their assistance in helping us access books, papers and so forth. We would also like to thank the ESRC for funding the research project and the Wenner-Gren Foundation for Anthropological Research for financing the conference from which this book derives. Our appreciation also extends to University College London for hosting the conference, and particularly Chris Hagisavva from the Department of Anthropology for providing expert technical support throughout. We are particularly grateful for the comments given by Sean Kingston and Colin Dibben.

List of Contributors

Lissant Bolton is Curator of the Pacific and Australian collections at the British Museum. She has undertaken research in Vanuatu since 1989, working collaboratively with the Vanuatu Cultural Centre. Her book, *Unfolding the Moon: Enacting Women's Kastom in Vanuatu*, was published by the University of Hawaii Press in 2003.

Chloe Colchester was Research Fellow in Anthropology at University College London and was a Research Associate on 'Clothing the Pacific: A Study of the Nature of Innovation'. She is currently a freelance writer.

Elizabeth Cory-Pearce is a doctoral candidate in the Department of Anthropology at Goldsmiths College, University of London. She is writing up her research on the ways in which things mediate social relationships and negotiate boundaries in Rotorua, New Zealand.

Anne D'Alleva is Associate Professor of Art History and Women's Studies at the University of Connecticut. She writes on art and gender in 18th century Tahiti. Her works include *Art of the Pacific* (Weidenfeld & Nicolson, 1998).

Vilsoni Hereniko is a Professor at the Centre for Pacific Islands Studies at the University of Hawaii. He is also a playwright, filmmaker and editor of the journal, *The Contemporary Pacific*.

Webb Keane is Associate Professor of Anthropology at the University of Michigan, Ann Arbor. He is the author of *Signs of Recognition: Powers and Hazards of Representation in an Indonesian Society* (University of California Press, 1997) and numerous articles on language and signification, material culture, religion, modernity and social theory.

Susanne Küchler is Reader in Anthropology at University College London. She has worked extensively on issues of remembering and forgetting in relation to Pacific art. Her works include *Malanggan: Art, Memory and Sacrifice* (Berg, 2002).

Michael O'Hanlon is Director of the Pitt Rivers Museum at Oxford. His fieldwork is with the Wahgi people in the Highlands of Papua New Guinea. His books on them include *Reading the Skin* (1989) and an ethnography of a museum exhibition, *Paradise: Portraying the New Guinea Highlands* (1993), both published by British Museum Press. His most recent book is *Hunting the Gatherers: Ethnographic Collectors, Agents and Agency in Melanesia* (Berghahn Books, 2000), co-edited with Robert Welsch.

Ruth B Phillips holds a Canada Research Chair and is Professor of Art History at Carleton University, Ottawa. Her research focuses on the art and material of north eastern North America. Her publications include: *Trading Identities: The Souvenir in Native North American Art from the Northeast, 1700–1900* (University of Washington Press, 1998); *Unpacking Culture: Art and Commodity in Colonial and Postcolonial*

Worlds, co-edited with Christopher B Steiner (University of California Press, 1999); and, with Janet Catherine Berlo, *Native North American Art* (Oxford University Press, 1998).

Paul Sharrad is Associate Professor of English Studies at the University of Wollongong, Australia where he teaches postcolonial literatures. He has edited *New Literatures Review*, published a wide range of articles, and has books on Raja Rao and Albert Wendt.

Marilyn Strathern is Professor of Social Anthropology at the University of Cambridge. Her ethnographic interests are divided between Melanesia and Britain, and latterly between new medical technologies, intellectual property issues and the audit culture. Living in Port Moresby in the early 1970s, she worked with migrants from Mount Hagen who stimulated her contribution here.

Lisa Taouma currently works as a television director for the Pacific Islands programme 'Tagata Pasifika' on TVONE in New Zealand. She has made a number of documentaries looking at social issues affecting Pacific people, including 'Otara Markets', 'Body Image Pasifika' and 'Tatau-Pacific tattooing'. She has an MA (1st Hons) in Art History from Auckland University.

Nicholas Thomas is Professor of Anthropology at Goldsmiths College, University of London. He has conducted wide-ranging research on art, culture and history in the Pacific. His books include *Entangled Objects* (Harvard University Press, 1991), *Oceanic Art* (Thames and Hudson, 1995) and *Discoveries: The Voyages of Captain Cook* (Allen Lane, 2003).

Graeme Were is Research Fellow in Anthropology at Goldsmiths College, University of London and was a Research Associate on 'Clothing the Pacific: A Study of the Nature of Innovation' at the British Museum. His ethnographic interests are museum collections, ethnomathematics and material culture.

Bente Wolff is Curator of the collections from Oceania and Indonesia at the National Museum of Denmark. She has done research in Papua New Guinea, Indonesia and the Solomon Islands. Her research interests are modern cultural cosmologies, identity, consumption practices and material culture.

Preface

Nicholas Thomas

In *Avant-Garde Gambits*, her influential critique of Gauguin, Griselda Pollock refers in passing to 'the shapeless sack inflicted on Tahitian women by missionaries' (1992: caption to Figures 25 and 26). This was to recapitulate one of the clichés of travel writing in the Pacific that took the inappropriateness of introduced dress, and specifically of the long 'Mother Hubbard' gown, to epitomise the insensitivity of the evangelical impositions that by the 1820s had had far reaching ramifications for clothing and many other aspects of life on Tahiti itself, and already in some neighbouring islands. From the early 19th century onwards, visitors who were not affiliated with the missions lamented the end of the voluptuous society they had fantasised about, and denounced the cultural blindness of the representatives of the London Missionary Society, who at once clothed the Polynesians and stifled their sensuality. Pollock's interests in the issue are certainly different. Yet it is odd that the observation should resurface in a discussion of Gauguin's work, since it is in some of his portraits, such as *Woman with a Flower* (1891, Ny Carlsberg Glyptotek, Copenhagen), that it is most evident that these garments have been not inflicted, but adopted by entirely dignified women who had found ways of making the Christian colonial modernity that was, by the 1890s, well established in the Pacific, their own.

This is not to say that Christianity was straightforwardly embraced rather than resisted by Polynesians. This is not to say that the foreign religion that was intimately associated with commoditisation did not indeed bring novel forms of oppression. It is or ought to be unnecessary to restate the thesis that this history was a matter of indigenous agency as well as imperial imposition. This is not a domain where there is anything to be gained from the installation of some new orthodoxy that takes the local appropriation of introduced forms to be axiomatic. What is needed, rather, is empirical study and analysis that establishes what changed and what was lost and gained with the momentous social changes associated with religious conversion, that affected virtually all parts of the Pacific Islands, like many other regions of the colonial world, during the 19th century or subsequently. In the Pacific case, these transformations generally preceded those associated with other forms of colonial intervention such as annexation and the establishment of colonial administrations; their effects were initially at least more pervasive. Yet the ramifications of missionary intervention remain under-researched, and certainly under-reflected upon.

This book arises from a research project on 'Clothing and Innovation in the Pacific'. The project responded in part to the fundamentally flawed character of judgments such as Pollock's, from the perspective of those who had spent time in Pacific societies, and become conscious – though this was in none of our cases an initial focus of research – of the manifold significances of cloth and clothing.

Though the theme had been eloquently addressed by Annette Weiner, colonial histories had generally remained secondary to her discussions, which were concerned above all to refine and elaborate upon the Maussian tradition of gift, value and exchange theory.

The rationale for the research project was not, of course, wholly negative. While, on the one hand, anthropology had in the past neglected or understated the significance of colonial intrusion, colonial histories had conversely been understood in restrictive terms as political and ideological operations rather than as material ones; where material objects were understood to figure within them, they were seen purely as bearers of Westernisation rather than as vehicles for innovations within indigenous practice. Yet there is much evidence – some of it presented and discussed in this book – for a far more creative and ambiguous process.

Pre-colonial Pacific societies were already heavily invested in cloth, which was a valuable, a ritual tool, a key exchange object, a locus of beautification, and an expression of collectivity, among other things. It is therefore not surprising that when Pacific Islanders were encouraged to adopt new forms of cloth they, in one sense or another, often took the fabric forms and ran with them, in diverse ways manifest in varied historical cases and contemporary practices.

The Pacific does represent an ideal region for exploring these questions and larger ones concerning what the 'art of clothing' offers anthropology and related disciplines, as a new domain of inquiry, and one inevitably engaged with Alfred Gell's provocative recent theorisation of objects and agency, that is taken up in a number of chapters of this book. The region is highly appropriate for this and other sorts of comparative study; related processes can be seen to have played themselves out in societies related ancestrally – despite their bewildering variety, there is a common underlying Austronesian heritage that links all Polynesian and most Melanesian societies, that engenders, at a deep level, certain parallels in uses of cloth across the region. To make this point is perhaps to affiliate this book with a long tradition of comparative analysis in Pacific studies, previously associated with overtly evolutionist studies such as Goldman's *Ancient Polynesian Society* (1970). Yet there is a notable difference. Those works employed an ultimately simplistic notion of laboratory-like comparison among societies that were indeed ancestrally related, but had been reshaped in complex ways by colonial histories that were not themselves comparatively addressed. Neither our wider project nor the studies in this book aim to reduce Oceanic cultural and historical variation to a general theory or transformational model. The intention is rather to fully integrate historical change into a comparative analysis that indeed takes advantage of regional affinities and parallels in elements of colonial modernity (such as the projects of the missionaries) across the region, but is directed rather toward the illumination of wider issues via the nuances of particular cases.

There is a final aspect of the project and this book that is worth emphasising. The processes of innovation in clothing that we are concerned with remain very much alive in the present, both at the local level, among rural and urban communities in the Pacific islands, and also perhaps most conspicuously among Pacific diasporas in New Zealand and elsewhere. Though the practices of a remarkably creative group of 'fashion activists' based mostly in Aotearoa were not initially intended to be a focus of the research, it quickly became apparent that the project had much to learn from the work of groups such as Pacific Sisters and that, in certain respects, these designers, artists and performance artists were addressing related questions through their own practice, to those that our project sought to explore. The conference that this book emerges from included a number of memorable presentations by Sofia Tekela-Smith, Lisa Taouma, Shigeyuki Kihara, Rosanna Raymond and Ani O'Neill that made it clear just how rich this kind of dialogue between academic research and contemporary artistic practice can be. Though that dimension of the conference cannot be really represented in any book, it has varied resonances that permanently change the way we engage in these sorts of inquiries and understand these kinds of issues.

References

Goldman, Irving (1970) *Ancient Polynesian Society*, Chicago: University of Chicago Press

Pollock, Griselda (1992) *Avant-Garde Gambits 1888–1893: Gender and the Colour of Art History*, London: Thames and Hudson

Contents

PART III: FASHIONING MODERNITIES

EPILOGUE

List of Illustrations

Introduction

Susanne Küchler and Graeme Were

Cloth and clothing play a uniquely important though often overlooked role in the way we experience the world. When we are born our bodies are wrapped in cloth to keep us warm, and throughout our lives we cover ourselves with various forms of clothing; before, finally, at the time of death, our bodies are again wrapped in cloth or dressed for the occasion. In fact, such is the human preoccupation with clothing that it is not surprising to learn of its enduring presence in anthropological studies where clothing features as an essential component of daily life and, at the same time, a telling trace of cultural negotiations of identity and difference. Yet, despite clothing's potential for social analysis, its study has long remained on the periphery of the social sciences, often only inviting specialist perspectives that zoom in narrowly on worn clothing's form and function.

Despite the lack of serious attention cloth and clothing invites from within the social sciences, something remarkable has happened to their position in academic writing, a change so profound that the scholarly benefits of this revived appreciation are only just beginning to be understood. Clothing is now the leading concern of a host of interdisciplinary studies whose theoretical scope and justification was marked by the appearance of an edited volume on *Cloth and Human Experience* (1989).[1] Its editors, Annette Weiner and Jane Schneider, could not have foreseen the resonance this study would invite when they set out to trace the diverse cultural evaluations of cloth and clothing as treasured possession and as key players in the shaping of social biographies.

The significance of *Cloth and Human Experience* lies in the fact that it drew attention to the importance of cloth as a material expression of genealogy. The book alerted anthropologists working in Melanesia to the seriousness of cloth and clothing, when they had repeatedly ignored the often ephemeral and highly fragile cloth in favour of the theorisation of male dominated exchange and ritual.[2] This new approach therefore liberated cloth from its superficial status and finally dispelled, once and for all, its classificatory role as a measure of social development (with the cultures of the Pacific placed at the lower end of the evolutionary scale as the region appeared bereft of clothing). As a result, this work formed the starting point for a series of novel studies that drew on the materiality

---

1   There is now a main journal in this field called *Fashion Theory* as well a book series on 'Dress, body, culture', published by Berg. An additional field has developed around the study of cloth, to which two journals are currently being dedicated: *Textile: The Journal of Cloth and Culture* and *Textile History*. There are also several professional associations related to this interest with their own journals: The Costume Society of Great Britain, The Costume Society of America, The International Textile and Apparel Association, and the Textile Society of America.

2   Anthropologists often regarded cloth and clothing as 'women's wealth', of little concern compared to the 'serious' work of men (see Weiner 1994).

of cloth and clothing to shed fresh light on the complexities of person-object relations (Eicher (ed) 1995; Perani and Wolff 1999; Banerjee and Miller 2003).

What is crucial to these new understandings of cloth and clothing is the concept of 'skin' and its pivotal role as idiom of personhood and identity (see O'Hanlon 1989; Strathern 1979, 1988). The functional association between skin and cloth in Pacific anthropology means that we can formulate bark cloth, body wrappings, clothing and so forth as 'second' skins, allowing us to question the conventional paradigm of a surface-depth model of personhood. One of the most ambitious studies to draw on these theoretical insights is Alfred Gell's visual and material re-assessment of the concept of self-decoration (Gell 1993). In his in-depth study of Polynesian tattooing, he theorises how the practice of 'wrapping in images' is tied to the experience of social and spatial distance, thus providing us with a theoretically informed view on what disparate body art practices across the region actually *do*. Most importantly, from the viewpoint of introduced clothing and associated technologies in the Pacific, his work underlines the contention that art, clothing and body decoration are not isolates but evens in the flow of relations, as intertwined as the relations between body, mind and person.

The alignment of clothing with practices of image making and self-decoration in the Pacific has uncanny parallels to developments in the theoretical analysis of European dress. Preoccupied with the vision of clothing as an illustration of social life, analyses of European clothing, like those in the Pacific, have been synonymous with the study of the body and the mind. Recent theoretical approaches have criticised this view of clothing as a mode of corporeality; critics argue that it devalues clothing, consigning it to a symptom of the body within. As Hollander rightly emphasises: we can no longer afford to treat clothing today as 'shifting ephemera on the surface of life' (Hollander 1993: xv); or as Wigley suggests, as 'trivial and fleeting expressions of a seriousness that resides elsewhere' (Wigley 2001).

In fact, clothing today provokes intense anxiety, as it has become the hallmark of an increasingly surface dependent identity (Clarke and Miller 2002). This condition was brought about arguably by what Emily Martin (1992) has termed 'the end of the body' – the emergence of changing technological modes of production and reproduction which separated bodily modes of being from social recognition (Strathern 1999). As what we wear no longer reflects an immutable, distinctive and distinguishable identity held within, our clothes suggest visual attachments across the material world more than categorical divisions between things. It is against the background of an identity that thrives on asserting connections and resemblances in the visual and material realm of the surfacing of the body that *the art of clothing* has emerged.

The present book unites these two theoretical strands: one focused on the Pacific and studies of personhood and exchange; the other on cultures of modernity. It takes as its starting point the suggestion that *the art of clothing* is not as new or as unique to us as we would like to assume, but has for long been a Pacific experience, vital to religious and political vision prior to the arrival of the mission. The investment of interest in clothing in the Pacific has become inseparable from our own colonial intervention and modernist aesthetic concerns.

As it shares its roots in Pacific anthropology with *Cloth and Human Experience*, this book invites the reader to rethink how the materiality of clothing comes to matter. This book thus presents a starting point for a comparative study of the 'art' of clothing, drawing attention to diverse technical practices that resulted in innovative uses, resemblances and textures inherent to clothing and its technology.

CLOTHING AND TRANSLATION

Clothing has been one of the key visual markers of the advent of colonialism in the Pacific, and was seen by Europeans as one of the signs of the acceptance of civilization by islanders. However, the way in which cloth and clothing was perceived and incorporated by islanders did not necessarily reflect these ideas, but involved the investment of existing indigenous preoccupations into new materials. Today, both imported and indigenous types of cloth and clothing are integral features of Pacific Island cultures and figure in exchange and religious practice; in fashion and in the decoration of domestic space; in public political activity; as well as in festivals, and the art and tourist market. The present collection of essays arose from discussions of this record by a group of researchers who understand clothing in the Pacific as acts of material translation – from which new ways of thinking and being arise (Colchester 2003).

Despite clothing's regional significance in the Pacific, its articulation has not been examined as a data resource. A wealth of historical archives, collections and photographic records has barely been touched, although it is known that this resource documents the transformative capacity of clothing and its role in linking modes of production – both local and industrial – to diverse audiences. Yet what precisely could this record tell us, when compared with Pacific Islanders' usage of clothing today, about the relation between clothing and innovation? Dissatisfied with the blanket definition of the 'hybrid' that sees clothing as articulating a mixing of the old and the new, the group looked for detail, both in historical and material evidence. What kind of clothing came into the Pacific via which route and what happened to it when it reached its destination? What can the fate of clothing tell us about the complex local strategies and competing historicities at play? What do collections tell us about how clothing came to transfigure or be transfigured by the body politic in the Pacific?

The ground laying question for our approach is asked by Webb Keane in this book: what does clothing make possible? Rather than treat clothing as a (material) sign of some (immaterial) meaning, Keane's theoretical exploration of clothing in culture (see Chapter 1) examines the qualities that render clothing 'effective' by considering what clothing can reveal besides meanings alone. With this notion of the question about the efficacy of clothing, we can ask why clothing took on such multifaceted significance in the Pacific. Is the relation of clothing to innovation in the Pacific determined by essentially 19th century preoccupations with a humanitarian notion of culture that positions man at the helm; or is there a deeper sense in which the two are related, conjoined by the materiality of the processes of which both partake independently? It is clear that how we answer these questions determines the comparative significance we can assign to our research into clothing.

Given the multifaceted nature of the Pacific, with its myriad of highly localised ways of being and thinking, the group's approach ran the risk of becoming bogged down in complex local scenarios that assign animacy to clothing in often highly idiosyncratic ways. What emerged as the common fabric of bringing together the local, historical and the contemporary clothing practices was the strategic transformation of clothing through the shifting of motifs onto new surfaces, the decomposition and re-assemblage of materials, and the shift in associations bound up with clothing through performance and art. The term that most closely reflects upon such material processes of transposition is *translation*.

The idea of translation – defined as the material afterlife and transformation of a thing that is intimately bound up with the way retrospective thought invests the future with the past – refers to Walter Benjamin's early 20th century writings on memory and art (Benjamin 1992). These writings provide one of the sharpest critiques of Enlightenment formal subjectivity, here understood as subjectivity without materiality. Benjamin contrasted the ways of being and thinking in Enlightenment culture – which he saw as driven by an autogenic spiritual entity – with the ways in which a 'surface identity' of things was capable of prompting spontaneous recognition and identification. This surface identity promoted a future-directed consciousness that fed off the immanent presence of the past in local and material objects and things. Benjamin's notion of translation – the material act of making connections visible in surfaces that resemble each other – has a contemporary tone and has been reconsidered in recent discussions of 'analogy' (see especially Stafford 1999). What is important for our purpose is his hypothesis that surfaces which successfully promote recognition and identification through acts of translation are 'corporeal', that is, they resemble the body's surface, *whether on or off the body*.

Translation thus can be argued to fabricate connections, to be a way of making attachments possible without recourse to a body. It ultimately allows one to craft one's identity visibly and materially as a connection, thus allowing for innovation and change, rather than constraining identity within the lonely prison of authenticity that shuns any form of attachment.

The data from the Pacific show that clothing does more than resemble the corporeal surface; it suggests possibilities of translation – and not just when it is covering a body. Most fibrous materials worn on the body in the Pacific are not tailored to the body, but resemble in their tent-like appearance other forms of clothing, such as fine mats or bark cloth. These are never worn on the body except during life changing events, when they are loosely wrapped around the body (see Vilsoni Hereniko's essay, Chapter 8). That clothing may be thought of as a social skin, its material density reflecting on the perceived complexity or status of social relations is one of the most pregnant insights derived from Pacific studies (Gell 1993; Weiner 1994). The essays brought together in this book explore, for the first time, how this insight can be used to re-examine what people really *do* with clothing. The clothing received by Pacific islanders was cut up, unstitched, unpicked and re-sewn to make new objects – and to give shape to new ways of indigenous thinking and being. Their resulting *art of clothing* was a profoundly Pacific experience, but the art of clothing itself resonates across every culture that, for diverse reasons, invests heavily in the materiality of the corporeal surface (see Ruth Phillips's essay, Chapter 11).

CLOTHING, MISSIONARIES AND CONVERSION

There can be little doubt that clothing makes visible the transformations that swept the South Pacific in the second half of the 19th century. The emergence of the Papua New Guinean *meri bilaus* – an ankle length, loose flowing 'Mother Hubbard' style smock, known in Hawaii as *holoku* – as well as the poncho-like Niuean and Tahitian *tiputa*, all trace their roots back to missionaries who imported new materials and ideas into the region. Yet the regional focus on variations in contemporary clothing styles often presents these complex material innovations as by-products of a series of interactions in the past, the origins of which are rooted in the advent of new social relations and the modes of deportment and domesticity they imply. In contrast, the contributors to this book have opted to treat these acts of creativity – the distinctive styles of cloth and clothing – as central agents in the process of change, and most radically, in some instances, as the instruments of conversion themselves. In other words, cloth and clothing are seen here as integral to new ways of thinking and being, rather than simply being derivatives of a new order that emerged. In the studies that follow, the authors describe how intense waves of missionary activity and colonial intervention inspired moments of creativity amongst Pacific Islanders, intellectual activities that flourished as a response to the new ideas flooding into the region. The extent to which this happened is something that missionaries as well as anthropologists have failed to fully appreciate.

To facilitate our understanding of the agency attributed to clothing, we should perhaps begin by reminding ourselves of the moral thinking and the set of intentionalities bound up with the wearing of clothes. For missionaries travelling to the Pacific from the 19th century onwards, clothing Pacific Islanders was an overriding concern. This is because the clothing of the body was seen as quintessential to the salvation of the soul and an ultimate sign of conversion to the Christian faith. The pretexts existed that God was closer to those clean and clothed, and that missionaries took the adoption of clothing to be indicative of the act of conversion; so they received Pacific Islanders' willingness to adopt clothing as an outward sign of religious conversion. The seizure of cloth and clothing by Polynesians and Melanesians may well have calmed the nerves of many missionaries, and presented them with proof that 'the grace of God can and does change the mould of a native's thought', to quote Reverend Mann, a Methodist missionary based in Island New Guinea in the early 1900s (Mann, 15 August 1920). Missionaries saw the folded cloth that they carried with them as a material that could easily be wrapped, cut, stitched or embroidered and transformed into an item of clothing to cover the body. Ready-made clothing – such items as calico skirts, shirts and so forth – that could immediately be worn as a covering on the body, simply provided a faster solution to the missionary stipulation requiring converts to appear at the mission clothed.

For many of the Christian missionaries, who had struggled to maintain a foothold in remote, untamed frontiers and were faced with constant threats of hostility, intimidation and violence, the adoption of clothing by indigenous people heightened resolve and boosted morale. The optimistic tone of the Methodist missionary George Brown gives us some idea of how indicative clothing became of the religious ideas brought into the region: 'I was glad to see Le Bera (the chief) clothed in a shirt and waistcloth, and his wives and daughters each wearing a handkerchief or small piece of cloth' (1908: 135–36). Indeed, it needs to be remembered that in Melanesia between the 19th and early 20th century, encounters were not always amicable; many traders only anchored close enough to shore to enable locals to paddle out in canoes and exchange food and goods. Many dreaded setting foot on the beaches of Melanesia, fearing attack. Since cloth and clothing provoked so much reaction in the region, missionaries carried them as acceptable gifts to placate local people, along with knives and axes as precautions. No doubt these missionaries were all too aware of the violent and bloody encounters experienced by fellow missionaries attempting to set up base there.

The missionaries' belief that clothing brought with it a new moral economy of body and mind correctly recognised the potential power of clothing, but failed to grasp why clothing was so efficacious. In fact, the reactions of the Pacific Islanders stemmed from the attribution of animacy to material things. This animacy can be traced in the way Pacific Islanders were fervently attracted to cloth and clothing and the inspiration they gained from its material quality: a quality that demanded immediate action by cutting, sewing and folding so as to harness the power contained within its woven surface. Arguably, one of the most documented of these changes in the Pacific has been the effect of cloth and clothing on traditional bark cloth techniques and their patterns.

The introduction of clothing impacted on bark cloth production, contexts, uses and pattern systems in different ways across the Pacific (see Kaeppler 1975). In western Polynesia, the manufacture and use of indigenous cloth was never interrupted by missionary activity. For example, in Fiji, the changing appearance of different kinds of bark cloth marked shifts in religious and political alliances between Fiji, Tonga and Britain that emerged during the period of conversion to Christianity. Meanwhile in Niue, the *hiapo* – a freehand painted bark cloth – exhibited dramatic variations and changes in pattern from the 1860s to the late 1880s, as a response to the introduction of European fabrics (see also Thomas 1999). On the other hand, in eastern Polynesia, the destruction of clothed wooden sculptures by members of the London Missionary Society halted the ritual use of bark cloth. This, however, did not signal the end of pattern systems and associated technical knowledge. Rather, European cloth and techniques of sewing liberated the work that went into the patterning of bark cloth, motivating a florescence of pattern innovation in the medium of ready-made cloth. The imprinting of designs was achieved through embroidery and appliqué techniques, using pre-coloured and pre-patterned material that led, through the folding and cutting of cloth, to quilt-like garments that were invested with new uses and ideas.

THE ART OF CLOTHING

A rich body of historical evidence supports contemporary ethnographic observations in documenting how abstract concepts, motivated by emotionally charged associations surrounding the animacy of cloth and clothing, become visible. Evocative examples are to be found in the spatial form of a winged dress or in the geometric patterning of a quilt, that have become the bases of re-visualisations of the differing ways in which new material relations are formed. In Vanuatu, for instance, Lissant Bolton describes (see Chapter 2) how the formal properties of missionary introduced women's dress inspired novel and sometimes island-specific clothing styles that are inseparable from traditional imagery, marking out new contexts for religious practices. Meanwhile in Fiji, Chloe Colchester (see Chapter 3) argues that the local uptake of a body wrap known as the *sulu* – derived from a traditional Tongan garment – reveals more about the relationship between Pacific Islanders' interpretation of Christianity and the place of clothing in local religious practice than about European missionaries' perceptions of dress.

Some of the contributors to this book single out the formal and material qualities of cloth and clothing – factors such as pattern, colour and texture – as sources of inspiration for motivating these acts of material translation. Indeed, Pacific Islanders' expectations of what clothing could *do* were magnified as both cloth and clothing arrived ready-patterned and ready-coloured. Pattern (as well as colouring) is attributed with the power of animacy in parts of the Pacific because it makes visible social, political, historical and symbolic ties; it is linked to concepts of spiritual power, and is often central to an object's religious efficacy (Campbell 2002; Gell 1998).

The question of what clothing does is taken up by Anne D'Alleva (see Chapter 4). Tracing how clothing became an important nexus of social interaction between Europeans and Tahitians, she describes how elite Tahitians used European clothing as a means to assert their political power, social status, genealogical ties and religious ideas. D'Alleva argues that in studying the hybrid wardrobes of the Tahitian elite – which contained a variety of both European and indigenous clothing – we can get a clearer picture of the strategies Pacific Islanders employed to deal with change, and the way they negotiated new and old forms of social and political power in the 18th and 19th century.

One such strategy that Pacific Islanders developed was to secure access to new pattern systems. Artefacts in museum collections and excerpts from historical archives are testament to this, explicitly showing that European patterns were often abstracted from items such as cloth and clothing and integrated within existing indigenous pattern systems. As Reverend Lawes records in his study of the Papuan Gulf (Papua New Guinea), the Motu people 'were glad to get new patterns from some of our printed calicoes and other English designs' for use in body tattooing (Lawes 1879: 370). It is reasonable to hypothesise that many patterns carried into the Pacific on the surface of cloth and clothing were analogous not only to tattoos but also indigenous designs on body ornaments and wooden carvings. The visual linking of indigenous and European patterns may have offered Islanders a motive for their selective seizure of clothing – on grounds of the operative qualities associated with different patterns. In the Solomon Islands, for example, men are photographed wearing what appears to be Union Jack patterned beaded belts (now residing in the collections of the British Museum). Yet, at a second glance, the viewer is struck by how the designs are reminiscent of traditional geometric shapes and patterns on local arts and crafts, leaving us to think twice about the driving force behind these modes of innovation. In focusing on the visual resemblances between things, we can see why patterned textiles took on such an influential role as agents connecting Europeans and Pacific Islanders, and thereby providing the material surface for inspiring novel ways of being.

We should also be aware that not all items of clothing and lengths of cloth were transformed; in some cases their mere presence was enough to signal status and prestige within religious polities – so they were left unaltered and unworn. Somerville, commenting on local trade in New Georgia (Solomon Islands), mentions that local islanders 'seem to make no use of their wealth however; the mere fact of possession is sufficient, and *kalo* (whale's teeth), shell rings, calico, clothes – any article of European clothing is a great prize – are simply stored up, and scarcely worn or used at all' (Somerville 1897). Indeed, Somerville references the use of calico in bride price payments in New Georgia, and shows that not only Europeans, but Pacific Islanders also saw its exchange value within local social networks (Somerville 1897: 394). Michael O'Hanlon draws out this point in his novel account of Western clothing in Highland Papua New Guinea. In his chapter, he describes how Western clothes are selected and arranged to attract, with no attention to the clothing's functional value (see Chapter 5).

While it appears from photographs that most cloth and clothing was simply worn in European style or wrapped around the waist like a sarong, some was radically transformed by Pacific Islanders by cutting or ripping into shreds. In New Ireland, for example, Duffield observed that 'the women took readily to clothing, but much preferred to make ribbons of calico petticoats to adorn their heads than to cover their bodies' (Duffield 1886: 116). In Santa Cruz, the islands to the south east of the Solomon Islands, Beasley describes how red cotton cloth was ripped into strips then interwoven to produce the red feather money of the island (Beasley 1936). Probably the most extreme material process of re-visualisation and radical transformation can be traced in appliqué quilts that are sewn across eastern Polynesia.

Although it is unknown when quilting precisely started in eastern Polynesia, we do know that in the early 20th century, discarded clothing, shipped from Victorian England to the Pacific for distribution by the missionaries, was cut up, unravelled and re-stitched or threaded into complex layered quilts resembling the layered bark cloth bedspreads and funerary cloaks indigenous to the region. The association of quilts with memory, protection and the sustaining of connections – in the Pacific and elsewhere – has been noted by generations of scholars and practitioners. Eastern Polynesian quilts emerged in the late 19th century and have continued to dominate women's work against the background of a burgeoning migrant diaspora. Loss, and a heightened concern with re-visualising connections, is today traced in the stitched patterns of large and elaborate appliqué and piecework quilts known as *tivaevae, tifaifai* and *kapa lau*. Quilts are produced by women across the Cook Islands, the Hawaiian Islands, the Society Islands and elsewhere in eastern Polynesia, where they are both substituted for bark cloth and are used in ways deeply invested in, yet unprecedented within, the new context of Christian domesticity. Diasporic demands, a Christian concern with time keeping and domesticity, and an existing tradition of fashioning genealogical markers has created a vibrant visual culture whose exemplars touch the core of anthropological theories of exchange. Reminiscent of Annette Weiner's (1992) famous treatise on exchange as an act of 'keeping while giving', quilts are stitched to be given away at funerals, at weddings and other events that mark stages of loss and severance in a person's life. Although often kept for years in treasure trunks far away from the homeland, the quilt's threads, apparent in multicoloured patterns on the surface of the quilt, connect those who have been parted and secure the 'road' along which variant returns are made.

CLOTHING, PERFORMANCE AND MODERNITY

Correlating historical evidence with ethnographic data, museum collection research and photographic records reinforces our contention that the adoption of cloth and clothing by Pacific Islanders was not purely a mimetic process. The collection of papers in this book reflects this position, stressing how local people operated on a strategic level in their appropriation of cloth and clothing, rather than simply conforming to missionary pressure or copying European fashion. Indeed, a number of authors in this book focus on the novel introduction of European cloth and clothing within traditional performances, something that highlights the strategic framing of Western material goods by Pacific Islanders.

Elizabeth Cory-Pearce demonstrates this (see Chapter 6) by describing how the appropriation of cloth and clothing in Maori ceremonial welcomes to British royalty in the early 20th century were strategically utilised as instruments to aid in the performance of kinship dynamics. Bente Wolff (see Chapter 7) describes the clothing worn by women in contemporary Mekeo society (Papua New Guinea) to comment on the way that traditional practices have been translated into new contexts; something that she attributes to the performance of 'being modern'. What is so interesting about these performances is their mode of innovation: on the one hand, the Mekeo women dress wearing Western fashion items, while on the other, the framework for these performances has not altered radically since pre-contact times. In this sense, Wolff stresses that the Mekeo are embracing modernity whilst at the same time the attention to a traditional customary framework ensures that the ritual remains efficacious.

Vilsoni Hereniko (see Chapter 8) traces the impact and ideas associated with contemporary Western clothing in traditional weddings. Drawing from his research on woven gods and female clowns in the Pacific island of Rotuma (Hereniko 1995), he discusses how, when he was a child living on the island, traditional wedding ceremonies provided a context for the ritual inversion of the social order. An old woman, dressed as a clown, would appear in front of the wedding guests and hurl mock insults at the chiefs and wedding officials, a performance considered vital for the success of the ceremony. Hereniko claims that this subversive role attributed to the female clown also extended to women weaving fine mats. As women weave the fine mats – imbuing them with ancestral power by attracting spirits – they taunt passers-by. These mats would then be wrapped around the bride and groom at the wedding ceremony, symbolically surrounding the couple with the *mana* of ancestral spirits. Hereniko ends by stating that the ancestral power imbued in these fine mats is no longer present at contemporary Rotuman weddings; since Western clothes are now generally worn, the ritual efficacy of wrapping in fine mats has been lost.

Hereniko's and Wolff's expositions on performance highlight the operative role of clothing as well as the disparate modes of framing ritual. In the Mekeo case, we can see how the performance provides a context for the wearing of Western fashion clothing, whereas in Rotuma, dressing the bride and groom in fine mats creates a stage for the ritual performance of subversion. Lisa Taouma's essay (see Chapter 9) takes the analysis of contemporary clothing further – into the theatres and art galleries of Auckland's diaspora communities, where she examines the multifaceted significance of clothing in performance.

Lisa Taouma's work – both written and screened for television – focuses on contemporary fashion parades amongst Pacific peoples in urban Auckland. It pays particular attention to how symbolic boundaries are challenged or inverted through innovative fashions and the clothing designs worn during performances. Her work shows how some Pacific artists challenge traditional artistic practices, transforming them in new contexts in a bid to undermine stereotypical images of Pacific culture. Taouma argues that these radical images provide a context in which to debate contemporary diaspora identities.

This book also shows how the link between clothing, performance and modernity extends towards other artistic practices as well as beyond the geographic region of the Pacific Islands. Paul Sharrad (see Chapter 10) guides us through the early years of Papua New Guinea's independence, providing us with insight into the colourful imagery conjured up in the literary works of Papua New Guinean writers. He discusses how, in the uncertain years after the end of colonial rule, urban men in Papua New Guinea celebrated their new found political freedom in new modes of expression. Sharrad describes how Western fashion clothes and a love for literature played an essential part in constructing the ideal of the sophisticated urban male during the period of the nation state's emergence.

In the final chapter in this book, the discussion is extended beyond the bounds of the Pacific Islands. In doing so, we aim to ask whether these acts of innovation and material translation are phenomena exclusive to Pacific societies. The chapter by Ruth Phillips (see Chapter 11) centres on the influence of European dress in the fashioning of local identities in the Great Lakes region of North America. Like Anne D'Alleva's essay, Phillips explores the significance of dress as a vehicle to reveal both local and colonial enterprises. Her chapter clearly underlines the inspiration behind this whole book in expressing just how new ways of thinking and being become manifest in clothing innovations and their associated technologies.

CONCLUSION

This book therefore pinpoints the way in which Pacific Islanders deal with change, while questioning notions of rupture, dis-analogy and progression that are often associated with moments of innovation. The book as a whole clearly demonstrates how the emphasis placed on clothing as a *product* of conversion masks the complexities that underpin the role of clothing as a mode of conversion. The chapters in this book suggest that Pacific Islanders did not initially share Christian ideas and values – but rather seized on clothing as a new material medium of ritual efficacy. Their innovative use of clothing may in fact be grounded in projects of material translation involving the formal qualities of clothing – an insight that allows us to reconsider the appropriation of clothing and the motivations that led to the selective adoption of particular clothing styles.

This central theme dominating the essays invites us to rethink our assumptions, not just about the nature of clothing, but also the nature of innovation itself. It reminds us that cloth and clothing serve not just as a metaphor for the body but also as a powerful surface, whose material properties enable the translation of new ways of thinking and being. How and under what conditions new technologies and materials are appropriated by the public is a question that is now more pressing than ever. This book offers a wealth of data and startling insights for those intent on answering this question.

References

Banerjee, M and Miller, D (2003) *The Sari*, Oxford: Berg

Beasley, HG (1936) 'Notes on red feather money from Santa Cruz Group New Hebrides' 66 Journal of the Anthropological Institute of Great Britain and Ireland 379–91

Benjamin, W (1992) *Illuminations*, Zohn, H (trans), London: Fontana

Brown, G (1908) *George Brown, DD Pioneer-Missionary and Explorer: An Auto-biography*, London: Hodder & Stoughton

Campbell, S (2002) *The Art of Kula*, Oxford: Berg

Clarke, A and Miller, D (2002) 'Fashion and anxiety' 6(2) Fashion Theory 191–214

Colchester, C (2003) 'Introduction' in Colchester, C (ed), *Clothing the Pacific*, Oxford: Berg

Duffield, AJ (1886) 'On the natives of New Ireland' 15 Journal of the Anthropological Institute of Great Britain and Ireland 114–21

Eicher, JB (ed) (1995) *Dress and Ethnicity: Change Across Space and Time*, Oxford: Berg

Gell, A (1993) *Wrapping in Images: Tattooing in Polynesia*, Oxford: Clarendon

Gell, A (1998) *Art and Agency: An Anthropological Theory*, Oxford: Clarendon

Hereniko, V (1995) *Woven Gods: Female Clowns and Power in Rotuma*, Honolulu: University of Hawaii Press

Hollander, A (1993) *Seeing Through Clothes*, Berkeley: University of California Press

Kaeppler, AL (1975) *The Fabrics of Hawaii*, Leigh-on-Sea: F Lewis

Lawes, Rev WG (1879) 'Ethnological notes on the Motu, Koitapu and Koiari tribes of New Guinea' 8 Journal of the Anthropological Institute of Great Britain and Ireland 369–77

Mann, Rev IJ (1919–41) 'Diaries and papers' PMB 630 Pacific Manuscripts Bureau, Australia National University, Canberra

Martin, E (1992) 'The end of the body?' 19(1) American Ethnologist 121–40

O'Hanlon, M (1989) *Reading the Skin: Adornment, Display and Society Among the Wahgi*, London: British Museum Publications

Perani, J and Wolff, NH (1999) *Cloth, Dress and Art Patronage in Africa*, Oxford: Berg

Somerville, BT (1897) 'Ethnographic notes in New Georgia, Solomon Islands' 26 Journal of the Anthropological Institute of Great Britain and Ireland 357–412

Stafford, BM (1999) *Visual Analogy: Consciousness as the Art of Collecting*, Cambridge, MA: The MIT Press

Strathern, M (1999) *Property, Substance and Effect: Anthropological Essays on Persons and Things*, London: Athlone

Strathern, M (1988) *The Gender of the Gift: Problems with Women and Problems with Society in Melanesia*, Berkeley: University of California Press

Strathern, M (1979) 'The self in self-decoration' 49(4) Oceania 241–57

Thomas, N (1999) 'The case of the misplaced ponchos: speculations concerning the history of cloth in Polynesia' 4(1) Journal of Material Culture 5–20

Weiner, AB (1994) 'Cultural difference and the density of objects' 21(2) American Ethnologist 391–403

Weiner, AB (1992) *Inalienable Possessions: The Paradox of Keeping-While-Giving*, Berkeley: University of California Press

Weiner, AB and Schneider, J (1989) *Cloth and Human Experience*, Washington: Smithsonian Institution Press

Wigley, M (2001) *White Walls, Designer Dresses: The Fashioning of Modern Architecture*, Cambridge, MA: The MIT Press

CHAPTER 1

THE HAZARDS OF NEW CLOTHES: WHAT SIGNS MAKE POSSIBLE[1]

Webb Keane

As the people of the Pacific took on new forms of dress, they might well have been advised to consider these words from early in Henry David Thoreau's book *Walden, or Life in the Woods*: 'I say, beware of all enterprises that require new clothes, and not rather a new wearer of clothes' (Thoreau 1971: 23). I want to start with this admonition since it seems appropriate – dare I say 'fitting'? – for several reasons. Written in 1854, these words speak to us from the heyday of the missionary endeavour. Voicing Thoreau's version of New England Transcendentalism, with its roots in Puritanism and ties to Universalism, they issue – however idiosyncratically – from the heart of Protestant modernity in a form that will be especially familiar to many of us today. It is perhaps no accident that, at least in America, Thoreau was revived as a guru in the Sixties when the likes of Henry Ward Beecher, Bronson Alcott and William Ellery Channing had long been forgotten.

Thoreau identified himself with the great philosophical traditions of renunciation and the radical return to foundations. But in contrast to those, his was informed by a certain utilitarianism. We identify what should be renounced by discovering what is functionally necessary and strip away everything else as superfluous luxury. 'The object of clothing,' he wrote, 'is, first, to retain the vital heat, and secondly, in this state of society, to cover nakedness' (Thoreau 1971: 21). Note the order in which he expresses these functions, and the qualification. A stricter theologian would insist that we are naked in any society, and even when alone. Thus, when Erasmus advised children on good bodily conduct in the 16th century, he reminded them that the angels are always watching (Elias 1994: 106). But Thoreau relativises the claims of modesty to 'this state of society' – to a particular historical moment, and to the presence of other persons.

And so Thoreau's moralism dwells not on modesty, as it might have, but on the ways in which clothing marks social distinctions, subjects us to the vagaries of fashion, and displaces our proper concern with our spiritual condition. He writes: 'there is greater anxiety, commonly, to have . . . clean and unpatched clothes, than to have a sound conscience' (Thoreau 1971: 22). Clothes form a material outside that distracts us from the spiritual inside, with the result that, in Thoreau's words,

---

1   I am grateful to Susanne Küchler and Graeme Were for their invitation to take on this topic, and to Daniel Miller, Judith Irvine, Adela Pinch and Christopher Pinney for their comments and provocations.

'We know but a few men, a great many coats and breeches' (Thoreau 1971: 22). In this ironic rhetoric, we may hear something in common with the words of Thoreau's junior by one year, Karl Marx. Recall how Marx famously appropriated 'fetishism', a concept that had until then been restricted to comparative religion, in order similarly to accuse his contemporaries of inverting the proper relations between animate and inanimate things.[2]

But there is more. Caring about clothing gives us over too much to the opinion of others. Thoreau's discussion of clothing ends with an attack on fashion (Thoreau 1971: 25), which forces us to acknowledge the authority of others, whether that be the distant arbiters of style or the opinion of our neighbours. For Thoreau, the distinction between inner and outer provides ontological support for his individualism, which sees in social relations a threat to personal authenticity. For both Thoreau and Marx, despite their obvious political differences, the misapprehension of material things is not merely a mistake – it has grave consequences. It leads us to invert our values, imputing life to the lifeless, and thereby losing ourselves.

Thoreau's remarks about clothing express some assumptions about clothes in the world from which the first missionaries took sail to the Pacific. They reveal an important link between the 19th century Protestant world of white churches, plain meeting houses and sincere speech, and the high modernist aesthetic of, say, the Austrian architect Adolf Loos a half century later. Thoreau would surely have welcomed Loos's assertion that 'the evolution of civilization is tantamount to the removal of ornament from objects of use' (quoted in Gell 1993: 15) with its celebration of function over appearance, and rejection of surfaces not just as superfluous, but as immoral.

We can find that quotation from Loos, by the way, in Alfred Gell's brilliant book on Polynesian tattooing, *Wrapping in Images* (1993). Gell's spirit surely hovers over the contributors to this book. For if the authors are animated by one shared, underlying concern beyond their regional speciality, it is perhaps in their efforts to go beyond certain intellectual habits. These habits were summarised by Nicholas Thomas (drawing in turn on Marilyn Strathern, for example, 1979, 1988) when he criticised anthropology for having 'continually reduced material artefacts to other relations or meanings in which they are embedded; our interpretations treat the objects as no more than an illustration of things that are external to it' (Thomas 1999: 5). I want to pursue this thought today, and suggest how clothing exemplifies certain general problems in the analysis of material culture.

My central claim is this: if we still find it difficult to treat objects as no more than illustrations of something else, as, say, communicating meanings or identities, it is because we remain heirs of a tradition that treats signs as if they were merely the clothing of meaning, meaning that, it would seem, must be

---

2   Cloth and clothing are central to Marx's discussion of the commodity form in the first
     volume of *Capital*. Moreover, as Peter Stallybrass (1998) observes, Marx's own practical
     ability to write this book in the British Museum, where proper dress was expected, hinged on
     his uncertain capacity to keep his own coat out of pawn.

stripped bare. As this tradition dematerialises signs, it privileges meaning over actions, consequences and possibilities. Yet we must be wary of merely reversing this privilege and thereby inadvertently reproducing the same dichotomy. Drawing on concepts such as indexicality and semiotic ideology, I'd like to suggest some alternatives.

Thoreau's spiritualism is most like Loos's modernism when he dwells on clothing as superficial luxury. He rather ducks the problem raised by modesty, that by concealing our skin, clothing reveals our morality. But herein lies a persistent tension in missionary efforts to clothe the naked. For in covering our nakedness and directing attention to our artificial surface, clothing threatens to supplant us. Mission history across the colonial world shows a persistent and troubling tension between the hope that clothing will change people, and the danger that people once clad will invest their clothing with too great a significance (Comaroff and Comaroff 1997: 223; Hansen 2000: 26, 30–32; Spyer 1998). On the one hand, proper dress is essential to the inculcation of modesty, propriety and civility. Yet how much should one hope clothing will transform people? Not so much that they forget it is but a surface that can be removed. There are many dangers. They may, for instance, become frivolous and vain, or embark on new forms of fashion and status competition. Colonial writing is replete with depictions of dandified or otherwise ridiculous natives. Morality thus depends on the correct understanding of the materiality of things and the immateriality of persons.

Protestantism often sees itself as treading the middle way between two extremes: a disregard for clothing on the one hand, and excessive regard for it on the other. This is quite evident, for example, in the Dutch colonial Indies. If the pagans of Kalimantan, Sulawesi, or Maluku were insufficiently clad, the most orthodox Muslims of, say, Sunda and Aceh were too much so.[3] Like Goldilocks, the judicious Christian should accord to clothing neither too little importance, nor too much, but just enough – a balancing act that invites perpetual anxiety.

Writing about Calvinist missionaries in the colonial Dutch East Indies, I have argued elsewhere that matter and materialism pose special difficulties for mainstream Protestants (Keane 1996). The effort to regulate certain verbal and material practices, and the anxieties that attend them, centre on the problem of consolidating a human subject that is at its core independent of, and superordinate to, the world of mere dead matter. What for anthropologists is a problem of social and cultural analysis – how to understand material things within human society – is faced by these missionaries as a practical problem: how to free humans from false relations to things as in fetishism, animism or naturalistic materialism. This view of signs has roots in an ontology that goes back before either Protestantism or modernity, to be sure, but it reaches a particularly strong and influential expression in their alliance, as expressed by Thoreau and

---

3 As Jean Gelman Taylor points out (1997), class and other distinctions in the colonial Indies were marked not just by what people wore, but by which parts of the body were exposed, at what time of day, and in what location. Differences in style also involved differences in which aspects of the body were emphasised or suppressed.

Loos. And this model of the sign underlies much of both missionary endeavours and our own social and cultural theories.

Of course it is hardly news to the authors in this book that clothing is more than a matter of 'mere appearances', and that we should be circumspect about purported distinctions between 'inner' and 'outer'. But I think we still have not sufficiently appreciated the extent to which this perception of clothing is rooted in a deeper set of semiotic assumptions and habits. Here I want to trace out some of the ways in which our discussion of clothing can be brought to bear on a rethinking of the concept of the sign in support of a more historically minded study of material culture.

To take clothes in particular, and objects more generally, as expressions of meanings that really lie elsewhere, is to depend on certain assumptions not just about objects, but about signs. Clothing seems most superficial to those who take signs to be the clothing of immaterial meanings. Like clothing, in this view, the sign both reveals and conceals, and serves to mediate relations between the self and others. These are the very grounds on which Thoreau and many other Protestants and modernists are suspicious of clothing and often of semiotic mediation altogether. In unmediated transparency they hope to discover unvarnished souls and naked truth. Here we have an example of what can be called representational economy. By representational economy, I mean the interconnections among different modes of signification. For instance, I have argued elsewhere that the ways in which people handle and value material goods may be implicated in how they use and interpret words, and vice versa (Keane 1996, 1997a, 2001, 2002). Their treatment of things and words both reflect certain underlying assumptions about the world and the beings that inhabit it. Such assumptions, for instance, will determine how one distinguishes between subjects and objects, with implications for what will or will not count as a possible agent – and thus, for what is a good candidate for being an intentional communication. Historically, changes in one will be reflected in changes in the other. Thus, they enter into a larger economy of mutual, often unexpected consequences.

Do new garments make a prince of a pauper? A woman of a man? It is not only missionaries who are unsettled by the question: how much change ought we to expect from a change of clothes? Transvestism, after all, is serious business. In Indonesia, the capacity of Buginese *bissu* to mediate between the world of the living and the dead, for instance, requires mixed-gendered dressing. And certainly new historical ambitions seem to demand new clothes. Across the Malay world, to convert to Islam required that one take on new kinds of clothing and food regulations, which is one reason people figured the same must be true of Christianity (Aragon 2000; Kipp 1993; Taylor 1997). Many Sumbanese assumed they needed Western clothes if they were to convert, despite the protestations of the Dutch missionaries; some still refer to this assumption today. By the end of the 19th century, young nationalists in the more urban parts of the Dutch East Indies were asserting their modernity and new capacities through sartorial transformations (Schulte Nordholt, 1997, especially the chapters by van Dijk, Danandjaja, Mrázek and Taylor). Numerous memoirs by members of the first generations of nationalists hinge on the moment in which they first acquired shoes and slacks (notably, women did not follow suit until well into the 20th century). Efforts in the 1930s by the Indonesian nationalist party to imitate Gandhi's *swadeshi* movement, and clothe its adherents in locally produced, indigenous styles, failed as the leaders persisted in their love of white suits, ties and well polished shoes. When Sukarno was held by the Dutch during the war of independence in the 1940s, the prisoners were allowed a few requests. His companions asked for books and newspapers. Sukarno, however, asked for a new Arrow shirt (Schulte Nordholt 1997: 19, n 17). Can we separate his leadership from such embodiments, which set the national fashion for men: Western suit jackets without ties, and black *pici*, Muslim caps?

Do such examples simply boil down to mere emblems of identity? I think not. Too much of the subjective pain and expectation of history centres on changes of dress. From Sumba to Sumatra, we find people's single most vivid recollection of the Japanese occupation during the Second World War was often not the violence, the hunger, the fear, but rather the disappearance of textiles and return to bark cloth. In Sulawesi, one man is reported to have refused to give up his tattered sarong in exchange for a cow (Aragon 2000: 144–45). I doubt anyone with those humiliating memories would consider clothing a mere surface.

We needn't look only to historical crises to see the power of new clothes. Think of how much anthropological fieldwork has depended on the hoped for – or feared – effects of cultural transvestism. My own experience is perhaps exemplary of the disquiet the question can provoke. Some mix of a life-long aversion to exposing my bony knees, and a postcolonial discomfort with the images of TE Lawrence clad as an Arab and Frank Hamilton Cushing as a Zuni, made me at first wary of donning Sumbanese dress. Most Sumbanese men wear a *hinggi* (in some dialects, *regi*), a rectangular cloth wrapped around the waist and upper thighs. It is held in a loose bundle with some assistance from a belt, one end left to hang down between the legs. The longer it hangs (yes, I'm afraid it's true), the higher the man's status claims. A smaller length of cloth (called a *rowa*) is wrapped around the head; different modes of tying facilitating a remarkable range of self-expression, far wider than that afforded by the tilt of a hat, and more adjustable than that of a haircut (see Keller 1992). Both above and below, I found all this a terribly insecure arrangement, threatening to expose, at the very least, my incompetence if not more.[4] My companions, however, would not let me get away even with such compromises as long pants under a symbolic waistcloth. With the sharp command *paborungumu!* ('gird your loins!'), they insisted I dress properly. And so I did. Yet, after two years I still hadn't come to feel entirely at home in this dress. And by sheer material logic I suffered from an additional impropriety: given my long legs and the size of the locally available cloth, I was forced to show myself at the lowest end of social order, or else leave so little material for securing it around my waist that I was at even greater risk of having the whole thing fall off me.

---

4 Even the habituated wearer can feel insecure; see Banerjee and Miller's evocative portrayal of the vulnerability of the sari wearer to slippage and exposure (2003).

Beware all enterprises that require new clothes indeed. The experience of comfort and discomfort has little to do with meaning, expression, identity, nor even, as Marcel Mauss (1979) would remind us, with some universal phenomenology of bodily experience. After all, most Sumbanese men feel at least as uncomfortable in pants and shoes (*kalabi jiawa*: foreign clothing) as I did in *regi* and *rowa*. No surprises here: we drape ourselves in habit, competence and constraint – with what clothing makes possible. Sumbanese cloth allows the comforting gesture of draping it protectively around oneself, as they say, like a hen huddled against the rain. The man's waistcloth leaves legs free to straddle a horse, his headcloth is good for everything, from wiping sweat off the neck to transmitting magical power (I knew one man who, as a child, was brought back from death when his father slapped him with his headcloth). Men and women's clothing has no pockets – another source of my discomfort – but special objects can be hidden in their folds and the very insecurity of this draping can be played to advantage. One man told me how he got rid of a powerful talisman that, while useful, was becoming dangerous. Knowing it would be even more dangerous were he intentionally to dispose of it, he folded it into his waistcloth and started on a long, cross-country trip. Somewhere, perhaps in crossing a river, the talisman was lost, as it were, accidentally on purpose. We could say he thereby elicits the very agency of the thing.

We should bear in mind the plasticity of the sense of comfort. Patricia Spyer (1998) points out that Dutch colonial observers sometimes exaggerated the discomfort of *Aruese* in western clothes, as if to insist on the irredeemable difference of native bodies, and on the limits of what new clothing could achieve. Indonesia's early nationalists struggled against these limits. Henk Schulte Nordholt remarks: 'Wearing a western suit with tie did facilitate a handshake instead of a humble *sembah* (a respectful Javanese gesture of greeting), and wearing trousers did lend itself to sitting on a chair instead of being seated on the floor' (Schulte Nordholt 1997: 15). And today's national style for Indonesian women, the so called *kain kebaya* (tight sarong, lace-decorated bodice, and high-heeled sandals) severely restricts free movement and imposes physical insecurity on the wearer (Taylor 1997: 113).

Of new clothing, then: what new practices, habits, intentions does it make possible – or inhibit? What projects does it invite? Nicholas Thomas (1999) observed that the adoption of the so called 'poncho' by western Polynesian Christians didn't merely express their new modesty; by offering new ways of covering themselves, it actually made it possible. What sense of protection does clothing afford – and against what threats? What Alfred Gell says of Polynesian tattooing, that it 'brings into existence and populates the world with subsidiary beings, spirit selves, which surround and protect the tattooed subject' (Gell 1993: 8), can *mutatis mutandis* often apply to clothing too.

Once you start wearing Western clothing, where do you get protection, and from what? What gives clothing its effects, or in Strathern's (1988) terms, what does it reveal and conceal, besides 'meanings'? This is a question we should ask of all material objects. For if we are to treat things 'in their own right', and not just as the tangible garments draped on otherwise invisible and immaterial ideas, we must consider their forms, qualities, practical capacities, and thus, their place within causal relations. For if objects are revelatory, it is not simply because people say so, nor even because the anthropologist can impute to people certain beliefs. And if things mediate our historicity, we cannot be content to ask only what meanings people attribute to them now. Let me be clear: I do not intend to eliminate words or beliefs from the story. But I do want to situate words in their right place; in their practical and consequential relations with other signs and activities.

To do this requires situating words and material things, their qualities, the practices they mediate, and the interpretations to which they give rise, within a world of causality. So I want to turn now to some semiotic principles that bear on the analysis of material things. In particular, I want to consider the place of logical-causal relations within representational economies. The goal is to understand the historicity and social power of material things without reducing them either to being only vehicles of meaning, on the one hand, or ultimate determinants, on the other. The term 'logical-causal' expresses a fundamental concept in Charles Sanders Peirce's (1955, 1958) semiotic model of the sign, indexicality. Indexicality refers to those properties of a sign by which an observer can make an inference about something actual (as opposed to possible – as in resemblance – or of a rule-like character, as in the conventional signs of language). These may involve proximity: an exit sign indicates the presence of a fire escape. But most interestingly they involve causal inferences: smoke indexes the presence of fire, a cauliflower ear indexes a life in the boxing ring.

Since semiotics is so commonly associated with a certain kind of unworldly, ahistorical and often rather simplistic idealism, some explanation of its pertinence to material things may be called for. First, a word on what it is not. One of the most dazzlingly original and insightful uses of the index is Alfred Gell's *Art and Agency* (1998). There, Gell identifies 'semiotics' (mostly) with 'language'. This won't do, he says, because he wants to attend to the qualities of the object itself. He writes: 'We talk about objects, using signs, but art objects are not, except in special cases, signs themselves, with "meanings"; and if they do have meanings, then they are part of language' (Gell 1998: 6). Fair enough, the problem here is that Gell too quickly assimilates 'sign' to 'meaning', 'meaning' in turn to 'language', and 'language' to something like 'coded messages'. In this, Gell seems to accept Saussure's (1959) structuralist model of language, as consisting of signifieds which are encoded in the form of signifiers, in order to be transmitted to someone else, who decodes them and thereby recovers the signified meanings.

Now, I agree with Gell that this model is of little help in understanding objects. But we can go further: it's not even a good account of language. Saussurean 'semiology' (not 'semiotics') also makes it hard to perceive the role that language does play vis à vis material things. First, it treats language as something that exists in a plane of reality quite distinct from that in which any non-linguistic things (material or conceptual) are found. It connects to those things only as objects of reference. Secondly, by seeing language only as coded meaning, Saussurean semiology fails to see the role linguistic practices play in the objectification of things, a point to which I will return. The problem is semiotics has too often been treated, especially in cultural studies, as merely about the communication of meanings, an excessively complicated kind of text interpretation. Perhaps for this reason, Gell's use of the concept of index doesn't develop its articulation with other aspects of Peirce's analysis of signs. As a result, I would argue he doesn't fully explore the social and historical implications of the index. Instead he seeks a direct road to cognition. I would like to show how semiotics can help us restore these social and historical dimensions to the analysis.

In contrast to those who treat signs as coded messages, Peirce located signs within a material world of consequences. He insisted that concrete circumstances were essential to the very possibility of signification. Thus he criticised Hegel's idealism with these words: 'The capital error of Hegel which permeates his whole system ... is that he almost altogether ignores the Outward Clash ... [This] direct consciousness of hitting and getting hit enters into all cognition and serves to make it mean something real' (Peirce 1958: 43–44). Peirce offers a way of thinking about the logic of signification that displays its inherent vulnerability to causation and contingency, as well as its openness to further causal consequences, without settling for the usual so called 'materialist' reductionisms. I want to argue that this openness should be central to any theoretically principled effort to understand the historical dynamics of social facts such as 'clothing'.

The Peircean model of the sign has two features I want to bring out here. First, it is processual: signs give rise to new signs, in an unending process of signification. This is important because the process entails sociability, struggle, power, historicity and contingency. Secondly is the considerable attention that Peirce devotes to the range of relationships (resemblance, proximity, causality and convention) not only between sign and its meaning, but also between both of those and (possible) objects of signification in the world. I stress these points because of the common charge that to take things as 'signs' is to reduce the world to discourse, to give in to the totalising imperative to render all things meaningful. This is not necessarily so.

Iconicity refers to a connection between sign and object on the basis of resemblance. Peirce observes that icons in and of themselves remain only unrealised potential. For one thing, an icon can resemble an object that doesn't exist – a map, say, of a fantastic land, or a cloud that looks like a unicorn. Since all objects have qualities, any given object potentially resembles something: this means any object can suggest possible future uses or interpretations. Peirce pointed out that the artist's preliminary sketch for a sculpture makes use of this characteristic openness of iconicity as a means of discovery, 'suggesting ... new aspects of supposed states of things' (Peirce 1955: 106–07). Moreover, since resemblance is underdetermined, icons require some further guidance to determine how they are similar to their objects. After all, even an ordinary portrait photograph is normally flat, immobile and much smaller than its subject (see Pinney 1997).

For our purposes, examples of these aspects of iconicity range from colonial subjects who turned western shirts upside down and wore them as pants, to European tourists who buy flat, rectangular, 'ikatted' Sumbanese waistcloths (hinggi hondo) and hang them on the wall as art. Resemblance, however, can only be with respect to certain features and therefore depends on selection. To hang a Sumbanese *ikat* as wall art requires one to overlook its bilateral inversion, since the images at each end are upside down relative to one another. Determining what features count towards resemblance commonly involves larger questions of social value and authority. This is easiest to see in colonial clashes. For instance, the Western sense of propriety in colonial southern Africa was offended by multifunctional apparel (Comaroff and Comaroff 1997: 270). Accustomed to one set of clothes for dining and another for gardening, one kind of textile to cover tables and another beds, Europeans were scandalised when Tswana used the same blankets as garments, ground cover, market bundles and baby carriers. In time, a successful hegemony would restrict such potential uses, constraining which iconic possibilities would be recognised in practice.

The point is this: iconicity is only a matter of potential. The realisation or suppression of that potential cannot be ascribed to the qualities of the object in themselves. There must always be other social processes involved that may involve varying degrees of self-consciousness and control. Semiotic analyses have tended to favour the more strictly regimented domains of royal or liturgical ritual, high fashion (Barthes 1983), or connoisseurship (Bourdieu 1984), but there are far less well organised dimensions to social life. Even in the more controlled domains, however, since those material qualities that are suppressed do persist, objects bring the potential for new realisations into new historical contexts (see Thomas 1991).

The key semiotic concept for understanding context and consequentiality is indexicality. Since iconicity and indexicality both require further instructions, their qualities are mediated by semiotic ideology, that is, a set of assumptions about signs and signifying practice.[5] Consider Thorstein Veblen's (1912) notion of conspicuous consumption – on the face of it a clear case of indexicality. One appreciates the value of a silk dress or high-heel shoes by recognising their lack of utility. But this recognition is mediated by what you assume about the world. High heels are not useful, for example, only if you believe they don't have magical power – or, say, that height is immaterial to selfhood. Here's my point of difference from Gell. For Gell, indexicality functions through abductions (1998: 14–15). These are inferences that rely on *ad hoc* hypotheses. This idea of abduction is useful because it offers an alternative to the full determinism of natural law, but doesn't require us to assume everyone goes around with a pre-existing code or social rule book in their heads. Gell treats the logic of abduction as a cognitive process, but while necessary, this is not, I think, sufficient. For one thing, abductions depend on historically conditioned preconceptions as to what might be good candidates for agents (people? Spirits?) and thus for intentional signs (spilled milk? Failed harvests? Rocks? Rain? Solar eclipses?). For another, abduction doesn't explain how and when discrete entities do or do not come to be recognisable as 'the same'. The capacity to recognise discrete entities as instances

---

5   The term derives from analogy with 'linguistic ideology' (Schieffelin, Woolard and Kroskrity 1998). To the extent that 'ethnosemiotic assumptions' (Parmentier 1997) include ideas about the place of language among other signs, linguistic ideology is perhaps a special case of semiotic ideology.

or tokens of types depends on the social organisation of interpretative possibilities. The inherent capacity of things to be iconic leaves them open to new possible objects of resemblance.

Take the social power of *ikatted* cloth in old Sumba. A century ago, *ikat* was a prerogative of nobility, and so to possess *ikat* was indexical of being noble. But this was only by virtue of sumptuary regulation, that is, mere convention sustained by social force (you could kill someone who violated it). Today, *ikat* motifs are thoroughly commoditised. Although nobles may still claim them, they no longer control their circulation. A motif-laden textile may, in some instances, be indexical of nothing more than a buyer's taste and the act of purchase (Forshee 2001).

But there's more to the story. Indexicality alone can't give any content to nobility. Moreover, the Sumbanese never essentialised nobility, as, say, a matter of bodily substance. So what makes a noble anything more than someone with more wealth than others? As it happens, Sumbanese nobles only wore black, or in some places, plain white; and in much of Sumba today these are still the favoured styles, which is why textile collections are so ethnographically inaccurate – who collects plain black cloth? It was the slaves of the nobility who wore the *ikats*. The displacement of that clothing from master's body to slave is iconic of the nature of nobility, as a quality that expands and transcends any particular embodied form. Detached from the possessor's body, the cloth reveals itself as more than clothing and its possessor as more than someone confined to the here and now. The indexical iconicity of displacement and expansion is reinforced by a formal parallel in linguistic practice. The noble's name is never uttered, but is replaced by that of the slave, the *ngara hunga* ('name which emerges') (Keane 1997b: 59–63). The naturalising effect wasn't merely a matter of communication – what slaves made possible was a way of being. Facilitating the capacity of nobles to extend themselves through the bodies and words of others, such displaced materialisations in effect dematerialised and thus spiritualised their object: noble rank. These indexical icons of rank emerged out of aesthetic intuitions and political actions, mutually reinforcing across different modalities (clothing, violence and linguistic habit). To be sure, the signs did communicate – but only as a function of their other capacities.

In general, for the concepts of icon and index to be analytically useful, they must be understood to face towards possible futures. What iconicity and indexicality begin to do is open up signification to causality, to the possible effects and new suggestions of material qualities. George Herbert Mead wrote that the self responds to inanimate objects socially: 'The chair is what it is in terms of its invitation to sit down' (1934: 279). The chair's iconicity, that is, forms a material instigation to certain sorts of action.[6] As instigation, it can only invite actions, not determine them: people in the colonial Indies may not have responded even if the Dutch had permitted them to rise from their floor mats. To realise some of the potentials suggested by iconicity, and not others, is the stuff of history.

6　We might include here the instigation to involuntary memory, provoked by such things as smells and shapes imparted to clothing by a former owner (Stallybrass 1996).

I have been elaborating here Peirce's important insight that icons and indexes in themselves assert nothing. What did Western dress worn by people of the Indies in the early 20th century index? What possibilities did people hope to effect by a change of clothes? Acceptance of European culture, a desire to be part of a sophisticated world, acquiescence to Dutch rule, assertions of equality to Europeans, hostility to Islam, rejection of village society, being modern, access to fungible wealth, or short sighted extravagance? And why did some of these attempts at cross-dressing fail and others succeed? When the Dutch, for instance, refused to acknowledge Indonesians' sartorial assertions of equality, they were helped by a semiotic ideology that told them that clothing is merely skin-deep, a message of little consequence.

But semiotic ideologies are vulnerable, not least by their exposure to the openness and what Daniel Miller has called 'the humility of things' (Miller 1987). Consider the effects of what I call bundling (see Keane 2003). A qualisign cannot be manifest apart from particular objectual forms. But once a qualisign is embodied in something particular, it is contingently (rather than by logical necessity or social convention) bound up with other qualities – redness on a cloth comes along with light weight, flat surface, flexibility, warmth, combustibility, and so forth. There is no way to eliminate (nor entirely to regiment) that factor of co-presence or bundling. This points to one of the obvious, but important, effects of materiality: redness cannot be manifest without some embodiment that inescapably binds it to some other qualities as well, which remain available, ready to emerge as real factors as it crosses contexts. Western slacks treat the legs independently of one another; this permits a longer gait than does a Javanese sarong, inviting athleticism and making them potentially iconic of, say, 'freedom'. In Indonesia, slacks have tended to be more expensive than the sarong as well, and thus indexical of relative wealth and, by extension, urban life (Kipp 1993: 201). But now that the sarong has come to be purposefully deployed as a conventional symbol of Islam (indexical only by decree), slacks also threaten to be indexical of the not-wearing of sarong.

These associations provide raw material for ideological consolidation. Middle class men in Indonesian cities today have a rule-governed sartorial repertoire: a neo-traditional outfit for weddings; safari suit for official meetings; long-sleeved batik shirt for receptions; shirt and tie for the office; sarong and *pici* for Friday prayers (Danandjaja 1997; van Dijk 1997). These are co-ordinated with bodily habituses: the Javanese *sembah*, sitting on mats and eating with hands while in neo-traditional clothes; firm handshake, direct eye contact, chairs and utensils in office attire; Islamic *salam* while in sarong. This cluster of habits, expectations and constrained possibilities is the outcome of several generations of semiotic regimentation and stabilisation. In addition to the direct effects of government regulations over its vast civil service, other responses reinforced them. For instance, a popular 'uniform fever' swept Indonesia in the 1970s, as people at the margins of citizenship sought to distinguish themselves from the anonymous masses by identifying themselves sartorially with the bureaucracy (Sekimoto 1997). Some people, for whom the wearing of uniforms was somewhat optional, such as university professors, took to wielding them as apotropaic talismans against corrupt police and vigilantes (Danandjaja 1997). It is against the background of such self-consciously communicative and highly systematised treatments of clothes that other modes of emblematisation, such as the taking on of more Middle Eastern styles of head covering by women emerge (Brenner 1996). Now, in these tightly regimented circumstances, a communication model of the sign actually does a great deal to explain style. But not all social life in all domains is so tightly controlled and totalised.

This consolidation, I think, is what Georg Simmel meant by saying that 'style is always something general' (Simmel 1950: 341), that is, a capacity for recognising 'the same thing' in further instances. This involves the effort to constitute general laws governing possible futures – something that often requires the work of language. For the practices of consolidation are often discursive, such as the ritual metaphors that emphasise some of cloth's qualities over others, or the government regulations that make uniforms the mark of citizenship. They may also require the textualising powers of language, its capacity to identify different things in different contexts as being 'the same' (Silverstein and Urban 1996). But the work of selecting and stabilising the relevant bundles of iconicity and indexicality, the semiotic ideology this involves, is a project that can in principle never be completed, or fully consolidated. As such, semiotic ideology is necessarily historical.

I want to conclude with the question of objectification and talk. Elsewhere, I have argued that a core component of the Protestant Reformation was a semiotic ideology that took words to be merely the outward expression of immaterial inner thoughts (Keane 1997a, 2002). Like language, goods too tended to become 'merely symbolic' or else merely functional; in either case, their sensuous qualities devalued and their significance dematerialised. The habit of treating clothing as superficial or as a mere vehicle of communication is one expression of this semiotic ideology. It is this view that Henry David Thoreau and Adolf Loos exemplify, each in his own way.

What are the conditions under which cloth does or does not come into view as a bearer of iconography, with meanings that can be treated as texts? Sumbanese *ikats* are only produced in a small number of villages, although they circulate through exchange and are highly valued across the island. Some aspects of meaning don't travel well: the fact that the smell of indigo dye vats is iconic of rotting flesh (Hoskins 1989) is quite significant in weaving villages but not elsewhere. Even in weaving villages, the explanation of motifs was restricted to male specialists, not the women who actually wove. In central Sumba, where weaving was carried out but the technique of *ikatting* forbidden, *ikatted* textiles were ritually, economically and socially potent, but their imagery drew little attention. The highly valued *patola* designs derive from the eponymous Indian cloth, but ritual specialists in central Sumba couldn't identify them, and knew only that the word meant something of great power. Sumbanese textiles lie at the boundary between cloth and clothing, their functions shifting by turns from wrapped garment to folded exchange valuable, open curtain, shroud draped on a corpse, shield against ritual heat, suspended banner, object of verbal exegesis, hidden relic, and nowadays, art on a wall. In the past, once a cloth was off the loom, there were few normal uses in which the imagery was laid out and made clearly visible as a whole – most uses revealed only fragments of the pattern, in constant motion. In practice, the qualities that come to the fore are brightness and busyness, fragility or durability (depending on context), capacity to block light and retain heat, softness, absorbency, ease of manipulation, and their bilateral symmetry (see Keane 1997b: 80–81).

Under what conditions, then, do iconology and exegesis become significant? We need to be sensitive to the historicity of semiotic practices. In old Sumba, the most common *ikat* motifs included *patola* designs drawn from Indian trade cloth, dragons from Chinese porcelain, and rampant heraldic animals from Dutch coins (Adams 1969). These require little exegetical knowledge beyond an awareness that they index the power of distance, conveyed through the capacity of objects to move across space and time. In recent decades, however, enormous attention has been drawn to motifs (but not, for instance, their repetition across the cloth, which gets overlooked). What has changed? Cloth is increasingly encountered as a plane parallel to the stance of the viewer. That is how they are displayed by sellers, illustrated in books, and hung on collectors' walls. They are visible as rectangular frames, taken in at a single glance, with a top and bottom. As frames for imagery, cloths become instances of the category 'traditional' art. They enter a series that also includes Balinese painting and Javanese shadow puppets, which encourages cross-reference among them. Commercial competition is also driving a focus on motifs, one of the main ways of differentiating producers and allowing them to display esoteric knowledge to the buyers. Discrete motifs become objects of discourse and readily circulate independently of waist clothes, to T-shirts and murals. This discourse plays a crucial role in objectifying cloth as bearer of motifs. Exegetical talk itself is becoming an indexical icon of male authority and of the 'tradition' embodied in the commodified cloth (Forshee 2001).

Whether one looks at such things as a failed harvest, torn cloth, or a minor stumble as evidence of spiritual disfavour, more mundane human malevolence, or as agent-less happenstance (see Keane 1997b: 29–32), depends on semiotic ideologies and the subjects, objects, and thus modes of agency, they presuppose. Thus the Protestant anxiety about the relative autonomy of the human subject from the material world constrains what will count as signs, as intentions, and as actions – excluding such things as the contingent materiality of things from the proper domain of the human. An analysis of the social power of things would thus demand an account of the semiotic ideologies by which things become objects. For these are the same processes that configure the borders and the possibilities of subjects.

Let me close by returning to the questions with which I began: what can we expect from a change of clothes? If Polynesian tattoos and Sumbanese *ikats* offered protective spirits against a dangerous world, what do our own clothes protect us against? Thoreau exemplifies an austere hope indeed, for we must rely on ourselves alone, and those selves only in the most disembodied form. A semiotic ideology that takes signs as mere clothing for immaterial meanings, and clothing as merely a covering for the covering of the solitary soul, leaves us protected against nothing but the elements. Perhaps it takes a spirit as rare as that of Henry David Thoreau to feel the need for no more shelter than that.

References

Adams, MJ (1969) *System and Meaning in East Sumba Textile Design: A Study in Traditional Indonesian Art*, New Haven: Yale University Southeast Asian Studies

Aragon, LV (2000) *Fields of the Lord: Animism, Christian Minorities, and State Development in Indonesia*, Honolulu: University of Hawaii Press

Banerjee, M and Miller, D (2003) *The Sari*, Oxford: Berg

Barthes, R (1983) [1967] *The Fashion System*, Lavers, A and Smith, C (trans), London: Jonathan Cape

Bourdieu, P (1984) [1979] *Distinction: A Social Critique of the Judgement of Taste*, Nice, R (trans), Cambridge, MA: Harvard University Press

Brenner, S (1996) 'Reconstruction self and society: Javanese Muslim women and "the Veil"' 23 American Ethnologist 673–97

Comaroff, JL and Comaroff, J (1997) *Of Revelation and Revolution: Volume 2, The Dialectics of Modernity on a South African Frontier*, Chicago: University of Chicago Press

Danandjaja, J (1997) 'From Hansop to Safari: notes from an eyewitness' in Schulte Nordholt, H (ed), *Outward Appearances: Dressing State and Society in Indonesia*, Leiden: KITLV Press

van Dijk, K (1997) 'Sarong, jubbah, and trousers: appearance as a means of distinction and discrimination' in Schulte Nordholt, H (ed), *Outward Appearances: Dressing State and Society in Indonesia*, Leiden: KITLV Press

Elias, N (1994) [1939] *The Civilizing Process*, Jephcott, E (trans), Oxford: Blackwell

Forshee, J (2001) *Between the Folds: Stories of Cloth, Lives, and Travels from Sumba*, Honolulu: University of Hawaii Press

Gell, A (1993) *Wrapping in Images: Tattooing in Polynesia*, Oxford: Clarendon

Gell, A (1998) *Art and Agency: An Anthropological Theory*, Oxford: Clarendon

Hansen, KT (2000) *Salaula: The World of Secondhand Clothing and Zambia*, Chicago: University of Chicago Press

Hoskins, J (1989) 'Why do ladies sing the blues? Indigo, cloth production, and gender symbolism in Kodi' in Weiner, AB and Schneider, J (eds), *Cloth and Human Experience*, Washington, DC: Smithsonian Institution Press

Keane, W (1996) 'Materialism, missionaries, and modern subjects in colonial Indonesia' in van der Veer, P (ed), *Conversion to Modernities: The Globalization of Christianity*, New York and London: Routledge

Keane, W (1997a) 'From fetishism to sincerity: agency, the speaking subject, and their historicity in the context of religious conversion' 39 Comparative Studies in Society and History 674–93

Keane, W (1997b) *Signs of Recognition: Powers and Hazards of Representation in an Indonesian Society*, Berkeley: University of California Press

Keane, W (2001) 'Money is no object: materiality, desire, and modernity in an Indonesian society' in Myers, FC (ed), *The Empire of Things: Regimes of Value and Material Culture*, Santa Fe: School of American Research Press

Keane, W (2002) 'Sincerity, "modernity", and the Protestants' 17 Cultural Anthropology 65–92

Keane, W (2003) 'Semiotics and the social analysis of material things' 23(2–3) Language and Communication 409–25, Special Issue, 'Words and Beyond: Linguistic and Semiotic Studies of Sociocultural Order' (Manning, P (ed))

Keller, E (1992) 'Head-dresses as a medium of self-expression in Laboya: Sumbanese attire in historical perspective' in Nabholz-Kartaschoff, M,

Barnes, R and Stuart-Fox, DJ (eds) *Weaving Patterns of Life: Indonesian Textile Symposium 1991*, Basel: Museum of Ethnography

Kipp, RS (1993) *Dissociated Identities: Ethnicity, Religion, and Class in an Indonesian Society*, Ann Arbor: University of Michigan Press

Mauss, M (1979) [1950] 'Bodily techniques' in Mauss, M, *Sociology and Psychology: Essays*, Brewster, B (trans), London: Routledge and Kegan Paul

Mead, GH (1934) *Mind, Self, and Society from the Standpoint of a Social Behaviorist*, Chicago: University of Chicago Press

Miller, D (1987) *Material Culture and Mass Consumption*, Oxford: Basil Blackwell

Mrázek, R (1997) '"Indonesian dandy": the politics of clothes in the late colonial period, 1893–1942' in Schulte Nordholt, H (ed), *Outward Appearances: Dressing State and Society in Indonesia*, Leiden: KITLV Press

Parmentier, RJ (1997) 'The pragmatic semiotics of cultures' 116 Semiotica, Special Issue

Peirce, CS (1955) *Philosophical Writings of Peirce*, Buchler, J (ed), New York: Dover

Peirce, CS (1958) *Collected Papers of Charles Sanders Peirce. VIII: Reviews, Correspondence, and Bibliography*, Cambridge, MA· Harvard University Press

Pinney, C (1997) *Camera Indica: The Social Life of Indian Photographs*, Chicago: University of Chicago Press

de Saussure, F (1959) *Course in General Linguistics*, New York: Philosophical Library

Schieffelin, BB, Woolard, KA and Kroskrity, PV (eds) (1998) *Language Ideologies: Practice and Theory*, New York: Oxford University Press

Schulte Nordholt, H (1997) 'Preface' in Schulte Nordholt, H (ed), *Outward Appearances: Dressing State and Society in Indonesia*, Leiden: KITLV Press

Schulte Nordholt, H (ed) (1997) *Outward Appearances: Dressing State and Society in Indonesia*, Leiden: KITLV Press

Sekimoto, T (1997) 'Uniforms and concrete walls: dressing the village under the new order in the 1970s and 1980s' in Schulte Nordholt, H (ed), *Outward Appearances: Dressing State and Society in Indonesia*, Leiden: KITLV Press

Silverstein, M and Urban, G (eds) (1996) *Natural Histories of Discourse*, Chicago: University of Chicago Press

Simmel, G (1950) [1923] 'Adornment' in Wolff, KH (ed), *The Sociology of Georg Simmel*, New York: Free Press

Spyer, P (1998) 'The tooth of time, or taking a look at the "look" of clothing in late nineteenth-century Aru' in Spyer, P (ed), *Border Fetishisms: Material Objects in Unstable Places*, New York: Routledge

Stallybrass, P (1996) 'Worn worlds: cloth and identity on the Renaissance stage' in de Grazia, M, Quilligan, M and Stallybrass, P (eds), *Subject and Object in Renaissance Culture*, Cambridge: Cambridge University Press

Stallybrass, P (1998) 'Marx's coat' in Spyer, P (ed), *Border Fetishisms: Material Objects in Unstable Places*, New York: Routledge

Strathern, M (1979) 'The self in self-decoration' 49 Oceania 241–57

Strathern, M (1988) *The Gender of the Gift: Problems with Women and Problems with Society in Melanesia*, Berkeley: University of California Press

Taylor, JG (1997) 'Costume and gender in colonial Java, 1800–1940' in Schulte Nordholt, H (ed), *Outward Appearances: Dressing State and Society in Indonesia*, Leiden: KITLV Press

Thomas, N (1991) *Entangled Objects: Exchange, Material Culture, and Colonialism in the Pacific*, Cambridge, MA: Harvard University Press

Thomas, N (1999) 'The case of the misplaced poncho: speculations concerning the history of cloth in Polynesia' 4(1) Journal of Material Culture 5–20

Thoreau, HD (1971) [1854] *Walden*, Shanley, L (ed), Princeton: Princeton University Press

Veblen, T (1912) *The Theory of the Leisure Class: An Economic Study of Institutions*, New York: Macmillan

PART I: CLOTHING AS THE ART OF INNOVATION

„Kathleen", Maori Guide, Rotorua. N. Z.

CHAPTER 2

DRESSING FOR TRANSITION: WEDDINGS, CLOTHING AND CHANGE IN VANUATU

Lissant Bolton

In Vanuatu, weddings are big time. With a phenomenal population growth – from 143,000 in 1989 to over 200,000 in 2003 – and an ever more juvenile population (over 50% are now under 18), the number of people of marriageable age is steadily increasing. The impact of this is beginning to show as an alteration in the extent and importance of wedding rituals, but at the moment it means mainly that weddings are the dominant ceremony in most areas of the country. The significant economic and social changes that have affected the archipelago since the end of the 19th century, and especially since the Second World War, have had their impact on these rituals. This paper is not about weddings in general, but rather focuses on one particular element of them: the question of what women wear to be married. Specifically, it makes a contrast between practice in two different parts of Vanuatu, comparing east Ambae, in north Vanuatu, with Pango, a peri-urban village adjacent to Vanuatu's capital, Port Vila.

The way in which wedding rituals are negotiated and achieved reveals a great deal about the core preoccupations and dominant idioms in a specific social context. To demonstrate this with a rather obvious example: the recent phenomenon of pre-nuptial agreements among the wealthy in the United States focuses on the two parties to the marriage only; in attending to the importance of property, the pre-nuptial recognises the bride's and the groom's potentially equal and competing rights to it. Such agreements assume the probability of divorce; and in attempting to control disputes in advance, indicate one of the key sources of fission in the relationship. If the arrangements and exchanges of property at marriage reveal some of the economic characteristics of a social group, then the degree to which wedding ritual is elaborated and the specific foci of attention within it, can illuminate how the relationships marriage creates are valued and understood. The paraphernalia of the ritual, and specifically the clothing, reflects on those relationships.

Wedding clothes are illuminating for what they reveal about relationships at marriage. They can also be analysed to reveal aspects of how things change. The adoption of expatriate goods and clothing in places like Vanuatu has often been popularly deplored, but old ideas and concepts are often invested in new materials. What is being negotiated when women on Ambae or in Pango dress to marry? What women wear to be married in east Ambae, a rural area in north Vanuatu, and what brides wear in Pango, a peri-urban village near the capital, Port Vila, on the central Vanuatu island of Efate, embodies specific indigenous concepts, local economic pressures and opportunities, and Christian denominational influences. In east Ambae, kinship is matrilineal and the denomination is Anglican. Pango, a village created as a consequence of the colonial incursion, has a flexible kinship system in which an earlier matrilineal system is increasingly being overtaken by more fluid, often patrilineally determined arrangements (Rawlings 1999: 81). Pango is Presbyterian.

When I was living on the island of Ambae in north Vanuatu in 1991 and 1992, weddings, in preparation or in the event, absorbed the energies of many women. In east Ambae, each wedding involves the exchange of wealth in the form of many hundreds of plaited *pandanus* textiles, most of which are made for the event by the couple's close female kin. In the past, the bride wore special *pandanus* textiles: now she wears new clothes, pinned all over with handkerchiefs, but still holds a textile over her head at certain moments. If she has access to one, the bride changes into a Western style white wedding dress for the brief church ceremony. In Pango village, weddings are now mostly held over the Christmas period, when holidays from work in town give people the opportunity to prepare and celebrate the necessary rituals. As on Ambae, Pango weddings involve the exchange of a great many textiles, but here the textiles are predominantly European cloth in the form of a specific style of dress, called an island dress. The bride wears a special white island dress to the church, one among many dresses that she puts on and off over the period of the celebration.

Why is an Ambaean bride pinned all over with handkerchiefs? Why do Pangoan brides wear a white island dress? In both places there is a complicated entanglement of indigenous ideas, missionary and other expatriate influences and available materials determining the form and use of wedding clothes. As they intersect, these factors influence clothing forms, colour and decoration, and affect the ways in which this clothing embodies wealth and status. The contrast between east Ambae and Pango helps to show how this happens.

In general, the adoption of expatriate cloth and clothing has not been discussed in relation to Melanesia. In some areas, as O'Hanlon discusses in this book, this kind of clothing is not given notable significance, although Regius does point to the significant meanings invested in contemporary women's dress in New Britain (Regius 1999). However, as has been demonstrated for the central and eastern Pacific, cloth and clothing have been used widely to embody and express a series of crucial cultural transformations (Colchester 2003). This chapter is intended to provide an ethnographically specific contribution to these developing discussions. It is based on research in east Ambae in 1991 to 1992 and 1994; and on a research project focusing on women's clothing throughout Vanuatu undertaken from 2001 to 2003.[1] Here I begin by providing some background to the

---

1   Both these research projects were developed and implemented in conjunction with the Vanuatu Cultural Centre, and in particular with Jean Tarisesei, whom I thank for all her assistance. About 20 Cultural Centre women fieldworkers have been involved in the second of these projects (see Bolton 2003a for an account of this program). I am indebted to Lenare Kalmet, Martha Yamsiu, Agnes Kaltabang and Jennifer Sope for assistance with the Pango material in this paper. The second project has been funded through the ESRC 'Clothing the Pacific' project. I thank the Economic and Social Science Research Council, and in particular my colleagues Susanne Küchler, Nicholas Thomas, Graeme Were and Chloe Colchester for their many and various contributions to my participation in this project.

introduction of cloth to Vanuatu, and to the nature of wedding rituals in east Ambae and Pango.

SOME BACKGROUND

Vanuatu is the political name for an archipelago in the south western Pacific. The archipelago lies roughly north to south over 850 kilometres of ocean to the east of northern Australia. It is a place of tremendous cultural diversity. The 200,000 people who live on the 80 or so Vanuatu islands speak 113 languages between them – and have as many different systems of knowledge and practice. Although predominantly Melanesian in character, there appears to have been ongoing contact with and influence from western Polynesia in the pre-contact era, involving invasions and settlement (Wilson 1999: 88). Before the colonial period there were trade links between many islands in the archipelago, but it had no overall unity. This lack of unity was complicated during the colonial era by the joint French and British administration: the Anglo-French Condominium of the New Hebrides, which lasted from 1906 to 1980. For the great part of that period, neither nation was much interested in the country itself, each being present mostly to protect the interests of their own nationals against the depredations of the nationals of the other.

During the 1970s the Independence movement introduced a rhetoric of cultural and political unity, based on the idea that the region's cultural diversity is grounded on a bedrock of similarity. This rhetoric was constructed in part on widely held ideas about the significance of one's place of origin. Place is a core identifier, the importance of which is now expressed in the national *lingua franca*, Bislama, in the phrase *man ples* (person of the place). This can refer to one's identity as a person from Vanuatu – a *ni-Vanuatu* – or it can refer to one's much more specific identity as belonging to an island (*man Ambae*) or to a village or hamlet (*man Pango*). The importance of belonging to one's place, narrowly to the local place, or now more broadly to the nation, is itself one of the ideas that facilitates the assertion of shared identity.

What is remembered in Vanuatu as 'the fight for Independence' had a crucial significance for the perceived ongoing relevance of local practice in the archipelago. The Independence movement argued that the diverse local practices throughout the islands are the same but a little bit different, positing unity in diversity to establish a distinct and common identity for the indigenous population against all incomers. The Bislama term used here is *kastom*. *Kastom* is sometimes translated as tradition, but it can, I think, be more accurately translated as the knowledge and practice of the place. In contemporary Vanuatu, *kastom* is a concept deployed to many ends and with many emphases, but originally it operated as one half of an opposing pair. In the colonial era there was a specific Bislama opposite to *kastom*, *skul*, meaning not just schooling but all that had been introduced, especially by missionaries. Today, *skul* is not much used, and there is no clear terminological opposite to *kastom*, except for generalities such as *fasin blong ol waetman* – expatriate ways. There remains a lingering binarism in how *kastom* is often used, expressing that inside/outside distinction. Specifically, there is no term for local developments that engage with what has been introduced. This has been the case for new institutions and positions, such as the role of chiefs, for the indigenisation of introduced ideas such as Christianity, as well as for adoptions of introduced materials, such as cloth (Bolton unpublished). One important example of this phenomenon is island dresses.

Island dresses (*aelan dres*)[2] are loose, wide dresses with a plain V neck and puff sleeves, often decorated with ribbons and lace and sometimes with two flaps attached to the dress at the hips, which are often described as wings. Since Independence, island dresses have been worn throughout the archipelago, although they are most commonly worn by central Vanuatu women. Although introduced in the context of the Presbyterian Church, they have a significantly local character. Missionaries brought a number of different dress styles to Vanuatu, which women today can still name, but now rarely make, such as *foapis*, *fulpis*, *franis fril* and *malmalkot*. By contrast, the basic structure of the island dress – the way the fabric is cut and sewn – seems to have been developed by a *ni-Vanuatu* tailor at a Presbyterian training centre on the small north Efate island of Nguna in the 1930s. The style was then introduced to the rest of the country by the wives of *ni-Vanuatu* lay teachers, trained on Nguna, who went to work in other islands.

The island dress style was most extensively adopted in central Vanuatu. In these areas, the dresses have their own local language name, and they have a remembered history of transmission that is entirely indigenous. In central Vanuatu today, women describe island dresses as *kastom dresing blong yumi* – as 'our own way of dressing' – even though they know that in fact they did have other ways of dressing before Europeans arrived. Island dresses are deeply incorporated into local practice in this part of Vanuatu; they no longer seem to be something from outside. The only way to express that is by identifying them as *kastom*. It is for this kind of reason that *kastom* is best identified, not as tradition, as practices from the past, but rather as the practices of the place.

If some adoptions become identified as *kastom*, not all do: practices and materials that have been introduced during the colonial era do not always achieve this status. In particular, wedding rituals in most parts of the country incorporate a number of practices which fall into this unidentified category. At a wedding I attended at Lovonda, east Ambae in 1994, for example, the main events of the day – the exchange of textiles and many other entirely Ambaean practices – were succeeded by a dance accompanied by mouth organ, guitar and English language songs. The dance was, someone explained to me, not *kastom* but was nevertheless something they do at weddings, and had its own Ambae language term: *volen*.

European cloth presumably appeared in the archipelago with the first explorers: de Quiros almost certainly left some on Espiritu Santo in 1606; the next recorded visitor, Bougainville, records distributing 'pieces of red cloth' in north east Ambae in 1768 (Bougainville 1967: 289, cited in Taylor unpublished).

2　Bislama spelling is still being standardised. In a previous publication (Bolton 2003b) I used the spelling *ilan dres*. I have now accepted the spelling preferred by the Vanuatu Cultural Centre: *aelan dres*.

However, Europeans only started appearing in the archipelago in any numbers after about 1820, and it was not until 1840 that planters and traders began to acquire land and settle there in any number. If traders exchanged cloth, missionaries introduced it with a moral imperative. The wearing of European cloth became a symbol of acceptance of Christianity (see Jolly 1996: 271; Lawson 1994: 91ff). The Presbyterians, who first appeared in 1848, rapidly became the dominant denomination, making converts through the south and centre of the archipelago. The Anglican Melanesian Mission worked mainly in the north of the country from 1849. Other denominations arrived later and squeezed in where they could. This regionalisation of missionary work has had a direct effect on female clothing in Vanuatu; for while the Presbyterians preferred to see their female converts in dresses, the Anglicans introduced blouses and skirts. Today, Anglican women still commonly wear skirts and T-shirts or shirts, while Presbyterians mainly wear dresses, now usually island dresses.

WEDDING DRESSES

Pre-Christian wedding rituals varied greatly through the archipelago, but there were a number of common concerns. Marriage in Vanuatu was and is generally virilocal, so that rituals emphasised the transition of the bride to a new place. They also emphasised the creation of new relationships between not just the bride and groom, but between the two groups of kin they represent. Although this was not the case everywhere, in many areas weddings involved a series of exchanges of wealth between these new kin, establishing debts and obligations that bound the two groups together in relationships of mutual interdependence.

The transition of the bride to a new place is still one of the main ritual foci of weddings on Ambae. If the big interest of the wedding for the greater number of participants is to contribute to and benefit from the exchanges of textiles that dominate the ceremony; the bride's family is equally concerned to send her to her new place well provided for and well protected. The first part of the wedding ritual takes place at the bride's hamlet, the second at the groom's. Much of what happens at the former is concerned with assisting the bride to make the transition to the latter. After the goods to be given with her have been gathered on her hamlet's central plaza – and she, the groom and certain other immediate kin have formally acknowledged them as a gift – the bride is taken aside by her close female kin.

The textiles which are exchanged at Ambae marriages are made from *pandanus* which women process and plait to produce a range of approximately 25 named textile types, each of which has specific uses and value – and each of which can be decorated in specific ways. Clothing textiles are part of this system. These textiles were formerly made using special techniques that softened the *pandanus* to make it comfortable to wear; now that textiles are only made to be worn at rituals and other special occasions, these techniques are in the process of being lost. The designs stencilled onto the surface of clothing textiles using a red vegetable dye are still known and made: they are used to mark the achieved status of the wearer. In the past, a bride was dressed in such *pandanus* textiles (*sakole*), decorated with the named designs that declared her own achieved status. This she always acquires in a ritual which takes place the day before the wedding, and which is her father's gift to ensure that she will be respected in her new home.[3]

Today an Ambae bride's kin dress her in a new skirt and blouse, pin new handkerchiefs to her clothing and rub her hair, face, hands and legs with oil. They sing to her, and feed her a last meal; then they place over her head a special plaited *pandanus* textile, a *qana hunhune*, which she holds over her head for the rest of the day as she is taken to her new home, and then formally made a person of that place. By contrast, the groom is largely indistinguishable among the other guests. Wearing a fairly ordinary shirt and trousers, he appears, somewhat sheepishly, to perform his allotted tasks in the ritual and disappears back into the throng thereafter.

However, fitted in at some point in the day's proceedings, the couple go to church to be married there also. For this, at several weddings that I attended, the couple don conventional western wedding clothing – the bride in a long white wedding dress, the groom in a suit. They are sometimes accompanied by bridesmaids in matching dresses. Often looking somewhat discomfited in these clothes, they perform the ceremony, pause for photos if someone has a camera, and then retire to change back into the clothes of the day. Usually this formal

Figure 2.1: Two couples posing for photographs with an Anglican priest after the church celebration of their marriages. Only one bride wears a white wedding dress. Narongleo, Longana, east Ambae, Vanuatu. March 1992. Photograph © Lissant Bolton.

---

3   I have described this process in more detail elsewhere (Bolton 2003a).

wedding outfit is borrowed and worn by a series of couples over time; a woman who cannot borrow such an outfit will wear a skirt and top.

Many Pango women are avid consumers of Australian and New Zealand women's magazines, bought in Port Vila: Euro-antipodean wedding practice is well known from these. However, in Pango, Western wedding dresses do not appear. Instead, women wear special island dresses for the church ceremony. These dresses are always white and are heavily decorated with white ribbons and white lace, but they retain the characteristic form of the island dress (see Figure 2.2 in the colour section). In 2003, they are made from synthetic silk; in past decades they were made from cottons and muslins. These island dress wedding dresses are a tradition that has had some duration. In Pango last year, I was shown a wedding dress from the 1970s, which a woman had carefully kept in her clothes box: she seemed slightly embarrassed to admit she had done so for sentimental reasons, to remember her own wedding. Although made in a light cotton fabric, the dress was identical in many respects to those being worn at present. In comparison to a wedding dress I bought last year for the British Museum collection, the older dress was different in small details only: the colour, cut and form of the decoration were all much the same.

As Pango weddings have been described to me (I have yet to attend one), island dresses are very important. They are used in a number of ritual contexts and are given as part of the exchanges made between the two families, along with yams, pigs and household goods. Before the wedding, a group of women belonging to the bride's kin, and a group of women belonging to the groom's kin, each makes for themselves a set of dresses, each team in a single fabric. Then each team goes into Port Vila to buy things needed for the wedding. Their distinctive and festive appearance in town signals to all long-term Vila residents that a wedding is in the offing. Island dresses also dominate the ceremony itself. The female guests all wear them. The bride does not just wear the white island dress; she wears that to church, and to go to her husband's house in the evening, but at other points in the day she wears another specially decorated island dress. When she wears the white dress, she must wear it with both a full petticoat, and a half slip, made new for her. These are usually decorated with the same lace as the dress itself, but remain unseen throughout. (See Figure 2.2 in the colour section.)

When she is brought to her husband's house, the bride brings a box of new island dresses with her, to give to his female kin; when she arrives she is herself given a series of new island dresses by her husband's family, which she puts on one after another. No other dress would be acceptable: a bride could not arrive at her new husband's house with a box full of dresses such as *malmalkot* or *franis fril*. Island dresses, in this sense, are a form of wealth, exchanged between the two kin groups, as plaited *pandanus* textiles are exchanged on Ambae.

REASONS FOR WEDDING CLOTHES

The aspect of wedding clothing that is easiest to disentangle is the form – the style of the clothing used. In both Ambae and Pango, there are accepted clothing styles that derive from missionary influence: blouses and skirts on Ambae, dresses in Pango. For Pango women, this is not just a matter of dresses, but of island dresses. Although many women enjoy wearing island dresses and take great interest in the subtle nuances of the style, there is a strong and explicit obligation to wear island dresses among central Vanuatu women. Not only is this style strongly associated with Presbyterianism, but also for these women the dresses are *kastom dresing blong yumi*, and to wear them is to assert one's identity as a woman from central Vanuatu. What is interesting to consider is how this particular introduced style achieved such importance. Why not *foapis* or *malmalkot*? The answer seems to depend on both practical and historical issues. The importance of island dresses is, at least in part, that they can be made without a pattern – the fabric is usually cut into five rectangles of varying sizes, which are then sewn together – and that they are very economical. They waste no fabric: only the material cut away to make the neck hole is discarded. These qualities facilitated the rapid dissemination of the style through rural areas. Also, loose, cool and readily adapting to every figure, they are a pleasure to wear, once one gets used to them.

Island dresses have also become connected with local practice at a number of levels. As I have discussed elsewhere, on Nguna, where island dresses were developed, they are conceptually equated with flying foxes (Bolton unpublished). Moreover, they have been adopted into local exchange networks, on Efate at least. There is a longstanding trade between peri-urban villages and north Efate in which island dresses are exchanged against plaited *pandanus* textiles, and men's shirts are exchanged against *kava*. This exchange is prescriptive: one may not exchange a dress for *kava*, or a shirt for a textile. An equivalence between European cloth and indigenous textiles in exchange occurs in many parts of the Pacific. In Vanuatu, this seems mostly to relate to indigenous clothing textiles, and especially to clothing textiles for women. On Ambae, one may substitute lengths of cloth for *sakole* – women's clothing textiles – in exchanges, but one cannot substitute it for anything else. I do not know, but consider it very likely that prior to European settlement, an Efate bride brought with her, and received from her husband's family, a number of clothing textiles, just as she now gives and receives island dresses. Island dresses are substituting for earlier clothing forms, I suggest, just as lengths of cloth can substitute for *sakole* on Ambae. There seems to have been a direct substitution.

Soon after Independence, island dresses were officially nominated as national dress for women in Vanuatu. This nomination was taken very seriously by women throughout the country. A recent innovation among central Vanuatu women has been to make island dresses in the colour of the national flag, in a patchwork of plain fabric. These are worn, usually as a uniform, by women performing or appearing in international contexts. But central Vanuatu women have taken this further by making 'flag dresses' in the colours of their provincial flag. Central Vanuatu is an administrative province called Shefa. The wearing of a Shefa flag dress is a complex assertion of place-based identity, framed in post-colonial symbols, and building upon the idea of island dresses as most specifically the *kastom dresing* of central

Vanuatu women. Given this level of identification, it is hardly surprising that Shefa women wear island dresses when they are married. Marriage is about place, about relinquishing one's own place and adopting that of one's husband and his kin. It is, I suggest, deeply important to wear clothing of the place to be married.

For Anglican women, the nomination of island dresses as national dress was also a serious matter; many Anglican women acquired island dresses to wear in the national contexts – meetings, training courses, conferences and so on – which, since Independence, they have had more opportunities to attend. A number of Anglican women have recalled for me how it was that they first acquired an island dress, and how they felt about wearing it – intrigued, but not quite comfortable. Nevertheless, on Ambae, while women may wear island dresses, especially when pregnant, they most usually appear in blouses and skirts. To wear an island dress is a matter of personal choice; since they are not made on Ambae, wearing an island dress is also a way of asserting one's connections elsewhere, or one's own experience of travel beyond the island. While the four weddings I attended don't represent an adequate sample, I doubt that one would ever see a bride on Ambae in an island dress.

Ambae women have not invested the significance into blouses and skirts that Shefa women have invested in island dresses. Their primary interest in textiles continues to be in the plaited *pandanus* textiles they make; as I have explained, a woman's status is still expressed primarily through these textiles. The textiles associated with a bride's status are the most important textiles worn at a wedding. Without that kind of strong significance attached to a specific dress type, it is not surprising that Ambae women follow Western conventions in participating in a church wedding. Pango women, by contrast, no longer make or even remember their former clothing textiles.

The second important issue, it seems to me, in what women wear to be married, is the question of colour. Both on Ambae and in Pango, the dress in which one goes to church is white. Anglican or Presbyterian missionaries in Vanuatu emphasised white as the colour for church, and especially for the sacraments. At the Anglican school, Torgil on Ambae, in the 1960s, for example, pupils had to wear white for communion, and this practice is also common among Presbyterians. Presbyterians also wear white for rituals like baptism. This use of white is a clear reference to the Biblical colour symbolism which equates white with purity; it is an obvious observation that the dressing of a bride in white emphasises both the sanctity of the ritual, and alludes, for missionaries, to the bride's ideally virginal state.

The church-based system of colour symbolism opposes white to black, and especially to black as the colour of mourning. But on Ambae, white is opposed to red, and has different symbolic associations. Ambaean plaited *pandanus* textiles are always dyed red (*memea*), today using chemical dyes stocked by trade stores on the island. Clothing textiles are never dyed a plain red but are always stencilled with patterns. The specific named patterns used on clothing textiles belong to the male public status alteration system, *huqe*, in which women participate until they are married. The opposite of red is white (*mavute*), the colour of an undyed textile. In the symbolisms of Ambaean life, white represents a capacity to absorb – people wishing to learn something important often sit on a white textile while they are taught. No east Ambaean would ever *wear* white. So wearing white to church is about observing the requirements of the church but doesn't make sense in any other way. It is not surprising that Ambaean brides get out of those white wedding dresses and back into a skirt and top, to return to the main part of the ritual.

In Bislama, and especially among women discussing island dresses, the word *kala* (colour) is often used to mean not colour, exactly, but pattern. Plain island dresses do occur but they seem to be nobody's preference, so that colour equates with pattern. Pattern and decoration are all important. However, when it comes to introduced cloth, I cannot remember that any woman ever discussed with me, as a matter of importance, or even as a matter of casual observation, the specific pattern on a dress. The colour and quality of the fabric are often discussed, the pattern never. But then there is currently no textile industry in Vanuatu. All cloth is imported, and it is imported already dyed, so that there is no way to determine the nature of the patterns. In Port Vila, where there are many trade stores supplying fabric imported from Fiji, Indonesia and Thailand, vendors do find some patterns more popular than others, although again this is partly to do with their colour qualities. In the islands, where trade stores stock a limited range, there is little opportunity to consider preferences. Patchwork, as in the flag dresses, is the only way to control pattern, and this is not currently a common strategy.

What it is possible to do is to control the details of the decoration of the dresses. Island dresses are very commonly decorated with bias binding, rickrack, ribbons and lace or at the very least with pleats folded in the fabric itself. In the period since the Second World War, it appears that some styles of decoration were specific to certain places, especially among the Port Vila peri-urban villages. A certain way of attaching lace and ribbons to the back of the bodice, for example, was distinctive to the peri-urban village of Ifira. In the past, Efate women wore a very distinctive kind of *pandanus* textile that was worn passed between the legs, and held in place at the waist by a belt. At the back, the length of the mat hanging from the belt was specially widened and fringed, so that it hung down and obscured the behind. These textiles are not well remembered on Efate, although a similar style on the island of Tongoa to the north is still recalled there. However, some information from Tongoa and my excursions into museum collections suggest to me that these textiles were plaited in patterns that were specific to kin groups, and probably, since central Vanuatu societies were to some extent hierarchical, to class. It would be consistent with practice through the archipelago if to some extent, such textiles also revealed the wearer's place. Pattern, in other words, was very probably as significant on Efate as it still is on Ambae. If the patterns on cloth cannot be controlled, then some control can be effected through decorative additions.

While this may be speculative, the importance of decoration cannot be denied. In the days when women were married wearing *pandanus* textiles, they also wore a belt, armbands and leg bands; into these were inserted small branches of sweet smelling leaves and flowers. Feathers were stuck in their hair. The right to wear each of these items had to be acquired and most had a specific meaning. These decorations are still used when women put on textiles to dance. When I asked why Ambae brides today are pinned all over with new handkerchiefs, a woman explained that they replaced the leaves and flowers. Leaves and flowers move and shimmer when they are attached to a moving body; pinned handkerchiefs and the ribbons that flow from island dresses seem to echo that aesthetic.

The dressing of the bride on Ambae is a rather tender moment. The way in which women gather around her, dress her, oil her, sing to her and feed her is explicitly a reference to the nurturing care that she will no longer receive from her kin. In the past, girls were often married before puberty; they were sent to live with their husband's mothers, to accommodate them to their new kin. The sexual relationship would be initiated later, when the girl was physically ready. The bride should be and still is carried like a baby, on the back of a close female relative, from her place to her husband's. The handkerchief pinning may also reflect something of that nurturing attention to the bride's body – a kind of caress of cloth – although this again may be unwarrantable speculation.

Figure 2.3: Claudine Tarisesei being tied onto her father's sister's back, in order to be carried to her husband's hamlet. Narongleo, Longana, east Ambae, Vanuatu. November 1994. Photograph © Lissant Bolton.

If island dresses are decorated to reflect an interest in pattern; and if the ribbons that flow from them also create the sense of movement that indigenous forms of body ornament created; the elaboration of island dresses may also reflect a concern with wrapping. As has been documented in a number of different ways, much of central Vanuatu seems to have been influenced by trade and possibly settlement from western Polynesia, prior to European settlement. In Polynesia, there was and is a widespread practice of wrapping of the body at significant moments of transition (see Gell 1993: 88–91, 183; Tcherkézoff 2003: 57; Hooper 2001). The wings on the island dresses may echo or allude to this kind of thinking, as may the insistence that the Pango bride wear both petticoat and half slip under her wedding dress; so also may the requirement that a Pango bride put on a whole series of island dresses as they are given to her by her husband's kin.

If there are aspects of clothing that relate to affect there are also aspects which relate to economics. Pango women in general are preoccupied with island dresses. As one woman observed, Pango men charge women with being like hermit crabs – always changing their house. Leslie Rabine observes of Senegal that 'in a crumbling physical, social and economic environment dress can provide a reassuring façade of illusory social stability and prosperity, a visual and sensorial shield against anxiety' (Rabine 2002: 33). Pango is not quite as economically straitened as the Senegal Rabine describes, but nevertheless the point has some potency. Elaborate dresses can present an illusion of prosperity for the wearer as for the viewer. They can also reflect a genuine prosperity, the affluence of conspicuous consumption. The addition of many ribbons and lace is an assertion of prosperity, since they have to be bought, and thus make the dress itself more costly.

At weddings on Ambae and in Pango, two kin groups give textile wealth to each other to create a series of new social relationships that support and assist the new couple. The gifts also affirm the wealth of those two groups to each other, representing a mutual display of affluence. That the bride should be dressed in those very textiles (as she was on Ambae, and still is in Pango) puts those economic realities at the very core of the ceremony. In Pango, the more elaborate the dresses the bride wears, the more evident is her family's prosperity, and the prosperity of her husband's kin.

As other chapters in this book demonstrate, clothing is often used strategically to make assertions to outsiders. It is saying nothing new to point out that clothing is also used to make assertions to others in the same group. What is interesting to me about what women wear to be married is not that this should be the case. Rather, it is the way in which more general preoccupations, concerns and aesthetics have been written into introduced fabrics; and the way in which people have worked around the limitations of introduced fabrics – the kinds of materials available – to achieve valued effects. The pinning of handkerchiefs and the wearing of island dresses are ways to address the preoccupations of the place with the materials of the present.

References

Bolton, L (2001) 'What makes *singo* different: north Vanuatu textiles and the theory of captivation' in Pinney, C and Thomas, N (eds), *Beyond Aesthetics: Art and the Technologies of Enchantment*, Oxford: Berg

Bolton, L (2003a) *Unfolding the Moon: Enacting Women's Kastom in Vanuatu*, Honolulu: University of Hawaii Press

Bolton, L (2003b) 'Gender, status and introduced clothing in Vanuatu' in Colchester, C (ed) (unpublished), *Clothing the Pacific*, Oxford: Berg

Bolton (unpublished) 'Stealing with the eye: mission dresses and the innovation of tradition in Vanuatu' in O'Hanlon, MDP and Ewart, E (eds), *Body Arts and Modernity*

Colchester, C (ed) (2003) *Clothing the Pacific*, Oxford: Berg

Gell, A (1993) *Wrapping in Images: Tattooing in Polynesia*, Oxford: Clarendon

Hooper, S (2001) 'Tribal image to divine image: reflections on Polynesian sculptures in the British Museum', William Fagg Memorial Lecture Presented at British Museum, 2 March

Jolly, M (1996) 'European perceptions of the arts of Vanuatu: engendering colonial interests' in Bonnemaison J *et al* (eds), *Arts of Vanuatu*, Bathurst: Crawford House Publishing

Lawson, B (1994) *Collected Curios: Missionary Tales from the South Seas*, Montreal: McGill University Press

Rabine, LW (2002) *The Global Circulation of African Fashion*, Oxford: Berg

Rawlings, GE (1999) 'Foundations of urbanisation: Port Vila Town and Pango village, Vanuatu' 70(1) Oceania 72–86

Regius, H (1999) *Between Catholicism and Bulu Sociality: The Visualisation of Culture in a West New Britain Society*, unpublished PhD thesis, University of Cambridge

Taylor, J (2003) *Ways of the Place: History, Cosmology and Material Culture in North Pentecost, Vanuatu*, unpublished PhD thesis, Australian National University

Tcherkézoff, T (2003) 'On cloth, gifts and nudity: regarding some European misunderstandings during early encounters in Polynesia' in Colchester, C (ed), *Clothing the Pacific*, Oxford: Berg

Wilson, M (1999) 'Bringing the art inside: a preliminary analysis of black linear rock-art from limestone caves in Erromango, Vanuatu' 70(1) Oceania 87–97

CHAPTER 3

OBJECTS OF CONVERSION: CONCERNING THE TRANSFER OF *SULU* TO FIJI

Chloe Colchester

The introduction of Christianity to the Pacific has typically been seen as having a devastating impact on the religious art of the Pacific Islands. Few indigenous art forms were to survive the initial impact of non-conformist missionary activity. In Tahiti, where the London Missionary Society (LMS) established one of its first outposts in 1797, religious arts such as dancing, miming, dramatic performance and ritual games, as well as sculpture and carving, all fell victim to missionary censure.

Both the LMS Methodists, many of whom were Evangelical Calvinists, and the Wesleyan Methodists (the two most prominent Protestant denominations active during the initial stages of the conversion of the Pacific) were heirs to the Puritan tradition: they shared an antipathy to images in institutionalised forms of divine mediation and disapproved of the arts, such as drama and dance, as a form of entertainment. Yet, when they were accused of destroying traditional art forms, the missionaries typically responded by arguing that it was the indigenous people who had taken the initiative (Gunson 1978: 189). This voluntary destruction of religious art by Pacific Islanders is surprising because it seems to have been replaced with little that could lift the mind from the physical here-and-now to another level of experience.

There was one notable exception to the general destruction of religious art and the widespread disruption of religious practices. In western Polynesia, the manufacture of indigenous clothing was not only sustained, but enjoyed an extraordinary efflorescence in the wake of missionary involvement. In Fiji, for example, mortuary rites, which involved spectacular displays and exchanges of bark cloth and other cloth wealth, superseded older religious practices involving sacrifice.

Indigenous clothing had already played an important part in missionary activity in the Pacific. The popular view that missionaries imposed European Christian clothes, such as 'Mother Hubbard' shirts and trousers, upon reluctant Pacific Islanders is highly misleading. For, although dress reform was central to the progress of the mission, reflecting the non-conformist preoccupation with sexual morality, missionaries seem to have been reluctant to encourage the indigenous population to attach too much significance to European dress.

The solution was to encourage the reform of indigenous dress. In Tahiti, missionaries promoted indigenous garments that conformed to European standards of modesty. When a few Tahitians were persuaded to accept the

Christian faith, more than 20 years after the beginning of the mission, it was suggested that they should be baptised in a traditional poncho-like garment made from bark cloth. As Charles Barff noted:

> We requested the men to get a *tiputa*, a wrapper reaching to the middle of the leg, and the women to get a *hu tiponoi*, a wrapper reaching down to the foot. In the above dress, the first 14 were baptised in 1819 … more than a 1,000 were all in the old costume, except oiling the body all over on the Sabbath. But from that day they all adopted the dress of the 14 at least on the Sabbath day, and have continued to improve in clothing from that time to the present. (Barff 1865, cited in Gunson 1978: 275)

As missionary activity was spread by Tahitian native teachers – from Tahiti and the Society Islands to other parts of the Pacific – *tiputa* went on to become associated with the foreign religion, together with the benefits that it promised. Tahitian native pioneers were expected to use their influence to break down traditional religious systems, and the reform of indigenous dress played a significant part in this. Yet the transfer of indigenous garments from one part of the Pacific to another came to reveal more about the relationship between Pacific Islanders' interpretation of Christianity and the place of indigenous clothing in indigenous religion, than about European missionaries' perceptions of dress.

Nicholas Thomas has already shown how Tahitian lay teachers, who constituted a missionary vanguard in Samoa and Tonga, tried to overcome the Samoans' reluctance to convert to Christianity and to adopt the Tahitian *tiputa* as a form of Sunday best. After five years of resistance, when the native teachers' attempts to impose these garments had largely been met with mockery and provocation, the case for adopting *tiputa* – and the foreign religion – was substantially improved when a small group of European missionaries came to visit the Tahitian missionary pioneers. As a result of this visit, *tiputa* became associated with the potential for a new kind of empowerment, as well as for the material benefits that might be expected to follow the adoption of the foreign religion. Yet precisely because this was an indigenous garment made from bark cloth, it is possible that *tiputa* could also recall the way that wrapping the body in coverings had been used traditionally to invoke divine intervention.

THE TRANSFER OF *SULU* TO FIJI

In Fiji, a different indigenous garment came to be accepted as a sign of conversion and as the standard form of Christian dress. This garment replaced local regional native dress, such as the short grass skirts called *liku* worn by women, and the white loincloths made from bark cloth called *malo*, customarily worn by men in many parts of the archipelago. It was a demure body wrap called *sulu*, a bark cloth garment that conformed to Victorian standards of modesty because it covered the legs, stretching down from the waist to the ankles.

Sulu were, like *tiputa*, a foreign form of indigenous dress. For, although body wraps made from lengths of calico went on to become a standard form of Christian attire in many parts of the Pacific, the bark cloth *sulu* introduced to Fiji was derived from a traditional Tongan garment. A *sulu* (called *vala* in Tonga) consisted of a rectangular piece of bark cloth stained ochre (known either as *gatuvakatoga*, *gatu* or *tutu* in Fiji). It was fastened in place with another bark cloth sash. In Tonga, this way of wearing bark cloth seems to have been reserved for people of high rank, and was typically worn on festive occasions (Kooijman 1972: 337).

Why did *sulu* come to substitute like *tiputa*, and what did this substitution involve? The challenge of this chapter is to see what the transfer of *sulu* to Fiji can reveal about the cumulative impact of missionary activity in the Pacific, and of the changing nature of religious experience promoted by rival missionary factions. For the introduction of this Tongan garment to Fiji seems to have coincided with a period when Wesleyan missionaries, who had overtaken the LMS as the dominant missionary faction in Tonga, began to rely heavily on the support of Tongan native preachers for their missions in Fiji.

The stories of the introduction of *tiputa* to Samoa and of bark cloth *sulu* to Fiji share many features in common. Yet there is no precedent, as far as I know, for the scale of the production of *gatu* in Fiji, which accompanied the introduction of *sulu* to the islands. In time, this would involve the establishment of new women's organisations for Tongan bark cloth production in Lau, Cakaudrove, Macuata, Bua, Lomaiviti, and across a substantial swathe of the Fijian archipelago. The scale of this activity is significant, and cannot simply be explained by the lack of European clothes, for the use of *sulu* made from *gatu* in indigenous ritual activity persisted long after European clothing became readily available.

The prominent place of *gatu* in Fijian ritual activity continues in Fiji today, although the manufacture of *gatu* went into decline in 1971 when Fiji claimed independence from British colonial rule. Nevertheless, despite the current climate of heightened ethnic nationalism in Fiji, *gatu* continues to be strongly linked to the lifecycle celebrations that are clearly associated with conversion to Christianity. For example, in Eastern Fiji, couples presenting their child for baptism will often hand it over to the minister whilst standing on a length of *gatu*. Whilst doing fieldwork on Vanua Levu, I saw photos of Tongan-style bark cloth, embellished with an image of the cross, covering the coffin of a chief. Fijians acquire *gatu* from Tonga (at great expense) to make shrouds for the dead. Long lengths of *gatu* are also spectacularly displayed and exchanged at chiefly mortuary rites (*vakataraisulu*) – an example of the way that *gatu* retains a prominent role in political rituals, which, at first sight would seem to have little obvious connection to Christianity.

THE ART OF INVOKING *MANA*

So far in this chapter, I have been building up a picture of the way in which certain bark cloth garments gained new significance during the initial phases of missionary activity in the Pacific. I have suggested that *sulu* became important because they could mediate different cultural perceptions: they were Christian clothes but they were also a kind of bark cloth which was displayed, paraded and

Figure 3.1: *Gatuvakatoga* prepared on the island of Moce for a *vakataraisulu* ceremony. Photograph by Simon Kooijman, © Rijksmuseum Volkenkunde Leiden.

exchanged in the novel contexts of Fijian lifecycle ceremonies. I now want to extend my analysis by suggesting that the processes of applying decorative patterns to *gatu* provide a unique insight into bark cloth's mediatory role; that is, into why *sulu* evoked associations between abandoned aspects of Polynesian religious practice and foreign Christian dress.

Perhaps it is inappropriate to speak of *gatu* patterns as 'decoration' since this suggests that imagery is superfluous to the 'function' of these artefacts. However, it should be noted that the mundane, domestic settings in which *gatu* is made today have meant that cloth treatment procedures are often perceived as a craft, rather than as a ritual process which is capable of altering the religious status of this fabric by rendering it *mana* or effective.

Let us look at two examples: the techniques of *gatu* decoration found on the small Lauan island of Moce in the late 1970s, as described by Simon Kooijman (Kooijman 1976); and the consecration of wrappings at the Oro cult in late 18th century Tahiti, as described by Alain Babadzan (Babadzan 2003). There are, of course, gulfs in space, time and historical experience between these two episodes, and I should emphasise that the connections that I draw between them are mine alone. Yet the treatment that *gatu* and wrappings undergo in order to alter their religious status have many striking affinities that merit comparison.[1]

---

1   See Küchler 2003 for a similar argument regarding the development of Tivaevae pattern in the Cook Islands.

Consider the various physical and ritual treatments that red feathers underwent in order to alter their religious status. They were carried to a sacred locus by a procession of priests and sacrifices were performed. Then the gods were invoked as the feathers were wrapped to the trunk of a staff-god, bound with layers of bark cloth and lashed into place with coir twine. After a significant period of time had elapsed, a second rite took place: the coir rope was unravelled, the bark cloth wrappings were removed and the feathers, now rendered potent (*tapu*), were distributed to members of the chiefly hierarchy. This regulated distribution of magically efficacious feathers affirmed the standing of the chiefly hierarchy. Why was it believed that this treatment would render the feathers effective (*tapu*)? Babadzan's brilliant analysis suggests that the manipulation of the staff-gods' wrappings of coir, feathers and cloth were a means of elaborating a series of analogies between the treatment of images, the exhumation and extraction of chiefly relics at chiefly mortuary rites, and beliefs regarding the creative transformation of ancestral substance (Babadzan 2003).

Now let us turn to Simon Kooijman's observations of the treatment of *gatu* on the island of Moce. His detailed description shows how a team of women prepare a substantial length of bark cloth that is laid – section by section – over a long length of wood called a *papa* (sometimes made from the disused outrigger of a canoe). In Lau, this length of wood is typically bound with relief images (*kupeti*), fishing net and coir binding. The superimposed cloth is rubbed firmly with a mixture of ochre and mangrove sap to produce a design on the surface of the fabric. This technique is reminiscent of making a brass rubbing and produces an interesting effect – giving the impression that the design has seeped to the surface, rather than being imposed externally. The cloth is then presented and exchanged and speeches are made (Kooijman 1972).

Figure 3.2: Women preparing a *papa* with fishing net and *kupeti* images on the Island of Moce. Photograph by Simon Kooijman, © Rijksmuseum Volkenkunde Leiden.

In contemporary Lau, as in contemporary Tonga, the relief images used to pattern cloth are often figurative, and the designs are highlighted with black lines. Furthermore, the design sections (*lalaga*) are typically numbered along the selvages of the cloth: three innovations that indicate, perhaps, how *gatu* has come to resemble foreign, factory-made fabric. For it is notable that the oldest examples of *gatu* held in museum collections, such as the sample collected by Joseph Rheinhold Forster in 1773[2] do not feature relief images of this sort, but are simply impressions of coir binding.

Babadzan's descriptions of the way objects are treated to secure divine intervention contribute a new dimension to the existing anthropological literature on Polynesian beliefs regarding the nature of *mana*. As Bradd Shore notes in his seminal essay on the subject, attempts to describe *mana* have hitherto tended to emphasise its abstract nature or its specific manifestations or *effects* – as opposed to the means of invoking it. Hence *mana* has been interpreted as 'luck', 'magical efficacy', 'creative potency' or as an 'activity principle in nature' which produces physical benefits, such as rainfall, a good crop harvest, the relief of sickness or improved prosperity (Shore 1989: 138). One marked exception, which anticipates Babadzan's study, is Raymond Firth's empirical study of *mana* in Tikopia. This indicated that a range of 'physical activities' such as dancing and canoe carving could serve to 'give a stimulus to the activity of nature ... using the theme of appeal to the gods as a medium of expression' (Firth 1940: 498).

It has long been recognised that chiefs in western Polynesia played a central mediatory role in securing ancestral *mana* and the prosperity of the land and people. Nevertheless, the place of exchange objects in such mediation has not always been made explicit; for as well as attesting to the spiritual condition of the chiefs or the people, the failure of a chief's *mana* was also interpreted as a failure of the votive art used to secure it. AM Hocart was interested in the way that historical shifts in the authority of different Fijian chiefly lineages were recorded by chiefly ceremonial titles that referred to cloth substitution. Thus, certain chiefs carried the title *na malo sivo* (literally, 'the abdicated [bark] cloth') and others *na masi vou* ('the new [bark] cloth').[3] These ceremonial titles indicate that prolonged periods of misfortune were not merely interpreted as a failure of a chief's *mana*, but as a failure of his cloth, and of his means of invoking it. As one of Hocart's informants specified: 'In Ndreketi in times of scarcity, they appoint a new cloth, a receiver of feasts ... A good chief is a good cloth under whom the bananas will ripen and everything will be plentiful' (Hocart 1952: 19).

OBJECTIONS TO CONVERSION

Beliefs regarding *mana* may therefore account for a certain pragmatism characteristic of Polynesian ritual politics during the period of conversion; and

---

2   Pitt Rivers Collections number 1886.1.1239.
3   Different types of bark cloth have been produced in Fiji. Cloths called *masikesa* (literally, 'the rubbed cloth') are distinctively patterned with intricate stencil patterns, and seem to have been substituted for different cloths called *malo*.

may explain why new cloths such as *gatu* were rapidly taken up when it was believed that a chief's *mana* had failed. Yet the missionaries' encounter with Fijian chiefs also gave rise to a discourse about religious difference, which slowed the conversion of the islands.

In Fiji, the relative poverty of the Wesleyan missionaries, their lack of generosity and their ambivalent relationship with Pacific traders, meant that they failed to advertise the immediate practical or material benefits that a chief could expect from conversion to Christianity. The records of the Wesleyan missionaries Thomas Williams and Richard Burdsall Lyth, who launched the ill-starred second mission station at Somosomo, refer to the infrequent visits of the trading boats. Their daybooks are full of moral outrage regarding the 'begging' or the 'theft' of their few possessions by members of the Somosomo nobility (attitudes that must have failed to endear them to the local population given the importance attributed to chiefly generosity).

However, Wesleyan and Fijian beliefs regarding the nature of divine intervention had certain things in common. For the suggestion that some spiritual condition was proven by the wellbeing and prosperity of the people concerned did not merely conform to Polynesian rhetoric, but also to the Wesleyan's view of divine agency being directly involved in the affairs of men. Indeed, Waterhouse's description of the turbulent events leading up to the conversion of the paramount chief of Bau, Ratu Cakobau, makes it plain that, in his view at least, the mission to Fiji came close to a standstill due to the missionaries' inability to demonstrate the superior efficacy of their God:

> Somosomo was their difficulty. Missionaries had laboured in that region for eight dreary years, but the opposition of the chiefs had compelled the half worn-out brethren to direct their labour to other channels. (Waterhouse 1866: 254)

Not long after the exhausted missionaries had abandoned the Somosomo mission, the Tui Cakau struck up a relationship with a trader who proved that he could secure material benefits independently of them:

> The king [of Somosomo] had secured the friendship of a merchant, William Owen esq … This gentleman, an old South Australian colonist, had commenced trading operations in that locality after a long dearth of vessels, and the people were thus enriched with their much-prized English muskets and British manufactures of all sorts. Proud of this change in their circumstances, the title Deliverer or Exalter of Somosomo was bestowed on Mr Owen by the chiefs. There was more in this circumstance than a stranger might suppose; for the old heathen king meant to declare by it his defiance of that God whose messengers he had despised. The city politicians, and Thakombau himself, began to think that Somosomo had rejected Christianity, without any degree of punishment being visibly attached to the present generation. (Waterhouse 1866: 254–55)

Six years later, 'no adversity had befallen the forsaken city' (Waterhouse 1866: 254). The Wesleyans' impatience stemmed from the fact that they believed that divine judgment was not reserved for some later date but was imminent.

What was the basis of the Tui Cakau's objection? The journal of Richard Burdsall Lyth, a doctor and Wesleyan missionary, contains an account of a dramatic incident that took place between the missionary and the paramount chief. It shows that, even during the very early stages of the mission to Fiji (that is, *before* the benefits of conversion could be put to the test), the encounter between missionaries and Fijian chiefs had begun to give rise to a discourse concerning the nature of religious difference.

Having heard that the Tui Cakau was suffering from a pain in his mouth, the doctor had decided to use the relative privacy of a medical visit in order to raise the issue of conversion:

> I thought it best to go to see him, that I might ascertain his complaint. I found him laid upon his mat and having enquired about his mouth, thought it was a favourable opportunity to speak to him about his soul ... So I spoke to him as faithfully and affectionately as I could – indeed my heart yearned over him. But he could not bear it. And interrupting me he said: 'Is Jehovah the God of the bad? As for you Englishmen you are liars – did I think that the Thakaundrove people would *lotu* [that is, convert]? No, they are a land of chiefs. Jehovah is only the God of heaven – but they are chiefs and their gods have to do with earth and *Bulu* [the place of the departed spirits]. I hate you for what you have now said.' I told him not to be angry, that what I said was true. He said I should be killed. He would kill me just now – and would Jehovah save me? I said I thought he would – on which he rose up – seized both my wrists and ordered his wife to club me. She prayed him to forbear but he ordered her to bring him his club. Seeing that she would not do as he bid her he let hold with his left hand and was about to strike me when she sprang in between us. (Lyth 1844: 154)

The passage indicates that the Tui Cakau's outrage was twofold: it concerned the missionary's attempts to bypass the chief's mediatory role, as well as the spiritual (as opposed to the earthly) nature of divine agency that the missionary was invoking for a cure. In other words, the paramount was not merely concerned with the material benefits to be secured from conversion so much as with the nature of divine mediation involved and the place of the chiefs in securing it.

Joseph Waterhouse's account suggests that the conversion of the Bauan paramount in 1854, which prompted the mass conversion of many different vassal states in Fiji, was motivated by many different factors, including the Tui Cakau's assassination, as well as the Bauan's defeat in battle against other rival chiefly factions. According to him, a letter from the King of Tonga arrived at a fortuitous moment, because 'it presented an opportunity of altering the national religion with credit to himself' (Waterhouse 1866).

Descriptions of the conversion of Cakobau suggests that Tongan influence also extended to the kinds of Christian clothes that were adopted. Waterhouse's account of the Bauan people's first service of Christian worship makes it plain that conversion was accompanied by a marked change in the dress of both the chiefs and the people:

> It was then resolved that the religion of Christ should be substituted for the vain traditions received from their fathers. Bales of native calicoes were opened, divided and distributed among those who wished to clothe themselves ... The change in the people was very striking. All had clean faces and were suitably clad ... and previous to the commencement of worship, the chiefs respectfully removed their snow white turbans ... Next day the temples were spoiled of their ornaments ... 'His new

religion shall not save Thakombau,' exclaimed some. 'It is only a fresh scheme to gain time; and when he recovers his position he will throw off his dress.' (Waterhouse 1866: 258–61)

Although Waterhouse's reference to 'native calicoes' does not specify that Tongan *gatu* was the 'suitable' clothing assumed for this service, this is suggested by other sources. Captain Denham's portrait of Cakobau, painted during HMS Herald's survey of the Fiji islands in 1854, portrays the paramount chief dressed in an ochre-coloured *sulu* made from *gatu*.

Writing in 1917, the Fijian ethnographer, Ratu Deve Tonganivalu commented:

Tutu: At the time when Christianity reached Fiji, they were used for clothing: but they are not much used for clothing nowadays, as cloth from abroad is used; they are still used as dresses in great gatherings and at weddings and they are worn by the native ministers when they go up for ordination. (Toganivalu 1917: 4)

OBJECTS OF CONVERSION

What was the significance of Ratu Cakobau assuming the new dress of the new religion? It is not my intention here to speculate upon the place of *gatu sulu* in the Tongan imperialist expansion in Fiji; though it should be noted that Berthold Seemann, among many other writers, believed that Tongan expansion capitalised on missionary activity (Seemann 1862).

Instead, I want to sustain the approach that I have adopted so far in examining the mediatory role of bark cloth. With this in mind I would like to draw the reader's attention to the Tongans' experience of conversion, inspired by Wesleyan missionaries, which immediately anticipated the transfer of *sulu* to Fiji.

Between 1830 and 1850, prior to the introduction of *sulu* to Fiji, Tonga had witnessed an extraordinary period of mass conversion, or Christian revival. Most non-conformist missionaries were evangelical – meaning that the essential religious experience that had fired them with holy zeal was the experience of conversion as a 'new birth'. Yet the attitudes of different non-conformist denominations as to the means of achieving spiritual rebirth differed significantly. For many members of the LMS, being 'born again of the spirit' was essentially a private experience, and though many of them hoped to win the hearts of Islanders through preaching the good news of Christian salvation, at least as much emphasis was placed on the civilising mission, on education and the promotion of parish life. The LMS missionaries' promotion of bark cloth ponchos (*tiputa*) as a form of 'Sunday best' was entirely in keeping with this approach.

By contrast, the Wesleyan mission in Tonga came to be associated with highly emotional Pentecostal revivals. These were occasions where the experience of rebirth, ostensibly inspired by the direct intervention of the Holy Spirit, became a mass phenomenon. Revivals often occurred in communal settings, typically at emotionally charged prayer meetings, which lasted throughout the night. Yet even by Wesleyan standards, the scale of the revivals that took place in Tonga between 1830 and 1850 was extraordinary – and its value was debated uneasily in missionary circles.

The first mass revival began in Vava'u in 1834, the year before the Wesleyan mission was extended to Lakeba in Fiji. Although the role of the revivalist preacher, Peter Turner, was undoubtedly influential, the revival was triggered by the emotional outburst of a Tongan native preacher, who later played a leading role in the mission to Fiji. I am citing Neil Gunson's account, which is based on the journal entries of the Wesleyan missionary David Cargill, because it details the experiential effects of 'being born' again in some detail:

> On 27 June 1834 Joel Bulu was 'powerfully wrought upon' at a love feast or testimony meeting. He 'wept aloud and fell exhausted on the floor'. Whilst in this swoon the Tongan preacher thought that a great light shone about him. This was the prelude to the revival … In the chapels the people became as 'dead persons'. They 'swooned away by complete exhaustion of body and the overwhelming manifestation of saving power'. Scores were carried out of the various chapels. Schools had to be suspended. On 29 July 1834, Turner wrote jubilantly that 'more than a 1,000 souls had been saved within the preceding five days'. (Gunson 1978: 233)

The fire of revival spread rapidly to Lifuka. Here the missionary James Watkin noted that: 'Chiefs are not ashamed to be seen weeping for their sins … the blind and the lame and some who are far from well crawl to the chapel that they may receive the blessing of forgiveness and a new nature' (cited in Gunson 1978: 234).

As Gunson notes, it seems that King George Tupou, who had already witnessed the first revival in Vava'u, appears to have had a hand in spreading the revival to Ha'apai and Tongatapu in 1835.

OBJECTS AND CONVERSION

I have argued that the nature of the religious experience involved in Wesleyan revivalism was distinct from the experience of Christian conversion promoted by the LMS. In this respect it is interesting to observe that the transfer of *sulu* and *gatu* to Fiji seems to have either coincided with, or else to have prompted, the introduction of a new chiefly mortuary complex to the islands, which replaced those older mortuary practices involving sacrifice that had met with missionary disapproval. This was the *vakataraisulu* ceremony.

Hocart was told about this chiefly mortuary rite, typically held a significant time after the burial of a chief, in about 1910. He was told that 'the name *vakataraisulu* was modern, and that it came from the West in Christian times and of old they had only a "net of the dead" or "net of death"' (Hocart 1929: 329). The phrase 'Christian times' presumably refers to the era of Cakobau's conversion in 1854; and since Hocart was stationed in Lakeba at the time, 'the West' can only mean Tonga.

The name *vakataraisulu* (literally, 'the permitting of clothing') has sometimes been interpreted as meaning the lifting of mourning and the resumption of ordinary (colourful) dress (Hooper 2001: 311). Certainly in contemporary Fiji, the lengths of *gatu* that are presented at these ceremonies are typically supplemented by serpentine lengths of floral cottons, which are subsequently cut up and worn by the participants at the rite. Thus, on one level, the greater emphasis upon clothing at mortuary rites may have been a reaction to the newly introduced Victorian custom of honouring the dead by going into mourning – that is, wearing black clothing – which either supplemented, or was a substitution for, older indigenous mourning practices.

As Stephen Hooper has argued in a recent paper, one feature of the mortuary rite that seems to have been temporarily suppressed during the eras of intensive missionary and colonial involvement was the practice of making a 'net of the dead' or *lawa ni mate* (Hooper 2001). These were memorial images made from coir rope whose appearance strikingly resembled the staff-gods of central and eastern Polynesia that had attracted the disfavour of the LMS missionaries.

Yet elsewhere Hocart's observations of the place of clothing in the *vakataraisulu* ceremony imply that, at least in 1910, *gatu* was still a means of achieving an important association between the experience of Christian revival or rebirth and older religious practices.

At this period it was still usual for girls and boys to run naked up until adolescence. Hocart noted that it was at the mortuary rites of chiefs that young teenage boys assumed lawful Christian clothing for the first time:

> It is as *iloloku* [an act of sacrifice] that all the little children put on clothes for the first time at the death of a chief. *It is clear that the Fijian mind associates the clothing of the dead with a boy's first assumption of clothes* ... The fictitious death of the mourners may explain 1 Corinthians xv: 29: 'Else what shall they do which are baptised for the dead if the dead rise not at all? Why are they then baptised for the dead?' Evidently the baptism of kinsmen was supposed to help the dead to resurrection by the identification of the living with the dead ... [But] the death ritual raises the dead to a higher rank than all the preceding consecrations; therefore the living humble themselves before him as vassals before the king. (Hocart 1931: 24, emphasis added)

Hocart is known to have followed his informants' statements as closely as possible, which may account for the very credible juxtaposition of biblical references and references to Fijian tradition contained here. His interpretation of the first assumption of clothes as a form of baptism or rebirth is supported by the fact that the verb 'to dress', *vakaisulu*, also means 'to convert'. Yet it is important to emphasise the range of associations that the presentation of *sulu* at these ceremonies had in 1910. The term *iloloku* refers to the practice of presenting human sacrifices – and later finger sacrifice – to honour the burial of a chief. This suggests that, at least in 1910, bark cloth continued to evoke recollections of practices of sacrifice, which had possibly been abolished within living memory.

How might the mortuary rites of chiefs have become associated with both the boy's first assumption of clothes and the experience of Christian revival or rebirth? Kooijman's photographs of the preparation of *gatu* and food for a *vakataraisulu* ceremony are particularly revealing here: they enable one to see that a number of separate and apparently discrete activities presaging the ceremonial exchange *per se*, may also be perceived as an integrated ritual sequence, culminating in the presentation and distribution of cloth. I suggest that by looking at these diverse activities *as a sequence*, and by paying attention to the way in which cloth is prepared and handled, it is possible to gain insight into the way that *gatu* could marry the experience of rebirth to the means of securing *mana*. (See Figure 3.3 in the colour section.)

Looking at the photographs one can begin to trace a series of visual analogies between discrete activities. For example, there is a formal correspondence between the way that women dress the grave of the deceased chief by covering it with new lengths of bark cloth, and the way that lengths of prepared bark cloth are decorated by applying the cloth to a wooden stave that has been bound with netting and pattern boards.[4] In a similar way, there is a formal analogy between the way that the new lengths of bark cloth placed on top of the grave are held in place with oiled stones, and the way that packets of food wrapped in leaves are placed on top of heated stones in earth ovens. Yet without some awareness of the analogies linking these preliminary activities, the *vakataraisulu* ceremony, involving as it does the dramatic presentation and distribution of the finished clothing and food, becomes little more than a sequence of exchange – the transfer of 'gifts' from one group to another.

The argument presented above is necessarily speculative. I have attempted to demonstrate that the association between the clothing of the dead chief with a boy's first assumption of clothes is highly arresting given the historical circumstances of the transfer of *sulu* and the *vakataraisulu* ceremony to Fiji. However, if the experience of mass revival in Tonga did prompt a degree of ritual change, it failed to achieve the reformation or cultural rupture envisioned by the missionaries. Although the ritual use of *gatu* may have been innovatory, its use in divine mediation was both conservative and politically expedient. Christian converts have often been tempted to set Christ up as a kind of super-king, whose power devolves upon earthly rulers. The *vakataraisulu* ceremony provides an instance of the way in which chiefs claimed to be privileged mediators of divine authority; for the interpretation of the rebirth of Christian converts through the medium of bark cloth preserved the role of the chiefs and their cloths as mediators in the transfer of *mana*, just as it incorporated the converts not merely into the mystical body of Christ but into a new body politic.

CONCLUSION

Bark cloth is not a relic, and I have suggested that it could only ever become effective through the elaboration of its associations with skin at chiefly mortuary rites. Without this associative logic, bark cloth is, as it were, only cloth. This is why it is important that *gatu* are still produced in mortuary contexts. Yet *gatu* are also made in other contexts, and it is to the impact of the changing nature of context

---

4   See Feeley-Harnik 1991 for a similar interpretation of the changing morphology and pace of Saklava burial practices in post-colonial Madagascar.

that I would like to draw the reader's attention in my concluding remarks. For if *gatu* become effective by virtue of the power of association, one must also ask if their effectiveness can be deflected and altered in changed circumstances.

In contemporary Fiji it is difficult to 'see' the visual and material analogies that I have described above. One reason for this is that all ritual activity involves a gendered division of labour, which means that men are barred from witnessing the preparation of cloth, whilst women are proscribed from witnessing the preparation of earth ovens in which *taro* and freshly slaughtered pigs are baked. Thus, interested observers are typically asked to witness either the men's or the women's activities – but are rarely encouraged to see both.

This difficulty may stem from certain Protestant assumptions regarding the nature of ritual performance and of the way that cloth is 'used' in it. It has been argued elsewhere (Toren 1999) that the Fijian concept of ritual activity, which is either termed *cakacakavakavanu* or *cakacakavuvale* (literally, 'work in the manner of the land' or 'work in the manner of the household ancestors') is far more pervasive, more all-embracing than conventional Western definitions of the terms 'ritual' or 'ceremony' would allow. Toren has shown that a range of seemingly quotidian activities, such as the way people sit at mealtimes or gather to drink *kava*, can be revealed as having a ritual aspect.

Such difficulties could be interpreted as evidence of a clever form of resistance, in which converts gain the ability to see themselves through the eyes of 'the Other'. In this interpretation, the slow performance of discrete, ritualised tasks shows how *sulu* are 'protective' in the sense of enabling island converts to sustain ancestral imagery whilst maintaining an outward show of moral conformity. However, the domestic settings of *gatu* production, the development of church-based women's associations for the manufacture of bark cloth, and the increasingly visible similarities between the appearance of bark cloth and imported island prints, are each instances of the way that the treatment of cloth has altered in ways that can no longer be described as sacred or empowering in the traditional sense. On the last evening of my fieldwork in Fiji, the man who was the local guardian of ceremonial valuables asked me how my research into Fijian bark cloth had gone. I expressed regret that I had not asked more questions about *mana*. He looked concerned: 'That is a *very* important subject', he said, and then added 'but *mana* is growing weaker'. I found the remark puzzling and was frustrated that circumstances meant that it was difficult for me to ask more. In this chapter I have attempted to investigate what his comment might have meant.

References

Babadzan, A (2003) 'The gods stripped bare' in Colchester, C (ed), *Clothing the Pacific*, Oxford: Berg

Colchester, C (1999) *Bark Cloth and Endogamous Reproduction in Natewa, Fiji*, unpublished PhD thesis, University College London

Feeley-Harnik, G (1991) *A Green Estate: Restoring Independence in Madagascar*, Washington: Smithsonian Institution

Firth, R (1940) 'An analysis of *mana*: an empirical approach' 49(4) Journal of the Polynesian Society 483–510

Freedberg, D (1989) *The Power of Images Studies in the History and Theory of Response*, Chicago: University of Chicago Press

Gunson, N (1978) *Messengers of Grace: Evangelical Missionaries in the South Seas 1797–1860*, Melbourne: Oxford University Press

Hocart, AM (1929) 'Coronation and marriage' 29 Man 104–05

Hocart, AM (1931) 'Death customs' in *Encyclopaedia of the Social Sciences*, New York: Macmillan

Hocart, AM (1952) *The Northern States of Fiji*, London: Royal Anthropological Institute Occasional Publications, No 11

Hooper, S (2001) 'Memorial images of Eastern Fiji: materials, metaphors and meanings' in Herle, A *et al* (eds), *Pacific Art: Persistence Change and Meaning*, Honolulu: University of Hawaii Press

Kooijman, S (1972) '*Tapa* in Polynesia', Bernice P Bishop Museum Bulletin 234, Honolulu: Bishop Museum Press

Kooijman, S (1976) *Tapa on Moce Island Fiji*, Leiden: EJ Brill

Küchler, S (2003) 'The Poncho and the quilt: material Christianity in the Cook Islands' in Colchester, C (ed), *Clothing the Pacific*, Oxford: Berg

Lyth, RB (1836–50) *Day Books*, Vols 1–4, The Mitchell Library, Sydney, Australia, B53–B536

Seemann, BC (1862) *Viti: An Account of a Government Mission to the Vitian or Fijian Islands, in the Years 1860–61*, Cambridge: Macmillan

Shore, B (1989) '*Mana* and *tapu*' in Howard, A and Borofsky, R (eds), *Developments in Polynesian Ethnology*, Honolulu: University of Hawaii Press

Thomas, N (2003) 'The case of the misplaced ponchos: speculations concerning the history of cloth in Polynesia' 4(1) Journal of Material Culture 5–20

Tonganivalu, D (1917) 'Ai yau kei na yaya vakaviti', *Transactions of the Fijian Society 1917*, Suva: The Fiji Society

Toren, C (1999) *Mind, Materiality and History*, London: Routledge

Waterhouse, J (1866) [1978] *The King and the People of Fiji: Containing a Life of Thakombau ... Previous to the Great Religious Transformation in 1854*, New York: AMS Press

CHAPTER 4

ELITE CLOTHING AND THE SOCIAL FABRIC OF PRE-COLONIAL TAHITI

Anne D'Alleva

In 1830, the Belgian trader Jacques-Antoine Moerenhout attended an assembly of high-ranking titleholders held by Queen Pomare in Papeete, Tahiti. Curiously, his attention seems to have been attracted as much by the wardrobes on display as by the political discourse:

> Went to the queen's palace where after a rather long wait the doors of an office were opened and the queen, her mother, and her aunt presented themselves, with very pretty hats and dressed in European fashion. What barbarism, and how could one engage these poor people to martyrise themselves so? Gentle and even elegant in her manners and in her bearing when she wore her national costume, [Queen Pomare] had now a bored air, gauche; she walked badly, raising her feet as if her shoes, which were nevertheless light … had weighted several pounds.
>
> After dinner the meeting was resumed, but the assembly no longer had for its subject the subscriptions in favour of the missionary society. It was about political questions or other matters having a direct bearing on the general interests of the island. The queen came there then in national dress, but what is more, in the ancient costume. Around her waist she had a piece of beautiful Indian [used here in the sense of 'native'] cloth which fell below her knees in the form of a skirt, and above a blouse gathered at the collar, with a collaret, and descending almost to her knees in the Chinese manner. This garment, which does not cling at all to the body, is very decent and is even better than any other to show off the form to advantage. (Moerenhout 1993: 115–16, 117–18)

Moerenhout's provocative description of Queen Pomare's costumes on this occasion serves to introduce some of the questions I have about Tahitian clothing in the 1820s and 1830s. This was 20 years or so after Queen Pomare's father, Pomare II, made an alliance with evangelical English missionaries that helped him to consolidate his position as *ari'i rahi maro 'ura*, the highest-ranking titleholder, able to wear the red feather girdle unchallenged. I am particularly interested in the complex and sometimes uneasy imbrication of European clothing and decorated Tahitian bark cloth clothing; most importantly the *ahu fara*, a shawl or cape, and the *tiputa*, a poncho-like tunic, both of which were made and worn by the elite. It seems to me that the hybrid wardrobes of the Tahitian elite, as designed and worn, have much to tell us about the ways that they negotiated new and old forms of political and social power at this time. (See Figure 4.1 in the colour section.)

Moerenhout, to my mind, certainly was not 'wrong,' then, to have been so fascinated by Tahitian clothing. I will argue here that elite clothing was at the nexus of interactions within and across gender; within and across class; and, perhaps most strikingly, within and across culture in Tahiti – and in the rest of the Society Islands archipelago – at this time. As the ethnographic accounts make clear, clothing, whether Tahitian or European in origin, was used by elite Tahitians to assert political power, social status, religion, wealth, artistic skill, taste, connection with the present and connection with the past. Take, for example, the explorer Otto von Kotzebue's description of the trade in clothing in Tahiti in the mid-1820s, which clearly shows that many such values are at stake, despite the writer's derisive tone:

> The high value which they set on clothes of our manufacture has already been remarked; they are more proud of possessing them than are our ladies of diamonds and Persian shawls, or our gentlemen of stars and orders. As they know nothing of our fashions, they pay no sort of attention to the cut, and even age and wear do not much diminish their estimation of their attire; a ripped out seam, or a hole, is no drawback in the elegance of the article. These clothes, which are brought to Tahaiti by merchant ships, are purchased at a rag market, and sold here at an enormous profit. The Tahaitian therefore, finding a complete suit of clothes very expensive, contents himself with a single garment; whoever can obtain an English military coat, or even a plain one, goes about with the rest of his body naked, except the universally-worn girdle; the happy owner of a waist coast or a pair of trowsers, thinks his wardrobe amply furnished ... Let any one imagine such an assembly [at church] perfectly satisfied of the propriety of their costume, and wearing, to complete the comic effect, a most ultra serious expression of countenance, and he will easily believe that it was impossible for me to be very devout in their presence. The attire of the females, though not quite so absurd, was by no means picturesque; some wore white, or striped men's shirts, which did not conceal their knees, and others were wrapped in sheets. Their hair was cut quite close to the roots, according to a fashion introduced by the Missionaries, and their heads covered by little European chip hats of a most tasteless form, and decorated with ribbons and flowers, made in Tahaiti. But the most valuable article of dress was a coloured gown, an indubitable sign of the possessor's opulence, and the object of her unbounded vanity. (von Kotzebue 1830: 155–57)

If, as Annette Weiner pointed out, the weaving or felting of cloth can symbolise the binding together of social relations, then I think we can also say that the cutting and forming of cloth into clothing, and the wearing of that clothing, can both symbolise the shaping of social relations as well as directly affect these social relations (Weiner 1989: 33). Clothing can reveal and conceal; it can declare alliance or independence; it can homogenise and it can distinguish human agents in society.

To indicate the powers exercised by cloth, and by extension, clothing, in late 18th and early 19th century Tahiti, we have only to look at the story of the god Tane's birth, as recited for the missionary JM Orsmond in 1823 by two Ra'iatean priests. At the beginning of the story, Tane is as yet unformed:

> O, shapeless, O shapeless! No face, no head, no nose, no ears, no mouth, no neck, no back, no chest, no ribs, no abdomen, no umbilicus, no thighs, no buttocks, no knees, no legs, no sole of the foot! O, what growth is this little child! O shapeless, O shapeless nothing! (Henry 1928: 364)

Figure 4.2: Jules Lejeune, *Costumes de l'Ile Taïti*, 1823. The standing female figure in the centre wears a bonnet of the type described by Moerenhout. *Service historique de la Marine,* Vincennes (SH 356, 29).

In the story, two parties of artisans or *tahu'a* attempt to give form to the child with their adzes, but fear overcomes them and they flee. Finally the god Ta'aroa intervenes:

> Then Ta'aroa caused skins to grow for the child, to give him qualities, to make him a great god [*atua mana*], a perfectly handsome man; the bark of the *hutu* to make the child hardy; the bark of the *atae*, for a rough skin for the child; the crust of the sea (salt), for a salt skin for the child; the bark of the coconut tree, for a porous skin for the child; the *purau* bark, for a skin full of fissures for the child; the bark of the *'ati*, for a variegated skin for the child … All these skins were placed on the child; the skin and its nature, the skin and its nature, for this child. (Henry 1928: 365–66)

This story suggests that bark cloth – for that is what is evoked by these bark skins – gives social and cultural shape to people, just as the bark skins gave shape to Tane. Bradd Shore, Alfred Gell and others have explored the importance of wrapping in Polynesian cultures, for wrapping did and does serve to invest people and objects with social and spiritual meaning (Shore 1989: 151–54; Gell 1993: 144–46). It is the wrapping of Tane in these barks and other substances that 'gives him qualities' and 'make[s] him a great god'. Indeed, the transformation achieved by Ta'aroa through the bark skins stands in direct contrast to the failure of the adze-wielding artisans, the *tahu'a*, to give Tane shape. This shaping of the body is especially important not only for the gods, but also for the elite, who derived their power from the embodied *mana* they inherited from divine ancestors.

It was clear from the first visit of Europeans to Tahiti, with Wallis's voyage in 1767, that clothing provided an important nexus of social interaction – that it shaped relations of power between groups and individuals. The participants in *taio* friendship exchanged not only names but also garments – wrapping each other in the *ahu fara*, *tiputa* or *pareu*, the special garments of the lineage. Through this name exchange and this wrapping in garments, the *taio* friends laid special claim to each other – they became not only friends but family and, most crucially, political allies (D'Alleva 1997: 73–81). The very first of these mutual investitures, which was enacted by Wallis's shipmaster George Robertson and Purea, a high-ranking Tahitian woman, presaged interactions that took place during every 18th century voyage of exploration, from Wallis to Vancouver. Robertson gave Purea a 'Ruffeld shirt' and showed her how to put it on, in a gift and gesture that, as he said, 'gained her heart'. When Robertson visited Purea on shore, she returned the favour, cutting for Robertson a 'suite of the country cloth' and dressing him in it, accompanying her gestures with a speech that Robertson, unfortunately, did not understand (Robertson 1948: 211, 214). Nonetheless, through Robertson's account I think we can understand that Purea saw this action as the mutual claiming and shaping of each other through the garment exchange of *taio* friendship.

Since, according to the story of Tane's creation, the skin *and its nature* were the key to giving him shape, my task here is to see the particular nature of these 'skins', the European clothing and the bark cloth clothing, *ahu fara* and the *tiputa*, made and worn in the 1820s and 1830s. I can partly do this through the accounts of contemporary observers, like Moerenhout, the missionary William Ellis and the explorer Otto von Kotzebue, who left detailed descriptions of what they saw and experienced in Tahiti. Yet clearly their accounts are not disinterested ethnography – if any such thing is even possible. In their descriptions of Tahitians and their wearing of Tahitian and European clothing, I see the play of certain tropes often used by European observers to come to grips with Tahiti and other native cultures: these texts reference the indigenous and the foreign, the authentic and the corrupt, tradition and innovation, dignity and clownishness. In fact, one of the challenges of this study is to read these works 'against the grain', as subaltern studies would have it, to read these works critically and creatively for alternative perspectives on the imbrication of European and Tahitian clothing (Guha and Spivak 1988). It is particularly difficult to negotiate the sentiments of condescension – as well as contempt, ridicule, pity and nostalgia for the authentic – which often mark these writings.

A minor incident that occurred during Otto von Kotzebue's voyage of exploration in the 1820s will show what I mean. During a visit to his ship, Queen Pomare and some of her female relatives found a cache of gold lace – von Kotzebue emphasises that it is *sham* gold lace – and, much taken with it, they demand it as a present. This started a fashion for gold lace on shore, and von Kotzebue reports that soon Tahitians were making extravagant offers for it; he particularly notes that husbands were driven to distraction trying to procure it for their wives. The supply of lace quickly ran out, and von Kotzebue goes on to write: 'The ladies who finally were unsuccessful in procuring the means of imitating a fashion thus accidentally introduced by the Royal sisters, *tout comme chez-nous*, actually fell ill and gave themselves up to the boundless lamentations of despair' (von Kotzebue 1830: 189).

But was this situation truly *tout comme chez-nous*? Von Kotzebue clearly interprets this incident in relation to the fashions and fads of European society women, which were silly and extravagant, as men everywhere – husbands particularly – apparently recognised. For him, the Tahitian women's response is risible – that they would get sick over this sham gold lace and indulge in 'boundless lamentations of despair' marks their racial and gender inferiority (we can almost hear him saying 'it's *fake* gold lace, for God's sake – who would want this stuff but an "Indian" or a woman?'). Now, even allowing that von Kotzebue may well have exaggerated this incident because it made a good story – one that humorously reinforces intertwining hierarchies of race and gender even as it rather generously and expansively allows a certain sense of universal male solidarity – there may yet be something to it. Whether or not it was real gold lace must have been irrelevant to Tahitians – the point is that it was real *European* lace. And while sham gold lace must have been a common enough thing for von Kotzebue, it would have been quite uncommon for the Tahitians; we can imagine them similarly laughing over the extravagant terms that Europeans sometimes offered in trade for common Tahitian items.

While von Kotzebue would certainly have taken very seriously the clothing hierarchies of his own world – just think about the exacting protocol surrounding military uniforms – he clearly cannot take seriously the clothing hierarchies of Tahiti, nor can he even begin to conceive that women might have been key players in political strategising through clothing. If Pomare and her highest ranking relatives wore something, then other elite women might well have wanted to have it too, as an assertion of their rank and privilege. It would not have done for Pomare to become too far elevated over other titleholders – especially at this time, when her political powers, in a developing amalgamation of the roles of European monarch and Tahitian *ari'i rahi*, were as yet unsettled. The European provenance of this ornamentation probably comprised a large part of its desirability, for to assert a connection to the European visitors, with their trade goods and guns, was an impressive thing indeed. Especially once it became clear how little there was of this lace to go around, its acquisition may have taken on added urgency. Perhaps a small thing, from the perspective of these titleholders, but worth some effort, just as the acquisition of a smart uniform was worth some effort to von Kotzebue and his contemporaries because it meant something in their society.

Of course, my work with the clothing of elite Tahitians at this time requires not only recourse to the archives, but also recourse to the garments themselves. If it is challenging to read the archives 'against the grain', it is also difficult to 'look against the grain', examining the surviving bark cloth garments for their unique qualities. (None of the European garments worn by Tahitians has survived, so I can only reconstruct their appearance via written accounts and visual images.) Each introduces its own peculiar history into the process: just as each observer had his own particular biases and interests, the bark cloth garments have their own histories and have undergone their own changes over 170 years or so. Most importantly, the dyes in the clothing have changed over time – originally, the buff-coloured background we typically see today was a rich yellow achieved with turmeric, and the dark brown was a brilliant magenta red, achieved by mixing the juices of several plants. In addition, the delicate floral perfumes that once enhanced the finest garments, adding another dimension to the experience of wearing them, have now faded.

When examining these bark cloth garments, there is a gap between the material record and the written record that must be negotiated. That is, the observers who wrote most extensively about these garments, their creation and circulation in society were not, as it happens, the people who collected them. I am most interested in this chapter, not in the garments in the context of *taio* friendship – in exchanges with Europeans – but as they were worn by Tahitians themselves, often together with European clothing. However, most of the garments extant in museum collections derived from *taio* friendships – that is, they were given as gifts to Europeans, rather than worn by Tahitians themselves. The surviving descriptions of garments suggest that there was no difference in those given to Europeans, but I cannot be sure of this.

In fact, the Tane story suggests that the particular characteristics of the bark cloth garments are important. In this sense, artistic style becomes a key issue: bark cloth design is intrinsic to the meaning of the work of art, intrinsic to its circulation

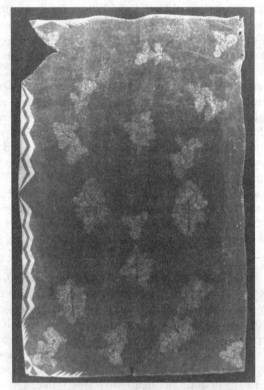

Figure 4.3: Large bark cloth (*ahu fara*). Given by Mahine Vahine, daughter of Tamatoa, the leading titleholder of Ra'iatea, to George Bennet of the London Missionary Society, 1821–24. Said to have been made by Mahine Vahine and her attendants. Saffron Walden Museum (1835.254).

in society. The design of these garments may express some of the issues – titleholding, prestige, lineage negotiations with outsiders – at stake in their circulation within and between genders, classes and cultures in Tahiti at this time. An anecdote related by the English missionary William Ellis, who spent the mid-1820s in Tahiti with the London Missionary Society, suggests the importance of artistic style in the making of clothing:

> In the manufacture of cloth, the females of all ranks were employed; and the queen, and wives of the chiefs of the highest rank, strove to excel in some department – in the elegance of the pattern, or the brilliancy of the colour. They are fond of society, and worked in large parties, in open and temporary houses erected for the purpose. Visiting one of these houses at Eimeo [Mo'orea], I saw sixteen or twenty females all employed. The queen sat in the midst, surrounded by several chief women, each with a mallet in her hand, beating the bark that was spread before her. [As] the wives and daughters of the chiefs take a pride in manufacturing superior cloth, the queen would often have felt it derogatory to her rank if any other female in the island could have finished a piece of cloth better than herself. I remember, in the island of Huahine, when a native once passed by, wearing a beautiful *ahufara*, hearing one native woman remark to another – What a finely printed shawl that is! The figures on it are [like] the work, or the marking of the queen! This desire among persons in high stations, to excel in departments of labour, is what we have always admired. This feeling probably led Pomare to bestow so much attention on his hand-writing, and induced the king of the Sandwich Islands to request that we would not teach any of the people till we had fully instructed him in reading and writing. (Ellis 1829: 185)

Let me note here that, although the passages I have quoted from Ellis and von Kotzebue make clear the importance of elite women in the creation of Tahitian clothing and in the strategic acquisition and wearing of both Tahitian and European clothes, I do not want to essentialise this association between women and clothing. Although high-ranking women did have a distinctive part to play in their intertwining roles as clothing artists and as diplomats and politicians, elite men also wore and distributed these bark cloth garments and acquired European clothes for themselves. (The *ahu fara* itself was more commonly, though not exclusively, worn by women, while the *tiputa* was worn by both sexes.) Thus, far from seeing these garments as invested with some kind of essentialised female power or female symbolism, I see elite women, like Mahine Vahine, who made the bark cloth *ahu fara* illustrated here, creating special garments that both they and elite men wore, either alone or in combination with European clothing, thereby helping to shape the dynamic political scene in Tahiti at this time.

As part of interpreting their circulation in society, I want to focus here on certain key visual qualities in these garments. The consistency among these garments – forms, colours, motifs and compositional structures that appear repeatedly – suggests a certain coherency in the framework of meaning in which they were interpreted. At the same time, individual artistic style was apparently recognised and valued, as William Ellis's story of the woman who recognises an *ahu fara* as being like the work of the queen, suggests. The distinctiveness of artistic style was recognised and valued among bark cloth artists, and perhaps even more widely.

Much of that interpretative framework and knowledge is missing now, so it is difficult to interpret particular motifs, like the geometric elements or leaf and fern prints, iconographically to any great degree. Although stylistic changes in bark cloth design are generally dismissed in the scholarly literature as merely decorative phenomena, the importance of cloth and clothing in wrapping and shaping the figure, and the significance of the gesture of wrapping and shaping in Tahitian culture, suggest that such changes were prompted by more than just the dictates of fashion. My guess is that much of that meaning was elusive and not available to every viewer, even in the original viewing and wearing contexts. Perhaps these garments were multiply metaphoric, employing what the Hawaiian people call *kaona*, or veiled references, which played out as a kind of unlimited semiosis (Kaeppler 1982). On one level, these motifs may simply have been pretty or fashionable, but on others they may have been invested with social, political or even spiritual significance.

Perhaps the most distinctive motifs incorporated into many of these garments are the flower, fern and leaf prints. These were made by dipping the botanical specimen in red dye and then pressing it on the surface of the cut garment; the appearance of these prints suggests that sometimes the leaves and ferns were trimmed before printing. Kooijman notes that such prints were not found on garments collected at the time of the Cook voyages; nor were they mentioned by any of the Cook voyagers, and he suggests that these botanical prints developed in imitation of printed textiles (probably of both European and south Asian origin) traded to Tahitians by the explorers (Kooijman 1972: 21, 22). In fact, in 1791, surgeon George Hamilton of the *Pandora* noted just this: 'Many of their figures were exactly the patterns which prevailed, as fashionable, when we left England, both striped and figured' (Edwards and Hamilton 1919: 115). The earliest extant piece with fern-and-flower printing is an *ahu fara* collected by Matthew Flinders on Bligh's second breadfruit voyage in 1792 and now in the collection of the British Museum. It is also important to remember that the first mention of such fern printing comes from Bligh's *Bounty* journal in 1788 (Bligh 1961: 417), meaning that fern printing developed, paradoxically, in the absence of European visitors between 1777 and 1788, when the *Lady Penrhyn* and the *Bounty* stopped there in short order. Perhaps these printed motifs provided a way for Tahitians at that time to assert among themselves their continuing connection with Europeans, as a reminder of the friendships they had contracted and the trade goods they had received, even in the absence of Europeans. Such printed bark cloth garments may even have supplanted, over the course of the 11 years in which Europeans were absent, the printed cloth and clothing that gradually wore out.

As much as they asserted a connection with European cloth designs, certain aspects of these motifs are distinctively local. After all, the printing technique itself, with the fern or leaf being dipped in dye and pressed onto the finished garment, was not used on the printed cloth traded to Tahitians; it was a local invention. These motifs were local because the plants themselves were, and these plants often had tremendous significance as medicines, ornaments, and spiritual offerings. While the prints on the Flinders cloth are small in scale, by the 1820s such prints are quite large and bold, much more so than the printed cottons typically worn by Europeans. They would have been quite visible at a distance, and legible as images of particular plants.

Fern, leaf and flower prints, as well as other motifs, were not dispersed evenly over the surface of the garments, as were the printed cottons that the Europeans traded to Tahitians. They are instead grouped on the cloth, and, along with the scale of the prints, this shows that the women who decorated these clothes clearly paid attention to how the design would look when worn. The designs that mix 'cloudy' areas of red pigment with fern and leaf prints on *ahu fara* may also have been developed with the drape of the garment on the body in mind. Depending on the folding and wrapping of the garment, those areas would expand and contract as it was worn, and the sharp, bright leaf imprints would emerge in all their crispness from these cloudy areas. Many *tiputa* or tunics show a particular emphasis on one shoulder or the other, or on the front of the garment versus the back. On this example, the front of the garment is decorated with botanical prints and geometric elements laid out in strict bilateral symmetry, while the design of the back is much looser, with loosely painted stripes and scattered botanical prints.

Of course these garments were not worn alone, but in combination with European clothing, both within the same outfit and at alternating times. Numerous sources attest to the appeal of European clothes for Tahitians of all ranks at this time, and much European clothing ended up in the hands of the elite. Among elite women, dresses were extremely popular, as were bonnets made locally in imitation of European styles. In the quotation above, von Kotzebue notes that *coloured* dresses were extremely popular – and, given the original brilliance of the bark cloth garments, this makes sense. Elite Tahitian men often wore coats, waistcoats and/or trousers – and military coats if they could get them. White bed sheets made a popular replacement for the *ahu fara*. Shirts and nightshirts were popular for both sexes, on both formal and informal occasions, especially striped or patterned examples. And, as Moerenhout indicates, for the Tahitian elite shoes were a necessary part of formal occasions, despite the discomfort.

I would argue that these combinations of Tahitian and European clothing were often self-conscious and significant, not the outlandish fancies of unsophisticated people as some observers seemed to think. On some occasions, such combinations of clothing may have been used to signal profound meanings. For example, I find it significant that at the assembly described by Moerenhout, in the quotation that began this chapter, Queen Pomare changed her clothes halfway through the event. During the discussion of questions relating to the missions, she wore primarily European clothing, while during the latter part of the assembly, which dealt with local politics, she wore bark cloth clothing in what Moerenhout calls the 'national dress' and 'ancient costume'. For Moerenhout this change of outfits maps onto a distinction between the inauthentic and authentic, the clownish and the dignified. For him, Queen Pomare is elegant and dignified in her bark cloth clothing, but clumsy and foolish in her European clothing. For me, that is not the relevant distinction here, however awkward Queen Pomare may have found her shoes to be. Her choice of a European outfit for the discussion of missionary affairs reflected the topic of discussion, and asserted, in a sense, her willingness and ability to move in that world and to be an authority in it – despite the discomfort of the shoes. Changing to bark cloth clothing – the 'beautiful piece of Indian cloth' described by Moerenhout – for the discussion of local politics, reflected the change in topic, and in a sense excluded the missionaries, because this was perhaps not something they could or would wear, and not something they had the authority to discuss. The bark cloth clothing may have strategically invoked tradition, the past, and thus Queen Pomare's pre-eminence as a high-ranking titleholder. Not surprisingly, the so called national dress that seems so authentic to Moerenhout is itself hybrid. The blouse with its collaret may or may not have been made from bark cloth, but it most certainly adapted a European form. The local now incorporated the foreign.

The French naval captain Bernard's account of a visit with Queen Pomare in 1840 provides a more sensitive account of her strategic use of European clothing:

> On the sixteenth we visited the Queen, Pomare Vahine, the gates of her house were guarded by two pairs of soldiers, recently appointed, whose headdresses of cardboard and ornaments of paper [bark cloth?] attested to the haste and difficulties which presided over their organisation: the chiefs, standing in line, followed, many of them distinguished by unusual epaulettes: the princess, seated on the floor of her apartment, completed the picture, her robe of yellow satin appeared from a distance, upon our entrance into the Fare, like the golden statue ... Our compliments transmitted via the consul, a movement of the sovereign's head directed an orator to address us, who made us welcome and assured us that it is always with pleasure that Pomare sees the French arrive at Papiete ... (Bernard 1840: fn 4 [my translation])

Unlike Moerenhout and von Kotzebue, Bernard does not focus on whether Pomare's gown was torn or old or too tight or too short – he perceives the effect of dignity she was trying to create instead. The yellow dress shining at the end of the large, semi-dark fare, the lines of titleholders with their epaulettes, the soldiers with their headdresses, all worked together to create a splendid picture, and her quiet authority – she directs the orator with but a nod of the head – was meant to impress. Indeed, Bernard goes on to note that 'she always carries herself with an unchanging seriousness'. The yellow colour of her dress – a colour often used in bark cloth and associated with the *ari'i*, the elite – may have deliberately referenced traditional authority even in a European dress. The regalia worn by the soldiers, titleholders, and the queen herself were a hybrid of European and Tahitian, putting into play new and old signs of authority and power.

Reading through the documents, and examining the material and visual record, I am struck by the performative quality of clothing. Clothing, as worn (as opposed to clothing that is stored away, displayed or given as gifts) has something of the quality of theatre. In combining European and Tahitian clothing, the Tahitian elite, both men and women, were in a sense 'dressing the part'. Their choices, as I see it, were self-conscious and deliberate, and if the effect on their European viewers was not always what they may have intended, I cannot find myself much in sympathy with Moerenhout's or von Kotzebue's ridiculing and deploring these costumes as the naïve choices of childish natives. What the role or

Figure 4.4: Jules Lejeune, *Le Mot d'Ordre/ Garde Royale de Taïti*, 1823. *Service historique de la Marine*, Vincennes (SH 356, 41).

roles being performed by these Tahitian elites actually were is the challenging question. With so few statements from them about what they were wearing and why, or how they perceived clothing – Ellis's comment from the woman on Huahine is a notable exception – I can only conjecture in the broadest ways about this, and about how the wearing of clothing may have helped the Tahitian elite negotiate the new and old forms of social, political and spiritual power that were at play in the 1820s and 1830s.

My understanding of the performative role of clothing in shaping the dynamic social and political scene of Tahiti at this time is in some limited but important ways informed by Judith Butler's theory of gender performativity (Butler 1990). I see the efficacy of this clothing as relying on citation and iteration, which Butler sees as key mechanisms in the formation of gender identity and expression. Butler explores how gender identity is formed through citation (for example, a little girl tries on her mother's clothes) and through repetition (a mother puts ribbons in her little girl's hair over and over again until the child learns to do it herself). So too in Tahiti we can see the elite citing the dress of Europeans when they wear waistcoats and shirts – and also citing their own dress traditions when they wear *ahu fara* and *tiputa*. Thus Queen Pomare wears European dress when discussing missionary politics and 'native' dress when discussing local issues: these are the 'citations' that are appropriate to each occasion. The practice of repetition is also key, for these types of garments were worn repeatedly, and I think the favouring of particular forms – the colourful dress, the shirt, the *tiputa*, certain motifs – worked to reinforce certain messages about the social and political power of the elite.

As helpful as these concepts of citation and iteration are, there are crucial differences in the work that Butler is doing and the work that I am doing here. Butler is primarily concerned with the formation and modulation of gender identity, but I am also concerned with politics – with what I might call identities in practice. The relations of power in each situation are also markedly different – the asymmetries of power that characterise gender identity formation (for example, children being persuaded and coerced into certain gender practices by their parents or teachers) do not characterise identities in practice such as the clothing performances of the Tahitian elite in the 1820s and 1830s. At this time the Tahitian elite were creating new forms of power and authority which drew on both the established powers of the *ari'i* and on styles of European authority (particularly the consolidation of military and economic power with genealogical pre-eminence) which had been introduced by both the voyagers and the missionaries. In other words, the largely hegemonic authority of the elite had been joined to much more coercive forms of authority (D'Alleva 1997).

Nonetheless, although Tahitians may have been exploring European forms of authority, and although this was a time when both English missionaries and the French military were attempting to influence and even control Tahitian affairs, this was *not* a colonial culture. The Tahitian elite was still very much in control of the power structures in Tahiti, even if these power structures were in flux and if the members of the elite themselves expressed a range of ideas about what these power structures should be. This is not citation that takes place from an inferior position, either culturally or politically. And while I do not want to underestimate the cultural influence of the English missionaries in Tahiti at this time, nor their very real political power, I will note that the elite often very easily resisted the missionaries and pursued their own agendas, co-operating only when it suited them. I think that marks an important distinction from both Butler's work and also from Homi Bhabha's work on mimicry in colonial cultures – another obvious point of reference here (Bhabha 1994). Bhabha writes that colonial cultures compel the colonised to imitate them – to adopt their laws, language, schooling, dress, religion, etc, and he explores the ways that this distorts culture and experience for both coloniser and colonised. The Tahitian elite, on the other hand, embraced European clothing and made it their own from the time of the very first voyages of exploration. Although missionaries tried to compel them to wear 'decent' clothing, the elite did so very much on their own terms. (I do want to note here that Tahitian commoners, under the linked authorities of the local elites and the missionaries had much more constrained choices and would have experienced this very differently.)

The elite's use of European clothing, their idiosyncratic blending of European and Tahitian garments, their refusal to adhere to the Europeans' ideas of what was authentic and ancient and indigenous to Tahitian culture; all of this may have seemed distorted to European observers, but I do not think it was to the elite themselves. This was not a colonial culture, and I do not think that process of self-othering that is so central to the power dynamics of colonial cultures had taken root among the Tahitian elite. Stuart Hall, drawing on Franz Fanon, explores the ways that the coloniser had the power to make the colonised see and experience themselves as Other (Hall 1990). Within a colonial regime, the colonised people internalise the criteria of the coloniser – they judge themselves as inferior, strange, uncivilised. Fanon says that this process produces 'individuals without an anchor, without horizon, colourless, stateless, rootless – a race of angels' (quoted in Hall 1990). I would argue that the derisive comments of Moerenhout, von Kotzebue and others like them, were as yet inaudible to Pomare II, Pomare IV, and the other elite. Instead of a race of angels, they were real men and women, vying for power, inventing new forms of authority, and creating and wearing their own distinctive blend of Tahitian and European garments as part of the process.

References

Bernard (1840) *Account of a Voyage to the South Seas*, unpublished manuscript, Aix-en-Provence: Archives d'Outre-Mer

Bhabha, HK (1994) *The Location of Culture*, New York: Routledge

Bligh, W (1961) [1789] *A Voyage to the South Sea, Undertaken by Command of His Majesty, for the Purpose of Conveying the Breadfruit Tree to the West Indies, in His Majesty's Ship the Bounty, Including an Account of the Mutiny on Board the Said Ship*, New York: New American Library

Butler, J (1990) *Gender Trouble: Feminism and the Subversion of Identity*, New York: Routledge

D'Alleva, A (1997) *Shaping the Body Politic: Gender, Status, and Power in the Art of Eighteenth-Century Tahiti and the Society Islands*, unpublished PhD thesis, Columbia University

Edwards, E and Hamilton, G (1919) *Voyage of HMS 'Pandora' Despatched to Arrest the Mutineers of the 'Bounty' in the South Seas, 1790–1791, Being the Narrative of Captain Edward Edwards, RN, the Commander and George Hamilton the Surgeon, with an Introduction and Notes by Basil Thomson*, London: Francis Edwards

Ellis, W (1829) *Polynesian Researches, During a Residence of Nearly Eight Years in the Society and Sandwich Islands*, London: Fisher, Son & Jackson

Gell, A (1993) *Wrapping in Images: Tattooing in Polynesia*, Oxford: Clarendon

Guha, R and Spivak, G (1988) *Selected Subaltern Studies*, Oxford: Oxford University Press

Hall, S (1990) 'Cultural identity and diaspora' in Rutherford, J (ed), *Identity: Community, Culture, Difference*, London: Lawrence & Wishart

Henry T (1928) *Ancient Tahitian Society*, Honolulu: Bishop Museum Press

Kaeppler, A (1982) 'Genealogy and disrespect: a study of symbolism in Hawaiian images' (3) RES 82–107

Kooijman, S (1972) *Tapa in Polynesia*, Honolulu: Bishop Museum Press

von Kotzebue, O (1830) *A New Voyage Round the World, in the Years 1823, 24, 25, and 26*, London: H Colburn & R Bentley

Moerenhout, JA (1993) *Travels to the Islands of the Pacific Ocean (1837)*, Borden, A (trans), Lanham: University Press of America

Robertson, G (1948) *The Discovery of Tahiti, A Journal of the Second Voyage of HMS Dolphin Round the World, Under the Command of Captain Wallis, RN, in the Years 1766, 1767 and 1768, Written by her Master George Robertson*, London: The Hakluyt Society

Shore, B (1989) '*Mana* and *Tapu*', in Howard, A and Borofsky, R (eds), *Developments in Polynesian Ethnology*, Honolulu: University of Hawaii Press

Weiner, A (1989) 'Why cloth? Wealth, gender, and power in Oceania' in Weiner, A and Schneider, J (eds), *Cloth and Human Experience*, Washington, DC: Smithsonian Institution Press

CHAPTER 5

UNDER WRAPS: AN UNPURSUED AVENUE OF INNOVATION

Michael O'Hanlon

I once wrote a book about the pervasive social significance that the decorated skin traditionally has among a people of Highland New Guinea called the Wahgi (O'Hanlon 1989). It is now sufficiently long ago that when I occasionally consult the book today, I do so with a sense of faint surprise at its contents. But the question I want to work towards now is: what is the significance of the more enveloping non-indigenous clothing mainly worn today in a society, like Wahgi, which is preoccupied by 'skin'? Do the same concerns translate across from one to the other integument? If not, why not? If so, do they do so directly, or are they transformed? While the answers I have to these questions are only provisional, the attempt to find them may reveal a little of the ethnography of introduced clothing and its significance in Highland New Guinea.

'Skin' in New Guinea (*nganz* in the Wahgi language) is, of course, a salient term, denoting both 'body' but also, and particularly, its surface. It is also of widespread metaphorical significance, reflected equally in mythologies of skin-changing and skin-changers (Leroy 1985) and in the titles of such academic works as 'No money on our skins' (Strathern, M 1975), 'Why is shame on the skin?' (Strathern, A 1977), 'Skin, personhood and redemption' (Lattas 1992), etc. What seems to emerge from much of this – and this is true not only of New Guinea but also more widely – is that part of the significance of skin is that it is both the inside of an outside, and the outside of an inside. In a dialectic of concealment and revelation, the body surface, and the skin in particular has the capacity to mark a whole set of potential disjunctions: between human and animal, the known and the unknown, male and female, the domestic and the public; or equally, the continuities between them and the absence of any such disjunctions.

What form does this general interest in the body surface take among the Wahgi people? There, one of the best known myths tells of the origin of pigs and hence of the grandest of traditional Wahgi rites, the Pig Festival, the one for which the most elaborate form of traditional attire is worn. The myth (of which there are a number of broadly similar variants) features two brothers, Mond and Mare. Where Mare worked hard and made houses and gardens, hedonistic Mond would decorate well and leave early in the morning, apparently to go courting. Eventually Mare decides to follow him covertly. Mare pursues his brother deep into the forest. There he watches from a concealed position and sees Mond remove his apron and bark belt, his cordyline rear covering, his headnet and his decorations and hang them on a branch. Thus disrobed, Mond gets on all fours where he begins to grunt and break ground like a pig, an animal hitherto unknown.

Mare, the voyeur of this transformative act, is perplexed and when his brother (now back in human clothing) returns home that evening he taxes him with this deception. Mond, the erstwhile pig, tells his brother that he, Mond, will die that night. His family are not to worry, he says, but to bury him in the middle of a vast enclosure. Mond duly dies, is buried by his wailing kin, and the following morning the enclosure – which has hurriedly been constructed – is full of pigs of enormous size.

The disclosure that Mond, beneath his traditional clothing, is a part-time pig – as well as the origin of pigs itself – has parallels elsewhere in Wahgi mythology: for example, in the courtship of Wusilamb, a promiscuously shape-shifting girl. But while appearance is deceptive in these cases, more typically the Wahgi view appearance as revelatory. In particular, the skin is felt to have the potential to reveal the true state of inter- and intra-group morality, and it is this I want to pursue here.

In Wahgi society, much knowledge is simultaneously regarded both as of vital importance but also as uncertain (O'Hanlon 1989: 134ff). The knowledge in question has to do with the true state of intra- and inter-group relationships as these have worked themselves out in a tangled and often violent past. Did A secretly poison B, his very own clansman? Is it possible that the man that C's father speared in long-past warfare was, unbeknownst to him, C's real or close classificatory mother's brother? Was the compensation payment made by clan D to their allies really adequate for the deaths the allies had suffered in supporting clan D in warfare? Did E, disaffected with his own clansmen, covertly hand over items of adornment to a rival clan, urging that they, not his own clansmen, be successful when decorated and massed for display?

In Wahgi thinking, much of the importance of such issues and suspected deeds has to do with the longer-term consequences they are feared to have. Their effect is not limited to an original impact but is thought to resonate down the generations. If A really did poison his clansman B, then B's children and their children risk continuing to be afflicted by misfortune until the originating act is revealed. The reason for C's wife producing daughter after daughter, but no sons, may lie back in C's father having unknowingly speared C's mother's brother in warfare as a youth. Inadequate compensation paid by clan D to their allies might explain the infertility afflicting girls married in from the one clan to the other half a century later, etc.

Consequently, knowledge of such moral breaches is felt to be crucial. Until the background is known, the necessary remedial steps cannot be taken (traditionally, this was often done by ensuring that the parties to the dispute ceased to eat food cooked on the same fire). A second reason why such knowledge is crucial is that it can be deployed by enemy clans in battle if they know something to your disadvantage. The problem, however, is that the vital significance of the relevant knowledge is matched by a high degree of uncertainty about its truth. Rumours abound of deathbed confessions which reveal the real reason for some cascade of misfortunes, or of some hidden deed slyly alluded to in a speech at a rival clan's ceremony. But few public forums for reaching a definitive verdict exist.

It is here that the body – more especially its surface – is traditionally regarded as highly significant. For breaches of intra- and inter-group morality are felt to manifest themselves literally *on the skin*, from which (it is felt) moral standing can be read off. The existence of internal treachery, of unreciprocated debts, the true state of relations with maternal kin, are thought to reveal themselves in the condition of the skin: in whether it looks glossy, glinting, glowing, clear and sparkling or dull, dark, ashy, flaky and sallow – there are more indigenous terms here than you can shake a stick at (O'Hanlon 1989: Glossary C).

The body, and 'skin' in particular, is felt to have this authenticatory capacity during the daily round, but especially on corporate ceremonial occasions when people decorate elaborately and dance before friends, rivals and enemies, adorned in pelts and plumes, belts and aprons. Here I should make the point that it is not only the skin surface itself that is felt to have this capacity to disclose. The fuller decorative repertoire reveals whether the complex additive ensemble of plumes, aprons, leaves and anklets manages to hang together during hours of dancing, how dancers' plumes and legs move, and whether their song (or, in more martial ceremonies, their war cries) resonate impressively, etc.[1] (See Figure 5.1 in the colour section.)

The question I want to ask is: does the authenticatory role with which the skin and indigenous clothing is credited transfer across to the non-indigenous clothing which virtually all Wahgi now wear, virtually all the time? To answer it, I need to provide the most thumbnail of sketches of the Wahgi take-up of exogenous clothing since their first contact with the West in the 1930s. Before doing so, I should acknowledge that my own fieldwork data on the topic suffers from the deficiency that this collection of papers is intended in part to address. Despite having spent nearly three years doing fieldwork with the Wahgi, and despite an explicit focus upon the significance of indigenous decoration, my data on the adoption and use of introduced clothing by the Wahgi, on the second-hand market which supplies much of it, and of any particular significance they see in such clothing, is only impressionistic. Oddly, as it now seems to me, I treated the final stages of the adoption by Wahgi of non-indigenous clothing (mainly second-hand Western clothes) – which I observed over the three periods of my fieldwork – merely as an unremarkable local instance of a phenomenon affecting indigenous people everywhere. I certainly did not devote to it the same methodical and systematic care as I did to the question of how individuals acquired items of indigenous dress and decoration, and their significance for them. It took Karen Hansen's (2000) volume on the second-hand clothes trade in Zambia to alert me to the potential anthropological interest of the topic.[2]

In providing my account I find it useful to periodise, dividing the years since the 1930s into three main blocks. The first of these is the 20 years from the point of

---

1   Patterns of fertility and deaths constitute a related complex of signs that the Wahgi view as potentially authenticating uncertain narratives – see O'Hanlon and Frankland (forthcoming).
2   In partial defence of this *lacuna* in my data, I should note that the Wahgi never raised with me the topic of their adoption of non-indigenous clothing as a preoccupying concern in the way that they did with 'skin'.

contact until the early to mid-1950s. It is clear from the early literature (Taylor 1933; 1933b), from photographs (for example, Baglin and de Courcy 1988) and from talking to people, that most people, for most of the time, continued to dress largely as they had before contact, for both everyday and for ceremonial wear. Everyday wear for men comprised a bark belt with a netted apron in front and cordyline leaves behind, with perhaps a head net. For women, it comprised a number of skirts suspended from a belt. The major form of bedding in this area was not bark cloth but *pandanus* matting. Ceremonial wear was an escalating elaboration of everyday wear. Depending on the occasion, it entailed adding plumes of many kinds, wigs, armlets, shells, pelts and coloured clays. Virtually everything worn (with the principal exception of some shell ornaments) was locally acquired or produced. Some was made by its users, but much more was exchanged or gifted. Partly this was a consequence of the sexes' reliance on each other for their respective productions (netting being largely a woman's task, while the production of armlets, belts and shell ornaments was a male affair). But also – if inventories of how such traditional decorative materials are acquired today are a reliable guide to past practice – there was a high degree of gifting of such materials, both between kin and as a reflection of friendship.

There were some exceptions to the overall 'little-change' scenario that I have suggested characterises the period from the early 1930s to the early 1950s. Those Wahgi men who went out as migrants on the Highlands Labour Scheme returned home with some non-indigenous clothing, either shorts and shirts or the lengths of material called in Tok Pisin *laplap*. Those Wahgi who worked as house servants for Whites similarly became acquainted with, and in some cases adopted, these items. Girls incorporated into their best dress unmodified sheets of the red fabric that served as an early trade good. Quantities of beads were adopted, as were imported decorative paints and enormous numbers of shells. Indeed, it seems relatively clear that the ceremonial occasions – photographs of which were used to represent 'untouched Highland New Guinea' in some popular accounts of the time – owed a good deal of their colour, scale and drama to the White world with which they were being contrasted, as more perceptive observers noted (Simpson 1962: 215ff).

The second of my periods stretches from the mid-1950s to the mid-1980s. Here the broad theme is the accelerating replacement of indigenous clothing by imported clothing for everyday occasions, and the gradual enclavement of 'traditional' dress until it became exclusively restricted to indigenous ceremonial use. Men adopted shirts, shorts and jackets, while women wore dresses, voluminous blouses and the lengths of fabric called *laplap*. Within this very broad pattern there was considerable variation as well as stylistic and generational differences. Older men and women retained a good deal of traditional dress. Older men in particular were content to combine indigenous with introduced items. For example, a shirt worn with bark belt and cordyline rear covering; or, in the case of my classificatory mother's brother, the formidable warrior Avun whose nose and mouth were much eaten away with yaws, a frilly, sky blue housecoat worn along with a pearl shell. (His disability gave this courtly man a terrifying appearance, not lessened for me by the frilly housecoat. Avun, thus attired, advancing to embrace me and declaiming as best he could through his missing lips *'Abapo! Abapo!'* ('Sister's child! Sister's child!') remains a powerful visual memory of early fieldwork.) There was also among older men a fashion for greatcoats and for bandleaders' hats, both presumably part of the surplus clothing offloaded in great quantities following the two world wars. Adopted dress tended to be more elaborate, and newer, the more public the occasion. (See Figure 5.2 in the colour section.)

As this second period progressed, younger men and some big men also increasingly took to wearing long trousers. This was one of the ways in which they set themselves off sartorially from their fellows. On public occasions this sometimes seemed to have its gastronomic counterpart in the consumption of sandwiches – my early fieldwork notes from 25 years ago include a number of accounts of events at which the big men involved in exchanges would sometimes separate themselves from their fellows in shaded pavilions where, dressed in long trousers, they would eat sandwiches. People were also buried more or less exclusively in non-traditional clothing by the end of this period.

How was this influx of non-indigenous clothing acquired? A certain amount was purchased as new in the supermarkets and stores that had sprung up in large centres like Mount Hagen. This particularly applied to the set of clothes that a bride is traditionally given to take with her when her bridewealth is handed over. However, the vast majority of clothing was obtained from the second-hand clothes stores that appeared even in quite small centres like Banz and later at local markets. Such clothing, whether new or second-hand, was mainly purchased with the income from selling coffee, a cash crop to which the Wahgi had taken with enthusiasm from the mid-1950s. Indeed, there was a noticeable switch of clothing in whole communities as a new season's coffee income came on stream. Individual identities – which had previously seemed inseparable from a particular hat, a much worn dress or an increasingly faded shirt – were transformed with the acquisition of new and more colourful clothing, and I had to learn new key markers for recognising people at a distance.

A certain amount of this clothing – whether new or second-hand – was purchased to be gifted. I mentioned the clothing made over to brides; husbands were also sometimes criticised for not making gifts of clothing to their wives, or for not buying adequate numbers of clothes for their children. There was also a certain amount of swapping clothing, especially among younger people: a distinctive shirt would be worn for weeks by one girl only to be adopted ('she just felt like giving it to me') by her sister-in-law. These qualifications apart, there seemed to be a far lower level of gifting or exchange of such purchased clothing than there was with indigenous items of wear. My impression is that most adults purchased the clothes they wore for themselves with income they earned, mainly from coffee growing.

The wearing of indigenous dress in this second period also became increasingly restricted to ceremonial occasions: to Pig Festival dancing; to food and bridewealth presentations; to the making over of compensation payments and to a variety of martial occasions, including warfare. There are considerable if limited appropriations here: neck ties were adopted by some dancers otherwise wearing largely indigenous ceremonial dress, and watches treated as a dancing accessory; warriors sometimes wore shorts which they felt were less likely than the traditional aprons to snag on bushes with potentially fatal results; the occasional woman would wear a bra rather than dance bare-breasted. The most obvious exception to the limiting of indigenous dress to use in traditional or quasi-traditional ceremonies was the encouragement on the part of Catholic mission schools that children should wear local dress to school once a week. This was in sharp contrast to the emphasis by other missions (principally the Swiss Mission and to a lesser extent the Nazarenes) that decorating and dancing were not congruent with a Christian lifestyle. (See Figure 5.3 in the colour section.)

My third rough period is from the mid-1980s through the 1990s (my ethnographic present). Introduced clothing is now more or less universal for all but the main participants in traditional ceremony. Such clothing is notably smarter than it was earlier, though I am unclear of the extent to which this is due to the kind of style-conscious self-making described by Hansen (2000) in her analysis of the second-hand clothes trade in Zambia. There has also been some decline in ceremonial activity for which traditional dress is worn, along with a broader national concern that such activity should not be hybridised by the inclusion of Western clothing: 'Remove your underwear and bras', Mewie Launa, the Chairman of the 2002 Goroka Show was reported more recently as saying in the national paper, the *Post Courier*: 'Why are women still wearing bras during singsings? Why are we still seeing underwear sticking out? Our parents never did that. This is not what our culture demands. Our culture is unique. It is in our blood. We should be proud of it and not mix modern culture with what we have always learnt.'[3]

This breakneck survey of the adoption by the Wahgi of introduced clothing raises a number of points of interest. But here I want to return to the question with which I started, and ask whether the moral revelations embodied in traditional 'skin' and appearance have been carried over into traditional dress. The answer is no: to the best of my knowledge, Wahgi appearance in non-indigenous dress is not an idiom in terms of which to seek revelation about the existence of moral breaches in the way that traditional dress was and to some extent still is. This is not because those concerns have gone away: people still remain preoccupied with whether clans harbour traitors; with the true state of relationships with maternal kin and with the possible effects in the present of long-past secret breaches of clan solidarity. It is interesting, then, that contemporary Wahgi dress and appearance has not been colonised by either older moral concerns or indeed by much in the way of fresh ones, save in limited areas.[4] After all, both the Australian colonial service and the missionaries 'moralised' appearance with their notions of

---

3   Mr Launa's remarks were reported in the weekend edition of the *Post Courier* for 20–22 September 2002, as read on the *Post Courier*'s website (www.postcourier.com.pg).

4   Eg, the ways in which Wahgi girls now wear net bags (whether over the shoulder, or round the neck instead of supported from the forehead) may be read as indicating that a girl is set on taking over her husband's role, is a prostitute, etc (O'Hanlon 1993: 72–73).

cleanliness, smartness and decorum – so there would have been a kind of elective affinity in the Wahgi doing the same.

I can think of three reasons why the Wahgi have not made introduced dress an authenticatory idiom that functions in the way that indigenous dress and appearance traditionally do. The first is the possibility that, along with the introduced clothing in which they now generally dress, the Wahgi have contextually assimilated those Western understandings that view appearance as concealing more than revealing. As I have outlined, for the Wahgi, appearance is in the main revelatory. In a world of uncertain rumours and secret accounts, truth is manifested on the skin, which can be 'read' for the reliability of those accounts. Of course, appearance can be regarded as revelatory in the West too, but I would hazard that on balance Western idioms – especially Christian ones – focus more often on the discontinuity than the continuity between inner personhood and external appearance. This is something that Bruce Knauft, working recently in Gebusi, also notes. He describes how even traditional Gebusi costume has now come to be regarded locally merely as the body's transient covering, without deeper context or social transaction. Equally, he says, 'the white shirt worn by Gebusi men on Sunday is *not* the index of one's spiritual authenticity. As the pastors continually emphasise, it is only in one's innermost heart and *not* on the skin that true dedication to God can be known' (Knauft forthcoming).

A second possible reason for introduced dress not assuming the kind of revelatory moral dimension that traditional dress possessed may have to do with the relative absence of a corporate dimension to modern dress. Traditionally, Wahgi skin, appearance and dress are regarded as most significantly revelatory on great massed occasions, when clan reputation and prowess are on the line. There are few such equivalent occasions in which people corporately adopt similar introduced dress and parade together. Perhaps the most potentially similar is school children's dress, though I have never heard the bevies of children making their way to school in the morning made the subject of the kind of evaluative moral commentary which decoration in traditional Wahgi dress provokes. There is, however, one suggestive point and this relates to the battle shields which were briefly revived for renewed inter-group warfare in the 1980s and 1990s (O'Hanlon 1995). Battle shields might not be thought of as an item of wear, still less of introduced wear, since they were a central part of traditional Wahgi warfare. But when shields were revived for the fighting that gripped parts of the Wahgi area, two changes were apparent in the decoration they bore. The first was that the decoration on many shields reflected the changes undergone by the Wahgi since warfare had originally been suppressed by the Australian administration in the 1940s. Shield decoration now included written material and images from advertising, including comic strip heroes such as the Phantom. Secondly, shield decoration, which had traditionally varied from warrior to warrior, had now become more corporate, so that the men of some groups each had a common design, rather as though they were members of a sports team. Indeed, team motifs featured on a good number of shields. Now the appearance of shields in battle, like that of the skin more generally, is felt to authenticate otherwise uncertain knowledge (for example, shields which look dull and ashy in colour may be taken to confirm that there is undisclosed treachery among the clansmen bearing them).

In other words, when there is a corporate dimension to modern dress (if that status is allowed to contemporary shield design), it does become an authenticatory idiom in the same way as 'skin'. (See Figure 5.4 in the colour section.)

A final possible reason for introduced dress not having become an authenticatory idiom may lie in the fact that where traditional dress was locally made and largely acquired through gift or exchange, contemporary introduced dress is purchased ready-made. So far as introduced fabric is concerned, there seemed to me to be a notable Wahgi indifference to modifying it, or mending it. Here there seems to be a marked contrast to some other, earlier and longer-colonised areas of Melanesia, such of Vanuatu. As Bolton (unpublished) has documented, there has long been a strong local tradition among ni-Vanuatu women of modifying introduced fabrics and of dressmaking. Different styles there reflect divergent mission histories, come to characterise different parts of Vanuatu, and are also 'stolen with the eye' in a constant process of copying styles considered attractive. I am unaware of anything comparable amongst the Wahgi. While there have been periodic attempts by Wahgi individuals from the 1950s onwards to acquire and use hand sewing machines (for example, Spencer 1960: 59), sewing by hand or machine, mending and other modifications of introduced fabrics has never to my knowledge really taken off. In the early 1980s, there was a flurry of talk among some North Wahgi women about establishing sewing clubs, with guidance from women from further east (the direction, as it happens, from which most Wahgi cults come), but the clubs never flowered. An extreme interest, dexterity and orientation towards innovation in the realm of net bag production (O'Hanlon 1993: 69ff), for example, has never apparently crossed to introduced clothing. Nor is there any tradition of taking purchased second-hand clothing to local tailors to have it adapted or fitted; consequently there are no such tailors to the best of my knowledge.

Traditional appearance, in contrast, could be described thus (borrowing the words of a north of England countryman once heard inspecting a 1950s Bentley): 'This were not manufactured, lad, it were *made*.' As I have indicated, individual items of dress were locally produced, and transferred as part of a nexus of individualised social relations. Before important ceremonies, individuals receive gifts of decorative items or of money to buy such items from specific kin. Some particularly elaborate decorative items amount, I have suggested elsewhere, to crafted second skins, overlaying one indigenous identity with another (O'Hanlon 1992). In short, traditional appearance is literally socially constructed in a way that is congruent with it becoming the focus for moral commentary, while the 'purchased' appearance does not seem to be, certainly not in the same way.

References

Baglin, D and de Courcy, C (1988) *The Jimi River Expedition*, 1950, Melbourne: Oxford University Press

Bolton (unpublished) 'Stealing with the eye: mission dresses and the innovation of tradition in Vanuatu' in O'Hanlon, MDP and Ewart, E (eds), *Body Arts and Modernity*

Hansen, KT (2000) *Salaula: the World of Secondhand Clothing and Zambia*, Chicago: University of Chicago Press

Knauft, B (unpublished) 'From self-decoration to self-fashioning: orientalism as backward progress at Nomad Station, Papua New Guinea' in O'Hanlon, MDP and Ewart, E (eds), *Body Arts and Modernity*

Lattas, A (1992) 'Skin, personhood and redemption: the double self in West New Britain' 63(1) Oceania 27–54

Leroy, J (1985) *Fabricated World: An Interpretation of Kewa Tales*, Vancouver: University of British Columbia Press

O'Hanlon, MDP (1989) *Reading the Skin: Adornment, Display and Society Among the Wahgi*, London: British Museum Publications

O'Hanlon, MDP (1992) 'Unstable images and second skins: artefacts, exegesis and assessments in the New Guinea Highlands' 27(3) Man (NS) 587–608

O'Hanlon, MDP (1993) *Paradise: Portraying the New Guinea Highlands*, Bathurst: Crawford House Press

O'Hanlon, MDP (1995) 'Modernity and the "graphicalization" of meaning: New Guinea Highlands shield design in historical perspective' 1(3) Journal of the Royal Anthropological Institute 469–93

O'Hanlon, MDP and Frankland, LHE (forthcoming) 'History embodied: authenticating the past in the New Guinea Highlands' in Ulijaszek, S (ed), *Fertility and Reproduction in Melanesia*, Oxford: Berghahn Books

Simpson, C (1962) *Plumes and Arrows: Inside New Guinea*, Sydney: Angus and Robertson

Spencer, M (1960) *Doctor's Wife in New Guinea*, Sydney: Angus and Robertson

Strathern, A (1977) 'Why is shame on the skin?' in Blacking, J (ed), *The Anthropology of the Body*, London: Academic Press

Strathern, M (1975) 'No money on our skins: Hagen migrants in Port Moresby' 61 New Guinea Research Bulletin, Canberra: Australian National University

Taylor, JL (1933a) *Mount Hagen Patrol Report*, 19 February 1934, Australian Archives A7034, Item 56

Taylor, JL (1933b) *Preliminary Report* [on Mount Hagen patrol], 30 August 1933, Australian Archives A7034, Item 56

PART II: CLOTHING AND THE PERFORMANCE OF TRANSLATION

"Kathleen", Maori Guide, Rotorua. N. Z.

CHAPTER 6

SURFACE ATTRACTION: CLOTHING AND THE MEDIATION OF MAORI/EUROPEAN RELATIONSHIPS

Elizabeth Cory-Pearce

Dear Lord and Father of mankind,
Forgive our foolish ways;
Re-clothe us in our rightful mind,
In purer lives thy service find,
In deeper reverence praise.
(from a hymn by JG Whittier, 1870–92)

… Maui
that smiling wide boy
flirting in Taranga's skirt
her maro
a cloaking device…
(from *Iri Descent*, a poem by Briar Woods, 2001)

This paper shall explore how Maori/European relationships have been mediated to some extent through clothing in both indigenous and introduced forms. To do this I shall begin with a brief description of what was already a complex indigenous dress system as it was encountered, experienced and described by late 18th century European explorers. Then I will move on to describe some ways in which clothing was introduced by Europeans and taken up by Maori – using 19th and early 20th century postcard photography and museum collections. I will finish with recent ethnographic examples of the use of introduced clothing materials and practices in ceremonial settings and in catwalk fashion. Whilst the temporal sweep of this chapter is broad, it maintains coherence by tracing a core theme: the ways in which introduced clothing and associated techniques have been incorporated into Maori dress and ceremonial practices, and used to mediate Maori and European social relations from contact, through colonisation and in the present.

DRESS IN EARLY MAORI/EUROPEAN ENGAGEMENTS

Initial European experiences of Maori dress were highly dynamic and dramatic ones. In the late 18th century, when off the east coast of Aotearoa, New Zealand for the first time, the *Endeavour* and her crew were charged on several occasions by Maori war canoes, whose crew members performed threatening posture dances, expressing what European observers referred to as attitudes of defiance. Such encounters were illustrated and described by Herman Diedrich Spöring and Sydney Parkinson (Joppien and Smith 1985: 36–37). They witnessed startling dances in which Maori were seen to be 'rolling their eyes about, lolling out their tongues, and in short, working themselves up to a sort of phrenzy' (Parkinson, 22 October 1769, cited in Joppien and Smith 1985: 168–69).

In these sketches and accounts, Maori men are frequently depicted and described as having long, oiled hair worn in a topknot with a large comb or a white feather or feathers inserted into it. According to William Brougham Monkhouse, also on the *Endeavour*, the men wore a variety of cloaks – from tough hard wearing rain capes, to finely woven shiny flax cloaks with borders woven in striking geometric patterns coloured cinnamon red, cream and black. More rarely, fine cloaks were ornamented with red breast feathers from the native parrot or strips of glossy white hair from the *kuri*, the dog introduced by Maori settlers.

Maori men were observed to have extensive tattooing, or to be more precise, skin carving on their faces, chests, buttocks and thighs. Wearing nothing beneath their cloaks except a 'Matt belt' that was 'principally intended for the purpose of sticking their *Patoo* [a hand held weapon] in' (Monkhouse 1955: 573), their striking pigmented skin designs could be easily revealed in their entirety. Men and women dressed their faces and limbs with a paint made from red ochre mixed with oil, the effect of which intensified the appearance of spiral designs carved into the face (Monkhouse 1955: 576).

Likewise, the spiral carvings on canoe prows and sterns were painted red with oily ochre, and fine cloaks were reddened by rubbing them with dry ochre. People carried various kinds of weaponry, the ends of which were often carved in the form of a face with bulging shell-inlaid eyes, protruding tongues and spiral tattoo patterns. The hafts of weapons were described as being bound with flax from which red feathers or white dogs' hair could be suspended (Banks Journal II, March 1770 cited in Joppien and Smith 1985: 210).

The significance of red was expressed in an exchange on 15 October 1769, in which Captain Cook desired to acquire the cloak worn by a headman of a canoe off the east coast, and offered an old black coat in exchange. Instead, the headman, 'observing a piece of red baize called out for that and it was immediately handed down to him' (Monkhouse 1955: 579–80). Whatever significance was invested in the colour red, this significance appears to have been translatable across different forms, from ochre to feathers, to novel cloth; and was applied to the surfaces of both persons and things. These descriptions and sketches of canoes (Joppien and Smith 1985: 176, 204), weaponry (Joppen and Smith 1985: 37, 209–10) and crewmen (Joppen and Smith 1985: 169, 191) reveal striking similarities in 'dress': feathers, carved skins or surfaces, wrapping and binding in flax, red ochre, flashing eyes and protruding tongues are features of appearance or dress that were evidently shared by people and things.

The visual analogies I make are supported by Monkhouse's description of a war dance that occurred on 14 October 1769, in which the headman of the canoe, 'in bending forward, throwing his Arms behind him, elevating his head, staring wildly upwards, and thrusting his tongue forward . . . exhibited a figure very like that expressed in the heads of their Canoes' (Monkhouse 1955: 577–78). These shared features are important because if people and things are alike in appearance it may not be plausible, in this time period at least, to assume a category of 'clothing' for persons as distinct from things. This is significant because, whilst those working in material culture studies and museum-based research may be familiar with approaching 'clothing' stored, displayed or depicted in sub-categories such as 'skirts', 'cloaks', 'ornaments', 'weapons' and so on, when people dressed in such things they may not have related to them in terms of such sub-categories or even in terms of the broader category of 'clothing' itself.

WOMEN AND PERCEPTIONS OF NUDITY AND SEXUALITY

Along the east coast in 1769–70, the crew of the *Endeavour* encountered women with far less frequency than men. Although women are described as being less ornamented than men, this may not be representative of their dress practices as a whole (Monkhouse 1955: 587; Joppien and Smith 1985: 174). The women Monkhouse met bore tattooing on the lip and chin, and were not nude but wore aprons of plaited grass, 'consisting of a number of platts or threads which form a pretty large roll: to this girdle are fastened the leaves of a plant by way of fig leaves' (Monkhouse 1955: 586). Interestingly, the men he encountered were 'totally without this part of dress', which suggests that women were more concerned to cover their pubic area than men. However, women were not anxious to cover their chests, in fact some 'readily uncovered their breasts' (Monkhouse 1955: 583), a condition which has often been assumed by Europeans to indicate immodesty or sexual licentiousness (Tcherkezoff 2003; Salmond 1991: 345–46).

Whether women in the Pacific displayed their bodies in a provocative manner or not, European men may have associated their 'nudity' (that is, bare breasts) with sexual availability. A general point of difference can be drawn here between Maori and European dress practices revolving around the social perception of what surfaces of the body ought, or ought not, to be revealed. Where such social perceptions are breached and a person becomes unsuitably dressed, they may be taken to be subversive and potentially dangerous (Gell 1993: 11–15). From a Christian viewpoint, the *Endeavour*'s crew may have found these unsuitably 'undressed' women dangerously attractive, and in subsequent times these Christian anxieties would be played out in the Pacific in missionary attempts to control those whom they considered to be unsuitably (un)dressed.

CHRISTIANITY, INDUSTRY AND DOMESTICITY

From the 19th century onwards, the promotion of Christianity in the Pacific, through organisations such as the London Missionary Society, encouraged a widespread need to clothe the body in line with Christian beliefs about modesty and dress (Colchester 2003). What I want to demonstrate here is how, from a missionary perspective, European clothing was introduced with an expectation that local social practices and cultural perceptions of the body could be changed because, as the hymn cited at the beginning of this paper suggests, Christian thinking posited a direct link between clothing the body and re-educating the mind.

Generally speaking, missionaries encouraged the uptake of European clothing such as long trousers and skirts, high neck blouses and restrictive undergarments that covered up as much skin as possible, shaping posture and limiting movement to some degree. In this sense, the clothing of this period can be conceived of as a form of body modification that inculcated certain Christian ideals of bodily concealment and psychological and sexual inhibition, in line with understandings of moral righteousness and purity.

In addition to wearing introduced clothing, entire domestic spaces required dressing: beds and pillows needed sheets and covers, tables needed cloths, and windows needed curtains and so on. From a European perspective, maintaining all these things was women's work and this required a particular range of sewing skills. These could be instilled through the practical making of things, for example, the needlework sampler. The sampler was less a decorative artwork than a technical exercise, a kind of needlework CV made by sewing samples of various stitches onto a rectangular piece of cotton or linen. This demonstrated competence in needlework and could be used to gain domestic employment. In addition to technique, samplers also demonstrated the ability to count and spell by embroidering letters, numbers and words in counted cross-stitch.

From around the mid-19th century, missionaries' wives often taught European domestic skills in mission schools. There is a sampler in Rotorua Museum made by Ellen Spencer, a missionary's wife stationed at Te Wairoa in the Rotorua region, where she is known to have taught local Maori girls to sew. Given that she made this sampler, it is likely that she taught needlework through this medium. She and other mission teachers like her may have encouraged an association between cloth, morality, and proximity to the divine, either directly by the embroidering of ecclesiastical quotations, or indirectly by inculcating Christian virtues such as patience, discipline and order through the tedious manufacture of needlework in general.

The Christian mission to dress converts was in Britain's commercial interest because, from a mercantile viewpoint, converting Christians in the colonies provided an emerging market for an expanding factory-produced textile industry. This conflation of religious and commercial interests should not be perceived only as a macro-structural process; it occurred through the livelihoods of particular families. For example, my family ancestors ran clothing factories in London and Manchester in the 19th century, importing textiles from China and India and producing clothing and fashionable trimmings for local sale and export. They were also devout practising Quakers. The scale with which 19th and early 20th century British manufacturers exported textiles to Aotearoa, New Zealand echoes into the present, for example in the continuing use of the term 'Manchester' to denote household linens today.

This point highlights that it was not just alienation of land and resources that pushed colonised people from a subsistence economy into a capitalist one. Peoples around the world entered into capitalist markets through the global circulation of commodities such as clothing. Money was needed to purchase such commodities, and from around the 1870s in the Arawa descent groups' region of Lake Rotorua, Maori could generate a monetary income through tourism.

Affluent European tourists were visiting the region to see striking geothermal scenery, such as the famous pink and white silica terraces near the Tuhourangi people's village of Te Wairoa. Here locals provided services for a fee, including guiding, canoeing to the terraces, food, accommodation and the performance of concerts.

The development of tourism stimulated a lucrative photographic industry and thousands of images taken in the region were circulated around the world in the form of the postcard. Today, remaining images in museums and private collections provide a rich historical archive that visually documents the uptake of European clothing from the late 19th century. Judging by the volume of cards around today, a popular subject appears to have been the practice of laundry washing in the natural hot pools in and around the Ngati Whakaue people's village of Ohinemutu and the Tuhourangi Ngati Wahiao people's village of Whakarewarewa. This outdoor 'domesticity' was an interesting novelty to Europeans and was frequently commented upon in travel writing, for example Payton (1888), and, with the development of the press, in pictorial newspapers that joked (with perhaps some irony) about the ease of simple native life, such as 'No trouble with the copper here!' (*The New Zealand Graphic*, 11 June 1904).

In the 19th century these activities might well have indicated the progress of civilization to European visitors, yet the outdoor and communal nature of laundry washing formed an important part of communal village social life that was not a simple reflection of European domesticity. As women elders today concur, outdoor laundry washing – and other practices that utilised the hot pools, such as cooking and bathing – emphasised Maori values such as: collective rights to village resources; being in a group (the kin group or *hapu*); a preference for openness and sharing rather than privacy and enclosure; and the observation of laws of *tapu* or ritual prohibition. The last point is particularly significant because clothing is associated with the body and thus becomes imbued with the bodily *tapu*, or ancestral sacredness, of the wearer. Clothing which is *tapu* should be kept apart from food and things associated with food, because food can remove and destroy *tapu*. This is why certain pools were reserved for laundry, others for bathing and others for cooking. Whilst missionaries, and Europeans in general, may have sought to change Maori perceptions of the body through encouraging the uptake of European clothing and related practices, in actuality this did not necessarily obviate Maori beliefs and practices.

CLOTHING AND POSTCARD PHOTOGRAPHY

After the uptake of European clothing in process, a significant section of society seems to have lamented this change, as is evidenced by the popularity of a particular style of postcard image available from the late 19th century. Here I refer to a number of romantic studio portraits of women, that in late 20th century critiques have come to be known, somewhat ironically, as the 'dusky maiden' genre. In these images, women are usually posed in a way that averts their gaze from the viewer. The pose tends to direct the viewer's attention to long flowing locks of hair and a bared shoulder, suggestive of a pre-civilised 'natural nudity' beneath the cloak. A photographer who was well known for producing these images, and was based in Rotorua for some time, is Arthur Iles. His series, *In Maiden Meditation*, typifies this genre. (See Figure 6.1 in the colour section.)

The nudity hinted at in this, and similar images, suggests an uninhibited sexuality that could attract buyers who liked to imagine native women in this way, but it was also a romantic and nostalgic genre. Critiques of 'dusky maiden' postcards as a white male commercial exploitation of sexually objectified indigenous women (for example, Sutton Beets 2000) cannot explain why many women bought these cards and sent them to women friends, as inscriptions on the backs of postcards reveal. Furthermore, male elders were also depicted in cloaks with a shoulder bared. Whilst these images are certainly romantic and nostalgic depicting the ageing 'chiefs' and 'warriors' of the past, male elders were not, to my mind, being sexually objectified. Without denying that sexual objectification and commercial exploitation took place, what I suggest is that it is necessary to consider other things happening at the time in order to engage more sensitively with the vast and multifarious photographic archives remaining today.

Considering that in turn of the 20th century, studio-based photographic portraiture the photographer was likely to have been able to exert a significant amount of direct influence over image content, it may be illuminating to consider other contexts in which photographs were taken, where subjects may have had a greater influence over the way in which they were presented to Europeans and to society in general. For example, where postcards depict people conducting particular activities, they wear clothes suited to that activity: when guiding tourists through the thermal region of Whakarewarewa, guides wore smart European dress, a red headscarf and various *taonga* or treasured heirlooms such as ear and neck pendants (see Figure 6.2 in the colour section); whereas, when washing laundry or cooking in hot pools, people wore standard European clothes and few or no precious *taonga*.

In a large number of images women engage directly with the camera, appearing confident and self-assured. And often the same women appear in a variety of dress styles in different postcards – at times in the latest Victorian fashions, at other times cloaked with a bare shoulder revealed, and at other times wearing a combination of Maori ceremonial *taonga*, such as cloaks, ornaments and weaponry, mixed with European-style jewellery and European clothing worn underneath.

These differences highlight the significance of context. To understand something of the way in which clothing was used to mediate Maori/European relationships, we need to look at the important context provided by large scale ceremonial welcomes – because these were occasions when Maori presented themselves to Europeans and to each other in a particular fashion. As with the tourist context, large ceremonial welcomes given to distinguished guests, especially European royalty and other dignitaries, tended to generate a lot of media interest. These welcomes produced a rich visual archive of postcards, newspapers, pictorial magazines, official accounts, souvenirs and memorabilia through which Maori responses to new clothing materials and the possibilities they offered can be explored.

CLOTHING IN MAORI CEREMONIAL PRACTICE

Ceremonial welcomes given to distinguished guests are auspicious occasions. Generally speaking, when guests come onto a regional descent group's *marae* (ceremonial meeting ground) they occupy a liminal position between 'inside' (hosts) and 'outside' (strangers). They are known as *manuhiri*, the word *manu* meaning 'bird' (Williams 1917: 206). To ritually welcome them, elders perform oratory to negotiate the potentially dangerous threshold between host and guest, and between living and dead, because when people come onto the *marae* they bring their dead with them. Upon completion of the *marae* ceremony, liminality is transcended and guests become part of the host group for the duration of their stay (see Salmond 1987 for an extended discussion of this ritual process). The elders performing this role are often adorned with feathers or feather cloaks evoking a bird-like stature. This may be advantageous when performing ceremonial roles, as birds occupy a liminal space – that between sky and earth – and have long been believed by Maori to mediate between the living and the dead (Lander 2001: 8).

In ceremonial events at the turn of the 20th century, generally speaking Maori men usually performed oratory and posture dances wearing woven cloaks, flax kilts known as *piupiu* or European blankets wrapped about the waist, with European clothing such as shorts and vests often worn underneath. Ceremonial dress for women consisted of *piupiu* wrapped over long European dresses, or skirts and blouses (see Figure 6.3 in the colour section). Women dancers also carried *poi*, balls made from bulrush and suspended from a flax cord. These were swung and rhythmically tapped against the body, creating optical patterns and aural percussion for entertainment and for training hand-eye co-ordination in the martial arts. In addition to this, people wrapped woven cloaks over their clothing, wore feathers in their hair and displayed stone, bone and wooden ornaments and weapons.

It is difficult to tell what cloaks were made from in the black and white photography of the turn of the 20th century period. By the mid-19th century, the travelling artist George French Angus had commented that introduced blankets were often worn by Maori like cloaks, and red ones were 'highly esteemed' and 'displayed by them on festive occasions' (Angus 1847: Plate 13). According to Angus, brightly coloured wool had become the preferred material for augmenting Maori clothing: 'Blue and scarlet caps, and variegated "comforters", brought by the traders, find a ready market amongst the women, who pick them to pieces to form the tufted ornamentation of their dresses' (Angus 1847: Plate 26).

A grand ceremonial welcome was given in Rotorua to the Duke and Duchess of Cornwall and York (later King George V and Queen Mary) on 14 and 15 June 1901. This particular event is pertinent because during the ceremonies many participants removed items of dress such as cloaks, belts, small hand held bags, weapons, personal ornaments and feathers and presented them to the Duke and Duchess in a great pile, in what was described at the time as a spontaneous and competitive act of gift giving (Loughnan 1902: 122–25, 131). Some of these gifted cloaks, belts and bags have been on loan to the British Museum from the royal family since 1902, and consistent with Angus's earlier comments, they demonstrate that weavers at the turn of the 20th century continued to experiment with the possibilities of a wide range of introduced materials and techniques. Highly colourful wools, cotton and exotic feathers, and sewing and embroidery techniques were combined with indigenous weaving techniques and materials such as plant fibres, dog hair and feathers in novel and exciting ways.

In addition to these creative practices, people modified ready-made European garments. Representatives from regional descent groups from across the whole country attended this event, and their choice of European clothing, as well as their song and dance style and composition, would serve to distinguish one group from the next as kinship dynamics were played out through hours of competitive performance of posture dances, poi dances, chants and songs (Loughnan 1902: 101–31, 368–76). This brings to mind the important point that clothing often mediates group relationships and is not just about individual expression.

However, I want to suggest that European clothing in Maori ceremonial performance enabled more than the expression of kin group identity. European clothing was modified and used in such a way that may have enhanced the quality of performance, which in turn could enhance the *mana* or prestige and standing of the descent group and their ancestors. For example, as part of the 1901 festivities, women of the Ngaiterangi regional descent group performed wearing long white blouses and skirts 'enriched with tufts of feathers' (Loughnan 1902: 94) 'from the neck of the blouse to the hem of the skirt' (*Auckland Weekly News*, 21 June 1901). Not only did the selection of uniform dress identify them as Ngaiterangi; by sewing feathers onto their clothing the performers could have been evoking the powerful metaphysical forces redolent in feathers, including *mana* (ancestral authority) and *tapu* (being potent and set apart) (Lander 2001: 8).

The practice would seem to be significant because 19th and 20th century oral sources record that when feathers are attached to inanimate things they are imbued with a life force or *hau*; this vital force being transferred via the mediating capacity of birds and feathers (Lander 2001: 7, citing Ngata and Te Hurinui 1970: 268–69). In this sense, feathers are protective and empowering, a kind of metaphysical armouring of persons and things. And the missionary association of sewing and embroidery with Christian morality and divine proximity – discussed earlier in relation to the sampler – could be interpreted within a local ontological framework that understood the binding of feathers and fibres as a conduit for ancestral and divine presences. This in turn suggests something of the spiritual significance of embroidering motifs onto cloaks, perhaps also acting as conduits for ancestral presences, such as the rainbow embroidered on a cloak currently in the British Museum.[1]

---

1   (BM Ethno Q82 Oc 709) Circumstantial evidence indicates this is likely to be one of the cloaks gifted at Rotorua in 1901, see Pendergrast 1996: 146 for an illustration.

Through excellence in performance and oratory, people can undergo a similar transformation in which they become pathways for the presence of their *tupuna* or ancestors. When this is the case, a performance will elicit *ihi*, an excitement or magnetism that evokes *wehi*, sending shivers over the body and making body hair stand on end. *Wehi* is the fear and awe elicited by psychic forces such as *ihi* and supernatural forces such as *mana* and *tapu*. People charged with *ihi* and *wehi* can enter a euphoric state known as *wana* that evokes fearful quivering and excitement (Marsden 1977: 144–48; Kruger 1984; Tapsell 1997; McLean 1996: 201; Williams 1917: 88, 562, 565).[2] The trembling that is characteristic of attaining these states would be visibly enhanced by the quivering motion of feathers attached to the body, or in this case to European clothing, an effect that could augment the awe-inspiring force of their performance.

Similarly, it was not only red wool and blankets that were popular to ornament cloaks or to wrap around the body like a cloak. Red clothing such as skirts, blouses and the guide's red headscarf mentioned before were also popular and used in interesting ways. Ngati Raukawa performers were likewise identifiable as a group distinct from other groups through their selection of a particular ceremonial uniform. In their case, the choice of clothing was particularly striking: the women wore red and white dresses in alternation to emphasise, quite deliberately, the precision and synchrony of their *poi* dance formations (Loughnan 1902: 94).

Precise unison has long been admired in Maori performing arts, and was noted by several early European observers, for example by Monkhouse (1955: 566, 569) and Parkinson (cited in Joppien and Smith 1985: 198). Around the turn of the 20th century, a term was in use – *te kura-takahi-puni* – that expressed great admiration for a powerful body of warriors moving simultaneously. This term directly associates unity and precision with redness and power through the concept of *kura*. *Kura* denotes both redness and something that is highly valued, such as red feathers and red ochre, and in the 19th century and most likely before, persons and things dressed in red were likely to be highly *tapu* and set apart (Williams 1917: 183–84).

This concept of *kura* points back to late 18th century observations of attributes shared between people and things, such as red ochre and feathers, outlined at the beginning of this paper. Other attributes that seem to have been significant in that period were the carving of skins or surfaces, defiant facial expressions and the girdles or waist-wrappings worn by women. I will return to these elements now, but this time in relation to more recent historical and contemporary ethnographic examples.

---

2   These writers all draw on the knowledge of elders whose understandings of Maori lore
    would be consistent with the early 20th century. Their accounts of these concepts accord with
    Williams' dictionary based on late 19th and early 20th century Maori oral sources.

CLOTHING AS A WAIST WRAPPING DEVICE

A notion adumbrated so far that I would like to draw out more explicitly is that of clothing as a wrapping device. By device I mean a thing that is both made or adapted for a particular purpose, and that can act as a tactical practice or strategy. Something like the practice of waist wrapping commented on by Monkhouse is described in 19th century oral sources. For example, women of high birth wore decorated aprons known as *maro kapua* that impressed their social status upon others. Their surfaces were embellished with *awe*, attachments made from white albatross feathers or long tufts of dog hair (Ngata and Te Hurinui 1970: 37 cited by Lander 2001: 17). Because *awe* also means 'strength, power and influence' (Williams 1917: 28), this suggests that *awe* strengthen a *maro*, which in turn suggests that *maro* strengthen and empower their bearers.

Waist wrapping was later described by the Arawa scholar, Makereti in her ethnography of life in the Rotorua region around the turn of the 20th century. Makereti stated that if a woman were to unwittingly reveal her pubic area to a stranger, this could incur an insult of such extreme shame as to cause the woman to take her own life (Makereti 1938: 124–25). Makereti would no doubt have understood the Christian notion of shame regarding genital exposure through her European schooling, but what I understand her to be referring to here is the condition of *whakama*, of a shyness or shame caused by *accidental* exposure that wrapping about the waist prevents. The practice of waist wrapping does not always concur with Christian notions of dress, bodily modesty and shame, because as a concealing device waist-wrappings also enabled their reverse: the power to reveal.

Oral sources recall a late 19th century incident in which a gesture known as *whakapohane* was ritually performed by Mihi Kotukutuku – an East Coast woman elder – to Mita Taupopoki, an Arawa elder; in which she flipped her skirt up in a deliberate act of exposure. Her gesture of contempt conveyed the utmost form of insult (Salmond 1987: 150–51).[3] This demonstrates how something wrapped about the waist can form an empowering device, both in terms of the insult and shame its operation prevents (*whakama*), and in terms of the potential to deliver insult its operation enables (*whakapohane*). Clearly, waist-wrappings do much more than enable 'modest' appearance in the Christian sense (although wearing a skirt does achieve this effect as well).

Wrappings worn about the waist continue to be important today. In fact they *enable* women to take part in ceremonial activities. A Maori woman wearing European-style trousers at a formal *hui* (ceremonial gathering on a *marae*) would most likely remain seated and not join in the *karanga* (welcome call) and *haka*

---

3   East Coast men performed a similar gesture to the *Endeavour*'s crew in 1769. Although the ship's crewmembers are likely to have had little or no understanding of local cultural practices at the time, Monkhouse seems to have intuitively got the point (1955: 575–76).

powhiri (the posture dance that beckons visitors onto the *marae*). Sometimes women dressed in trousers quickly wrap something at hand around their waists to create the appropriate ceremonial attire. This could be a shawl, a blanket or even a jacket, demonstrating that it is waist wrapping that enables ceremonial participation – whether this is done with an item of European dress is incidental.

To further consider the notion of wrapping and empowerment in relation to introduced clothing materials, I want to bring in a contemporary non-ceremonial example of clothing design and practice to draw out several important points. Jeanine Clarkin makes contemporary Maori fashion, and her designs often incorporate and rework the standard Western domestic apron form. In a recent catwalk fashion show, these were worn wrapped over European-style skirts worn over trousers, demonstrating an ongoing concern with wrapping the hip area in Maori women's dress practices.

Jeanine Clarkin describes her work as a direct engagement with her experiences of living in a colonised country, where in predominantly European social contexts Maori can feel alienated and uncomfortable. Yet, when Maori host events on their kin group *marae*, such occasions normally generate great pride as the provision of generous hospitality can raise the *mana* or ancestral standing of the group considerably. Correspondingly, the organisation and provision of hospitality, and in particular of food, is an important task. It is also a task in which women usually play key roles, hence today the *marae* kitchen and dining areas are spaces in which Maori women often feel confident, at ease and in charge. They are also spaces in which aprons are frequently worn, which is why Jeanine Clarkin sees the apron as an enabling device for bringing the pride and assurance women feel in *marae* kitchens out into any given social context.

Some of her aprons have magnified *moko kauwae* designs printed across the front. But unlike the typically miniaturised designs on mass-produced souvenirs, Jeanine Clarkin uses Maori imagery on a scale that is big, bold and positively affirmative of Maori values and practices (see Figure 6.4). For centuries Maori women have worn *moko kauwae* (facial tattooing) on the lip and chin. The *moko kauwae* is a mark that acknowledges women as repositories of important skills and knowledge particular to their regional descent group. More generally speaking, they are understood as a positive affirmation of *mana wahine* – of the strength, authority and influence of women (Te Ao 1998).

This difference between the specific and general effect of *moko kauwae* is what I refer to as their 'inside' and 'outside' effect, where inside and outside refers not to the individual body, but to belonging, by descent from a shared ancestor, to a regional descent group. What I mean by 'inside effect' is the detailed meaning that can be contained within *moko kauwae*, which is usually restricted, passed on within the kin group and not to outsiders. It is the inside effect which makes problematic the mass production of clothing, souvenirs and other things bearing Maori designs, because the right to display certain designs is not automatic, but this is a subject for another work.

However, markings made on the face are hardly private, they are exposed. Outsiders can see them, but they are not privy to inside knowledge and so

Figure 6.4: Black denim apron with silver *moko
kauwae* design. Jeanine Clarkin Fashion, Auckland,
November 2001. Photograph © Elizabeth Cory-Pearce.

experience them differently. They experience what I call 'the outside effect', and
this is what I understand Gell (1993) to have theorised: the social function of
tattooing as a defensive wrapping. The distinction between inside and outside is
important because tattooing does not necessarily armour and defend the
individual from attack by anyone and everyone, including their own kin.
Similarly, it does not follow that tattoo designs are intended to communicate
restricted meaning to anyone regardless of descent (Gell 1993).

What I discuss here is the outside, or 'apotropaic' effect (Gell 1998: 83) of
surfaces rather than their encoded meaning. *Moko kauwae* are visually complex
patterns that can trap the onlooker in the twists and turns of their design and
therefore afford the wearer a kind of optical protection. Perhaps it is not a
coincidence that these designs are magnified and relocated from the chin to the
chest, given the European fascination with women's chests discussed earlier.
Furthermore, in some of her apron designs, Jeanine Clarkin augments the
cognitive complexity of *moko kauwae* by overlaying the design with a shimmering
bright translucent material that moves with the wearer's body, enhancing the

optical motion of the pattern and increasing its protective effect. Catwalk models amplify this armouring effect by performing posture dance moves such as *pukana*, an expression of defiance in which the mouth is upturned and the eyeballs are rolled down and side to side with incredible dexterity. The notion of clothing as a wrapping that is defensive and empowering is further conveyed in the names Jeanine Clarkin gives to her designs, such as *Wahine Toa*, or 'Fighting Woman'. The whole effect – form, imagery, materiality and performance – challenges onlookers, recalling impressions made by Maori in early encounters with Europeans, rather than the demure impression constructed by Arthur Iles and other colonial studio photographers.

This point brings me back to the notion posited at the beginning of the chapter, of clothing as part of a broader category of wrappings that dress both people and things; and to the suggestion that the relationships between them may become apparent through performance and practice. It is perplexing to attempt to engage with the oral, aural and visually dynamic complexity of clothing as activated through performance and practice, when clothing is encountered through still and silent collections, archives and texts. Because of this, I feel that oral sources and ethnographic experiences are invaluable as they inform historical archives and museum and pictorial collections. In fact, these things dialectically inform each other, bringing past events to life and giving an understanding of the historical depth and dynamism of things encountered in the present.

SURFACE ATTRACTION

Since pre-European times, dress has been part of a complex presentation of self and social group that mediates social action and effectiveness in accordance with the prevailing context. With the introduction of Christianity and European colonisation came new understandings of the possibilities of introduced clothing to enable social interactions explored through performance and practice. Whilst these may accommodate certain Christian and European beliefs and practices, it cannot be assumed that Maori people, and women in particular, made use of such clothing solely to cover themselves in accordance with introduced notions of modesty, purity and reverence.

The accommodation of European dress was in certain respects like putting on a second skin, a wrapping that provided a material surface over which various wrappings, attachments and colours could be applied, making use of both local and introduced materials and techniques to achieve the desired effect. The attractiveness of these surface embellishments may reside in their potential to strengthen, protect and empower the person and the group physically, psychologically and spiritually. It may reside in their capacity to act as vehicles for ancestral and divine forces that transform persons and things from dormant into actively charged states, demonstrating the significance of clothing in mediating social relations.

When Alfred Gell argued that tattooing formed a more permanent defence of skin because it is inserted into the skin rather than merely covering its surface, he effectively elevated the significance of tattooing over clothing by reifying a distinction between persons and things and reasserting a prioritisation of depth over surface (Gell 1993: 38–39). Because these distinctions were ones he sought to transcend, my understanding is that he has recapitulated his own critique in this respect.

Yet Maori cloaks, ornaments, weapons and tattoo designs are like heirlooms – treasured things handed down family lines – and in this sense they cannot be considered to be less permanent than tattooed skin. Certainly some have a greater material longevity than others, for example a greenstone weapon can be handed down through many generations long after a flax cloak has disintegrated. People desire these things because they can act as material conduits for the direct transmission of power and authority from ancestors to descendants. They become socially effective precisely because the relationships people have with them transcend the boundaries between persons and things, individuals and groups, the living and the dead.

Acknowledgments

This chapter is from a paper drawn from my doctoral research funded by the ESRC. I am indebted to my mentors and hosts, Kaumatua Wihapi Winiata and Kuia Huhana Mihinui, for their guidance and wisdom. Similarly, I thank: June Northcroft Grant, Dell Rae and Zella Morrison-Briars and Whanau for sharing many valuable insights into life in Whakarewarewa and Ohinemutu; Kathleen Pearce for her research into our family history in the textile industry; members of Te Matarae I Orehu, Ngati Rangiwewehi, Te Waka Huia, Ngati Ranana, and Te Wananga O Aotearoa (Rotorua) for unforgettable experiences of life on the *marae* and performing arts; Jeanine Clarkin for sharing her work and permitting me to write about it; Maureen Lander for inspirational conversations about feathers; Anne Somerville for her knowledge of Ellen Spencer and for assistance with photographic and clothing collections; and Jill Hassell for assistance with the Royal Loan Collection.

References

Angus, GF (1847) *The New Zealanders Illustrated*, London: Thomas McLean
Colchester, C (2003) 'Introduction' in Colchester, C (ed), *Clothing The Pacific*, Oxford: Berg
Gell, A (1993) *Wrapping in Images: Tattooing in Polynesia*, Oxford: Clarendon
Gell, A (1998) *Art and Agency: An Anthropological Theory*, Oxford: Clarendon
Joppien, R and Smith, B (1985) *The Art of Captain Cook's Voyages, Volume 1: The Voyage of the Endeavour 1768–1771*, New Haven: Yale University Press
Kruger, T (1984) 'The Qualities of *ihi, wehi* and *wana*' in Mead, S (ed), *Nga Tikanga Tuku Iho a te Maori: Customary Concepts of the Maori*, unpublished Maori Studies Source Book, University of Waikato
Lander, M (2001) '*Manu* as medium' in Wood, B and Lander, M (eds), *Glorified Scales*, Auckland: Maureen Lande

Loughnan, RA (1902) *Royalty in New Zealand. The Visit of their Royal Highnesses The Duke and Duchess of Cornwall and York to New Zealand, 10–27 June 1901: A Descriptive Narrative*, Wellington: John Mackay, Government Printer

Makereti (1938) *The Old Time Maori*, London: Victor Gollancz

Marsden, M (1977) [1975] 'God, man and universe: a Maori view' in King, M (ed), *Te Ao Hurihur, The World Moves On: Aspects of Maoritanga*, New Zealand: Hicks Smith Methuen

McLean, M (1996) *Maori Music*, Auckland: Auckland University Press

Monkhouse, WB (1955) [1769] 'Journal of William Brougham Monkhouse' in Beaglehole, JC (ed), *The Journals of Captain James Cook, Volume One: The Voyage of the Endeavour, 1768–1771*, Cambridge: Cambridge University Press/Hakluyt Society

Ngata, AT and Te Hurinui, P (1970) *Nga Moteatea, The Songs: Part Three*, Wellington: The Polynesian Society

Payton, EW (1888) *Round About New Zealand, Being Notes From a Journal of Three Years Wanderings in the Antipodes*, London: Chapman & Hall

Pendergrast, M (1996) 'The fibre arts' in Starzecka, DC (ed), *Maori Art and Culture*, London: British Museum Press

Salmond, A (1987) [1975] *Hui. A Study of Maori Ceremonial Gatherings*, Auckland: Reed Methuen

Salmond, A (1991) *Two Worlds, First Meetings Between Maori and Europeans 1642–1772*, Auckland: Vikin

Sutton Beets, J (2000) 'Images of Maori women in New Zealand postcards after 1900' in Jones, A *et al* (eds), *Bitter Sweet: Indigenous Women in the Pacific*, Dunedin: University of Otago Press

Tapsell, P (1997) 'The flight of Pareraututu: an investigation of *Taonga* from a tribal perspective' 106(4) Journal of the Polynesian Society 323–74

Tcherkezoff, S (2003) 'On cloth, gifts and nudity: regarding some European misunderstandings during early encounters in Polynesia' in Colchester, C (ed), *Clothing the Pacific*, Oxford: Berg

Te Ao, N (1998) *Kauwae: Maori Women's Contemporary Visual Art*, Gisborne: Gisborne Museum Press

Williams, HW (1917) *Williams's Maori Dictionary, A Dictionary of the Maori Language*, Wellington: Marcus F Marks, Government Printer

CHAPTER 7

DISCO, DOG'S TEETH AND WOMEN IN UNIFORMS: MODERN MEKEO DRESS CODES

Bente Wolff

The Mekeo in the lowlands of Papua New Guinea have become wealthy on growing the 'Mekeo gold' of betel nut for the urban market in Port Moresby.[1] The increased incomes have lead to an extension and modernisation of the formal dress codes marking a person's position in the shifting social relations that he, and even more so *she*, is part of. Some of the clothes are locally referred to as 'modern', for example volleyball outfits, bachelors' fashion clothes, women's clan uniforms and young girls' plastic skirts for disco dancing. Others are described as ancestral 'custom', for example, dancing costumes made of feathers, dog's teeth and shells. The very classification of things as being either modern or traditional in itself indicates a modern ideology, in which time equals change and the future is contrasted to the past. However, for the Mekeo, modernity (the present/future) does not necessarily imply a potential loss of tradition (the past). Rather than countering or threatening ancestral tradition, objects of modernity and development are regarded as complements to and, indeed, the fulfilment of tradition.

Numerous Mekeo myths relate how they were the first to own modern goods. But the god(s) possessing the knowledge to produce modern goods left the Mekeo and went to Europe or America, where white people received the advanced technology (Bergendorff 1996a: 217–25; Wolff 1995). Modern imported goods are thus not regarded as completely new or foreign. Rather, they represent something lost, which may be reintegrated into the local ancestral inheritance of the people of the clan, their customs, land resources and powerful spells for gardening, hunting and love. Also, in basic economic terms, there is a direct connection between ancestral inheritance in the form of land used for betel nut production and the goods that are bought with betel nut profits.

Clothing is a case in point that illustrates how the understanding of modernity as an extension of ancestral tradition is practised. After briefly describing different dress codes that signify the individual's marital status, I will focus on the formal clothing at some larger social events that took place in Eboa village in the early 1990s – when betel nut prices peaked. The situation at that time gave privileged conditions for the study of the cultural rationales behind local consumption strategies, as people could 'realise cultural projects that would

---

1   The term 'betel nut' refers to areca nuts and betel nut 'peppers' that together are chewed with lime.

normally not be visible under the constraints of scarcity' (Miller 1994: 73). The following examples are: a customary mocking feast adapted to the form of a disco party; a fundraising feast for women dressed up as modern young men; a volleyball tournament; and a large-scale feast at which the guests were dressed in feather headdresses and shell valuables, and the hosts wore uniforms. These events were all costly celebrations of the hosting clan's strength, in terms of unity, money, beauty and the power to surprise. They were steps in the process of reaching the full potential of local tradition by (re)integrating the signs of modernity into ancestral custom.

Towards the end of this paper I shall briefly present some more recent changes in the same village. It seems that the big clan celebrations of the early 1990s were followed by disappointment, in terms of the actual effect that people felt their investments to have. Today the attempts to modernise tradition are being challenged by an open antagonism to tradition on the part of adherents to two new churches who refuse to wear the customary feasting costumes.

CLEAN OR DIRTY, FAT OR SKINNY: MARRIAGE AND APPEARANCE

The Mekeo live in exogamous patri-clans, and, as it will become evident, clothing and appearance mark the position of the individual in relation to his or her immediate in-laws and to the clan as a whole. Affinal relatives are in a relation of formal inequality, in which 'wife-givers' are superior to 'wife-takers' and a woman is regarded as inferior to her husband's clan. A married man is not only an inferior in-law (*ipangava*) to his wife's native clan, but also to her mother's and maternal grandmother's clans, who are the wife-givers of previous generations. Likewise, a married woman is *ipangava*, not only to her husband's clan, but also to the clans of his mother and maternal grandmother. As an *ipangava*, one has to work for one's superiors whenever it is required. For the married woman, who lives in her husband's clan, it means that she is in a permanent position of worker. A married man works for his superior in-laws only when called to assist at funerals, house building, feast preparation and other projects. In return for their services, the *ipangava* must receive payments in food from their superior affines.

Marriage is contracted by a young couple eloping to a house belonging to the groom's kin. Here the bride must spend the first months lying passively inside the house, except for the evenings where she is presented on the veranda dressed in the customary attire of grass skirt, flowers, and bride price valuables of shells, bird's feathers and dog's teeth. She is kept away from the sun for her skin to become white, and her in-laws give her new clothes, bathe her, rub her skin with oil and comb her hair. The purpose of keeping the bride in the house for so long is to make her gain as much weight as possible, and she is virtually force-fed by the other clanswomen in order to attain this goal quickly. After having reached a considerable increase of weight and a light tone of skin, she is dressed in all her fineries and formally presented in the church on one of the major church days. The local explanation of the bride's treatment is to show her relatives how well her new family provides for her, but the fattening and the new clothes also contain a strong element of symbolic rebirth in the form of skin change.[2]

Termination of married life is marked by an exact inversion of the arrangements made for the young bride. When a married person dies, the surviving spouse is forced to live in seclusion in a small hut near the dwelling of the dead partner's closest kin. A widow remains in her husband's clan where she has lived throughout her married life, but a widower must move to the native clan of his wife for some months or even years. The widow or widower is dressed in black and is not supposed to wash or cut their hair (even the male beard). He or she must fast and usually shows a marked loss of weight shortly after the partner's death.[3] The seclusion and fasting is part of a bodily strengthening at a time of dangerous transition from married to single life. But it is also the in-law's punishment of the surviving spouse for not taking sufficiently good care of the partner. He or she is, as a local idiom has it, 'put in jail' by the in-laws, who will only release the captive after having been financially compensated for their loss of a relative (Mosko 1985: 156ff; Hau'ofa 1981: 171). (See Figure 7.1 in the colour section.)

The bachelor shows similarities as well as differences to the two previous categories. In contrast to the bride he is supposed to be as skinny as possible; unlike the mourner, he dresses up to look handsome and dazzling. The terms for his appearance are *pakai*, which also means 'love magic', and *stailo* (from the English 'style'). His hair is cut according to the latest international fashion and he wears baggy jeans and other fashionable clothes, sunglasses and a hat or cap. The appearance of the Mekeo bachelor has certainly changed over time, but what remains constant is the general idea that, along with certain powerful words and substances, a dazzling appearance is essential to a man's ability to attract and court girls (Hau'ofa 1981: 117–18). (See Figure 7.2 in the colour section.)

With the exception of the bachelor, the above examples show how other people are responsible for a person's formal appearance, by being in a position to order inferior in-laws to wear certain clothes and control their food intake. This principle not only applies to the individual's change of marital status, but also to the dress codes marking the person's position in the clan at larger collective events. The next examples illustrate how the system of dress codes has been expanded by the addition of modern clothes that mark the shifting positions of married women as, respectively, subordinate in-laws and celebrated guests of honour.

---

2   As opposed to Mosko's observations from the North Mekeo (Mosko 1985: 73ff), increasing her procreative capacity was not a direct reason for fattening the bride in Eboa. The groom was expected to sleep outside the family house at night and to spend only very limited time with his new wife during the day.

3   Other mourners, especially close female relatives by descent, and sometimes those by marriage, shave their heads and dress in dark clothes (blue, brown or purple) until their mourning is lifted by the chief of a neighbouring clan.

DISCO DANCING AS A PUNISHMENT

Superior in-laws not only expect work services from their inferior affines, but also a respectful attitude. Any disobedience, mistake, or complaint on the part of a single *ipangava* may call the superiors' punishment upon all the *ipangava*s in the form of a mocking feast, called *ipaipa*. An *ipaipa* normally consists of the (superior) hosts 'paying' their (inferior) guests with enormous amounts of greasy food. The guests are forced to try to consume all the food, even if the amount is much larger than any person could possibly eat (Hau'ofa 1981: 132–40).

In 1991, a modernised and milder *ipaipa* took place in the village of Jesubaibua. The feast sponsor was a man who owned some full-grown pigs that would soon begin to lose value. Instead of selling the animals, he organised an *ipaipa* for all the female *ipangava*s of his clan.[4] It followed the general principle of turning something otherwise regarded as a pleasure into a punishment through exaggeration. In this case, however, the guests were summoned at daybreak not to overeat, but to attend a disco party. The customary outfit for a women's *ipaipa* is the grass skirt, but here the women had been instructed to dress up as young girls attending a disco party.[5] They therefore wore so called 'plastic grass skirts', made of long pink and blue plastic cords – and put make-up on their faces and plastic flowers in their hair. They each paid an entrance fee of approximately US$12 and danced for a full day under a tropical sun, while three local bands took turns accompanying them. Finally, the women were allowed to leave in the afternoon, each with a gift of raw pork from the host. By then they were exhausted, but they clearly also had enjoyed the disco, which was either a whole new experience to them, or something they had been prevented from doing since their marriage. (See Figure 7.3 in the colour section.)

At a first glance the disco party may appear to be a local emulation of an urban, universal fashion phenomenon. However, the structure and meaning were very clearly local. Kin relations determined participation in the disco-*ipaipa*, and although some of the women were so distantly related to the host that they did not even know him, their relation to him as inferior in-laws meant that they could not decline the invitation.

TROUSERS, BEER AND CIGARETTES: WOMEN IN MEN'S CLOTHES

The structural inequality between in-laws is reversed in relation to a married woman's native clan and the clans of her mother and maternal grandmother. When formally invited to festive occasions in these clans, the married woman is

---

4   Thus the invitation was aimed at women married into the host's clan and wives of men whose mothers or maternal grandmothers were born in his clan.

5   Disco parties are frequently held at nights for the unmarried village youth. They are organised by an individual sponsor with the aim of generating profit from the entrance fees. There are no formal rules or prescriptions in terms of who can participate; every paying guest is welcome. Other villagers, ie, married people and children, watch the party from outside the dancing enclosure as a form of entertainment (Wolff 2001).

treated as a guest of honour, whereas her husband is the *ipangava* who may be called as a worker or mocked at an *ipaipa* by *his* superior in-laws.

When married women are invited collectively to their native clan they are called 'child women' *(imoi papie)*. They dress up as men to mark their position as true clan members by birth, rather than as temporary members by marriage.[6] A common occasion for inviting the child women is Christmas sports competitions between the child women – who have the advantage of wearing trousers or shorts – and the women married into the clan, who race and play ball dressed in grass skirts. Likewise, unmarried girls may dress up as men to mark their true clan membership and mock their own mothers as inferior in-laws at an *ipaipa* (Hau'ofa 1981: 139). (See Figure 7.4 in the colour section.)

In 1991, the clans invited their child women to bring cash contributions to the construction of new clubhouses. Some of the women wore the 'classic' men's attire of a *laplap* (long wrap-around), but the majority had decided to dress up as bachelors in jeans, shorts, T-shirts, sunglasses, hats and other objects of *stailo*. They placed the bank notes conspicuously on sticks that they waved in the air, or they attached the money to their hats and clothes. They were served beer and cigarettes, modern items otherwise reserved for men, thus further testifying to their male (or rather gender-neutral) status in their native clan.[7] Again, the ceremony itself was a customary one, but it was aggrandised and modernised by the beer, cigarettes, fashion clothes and bank notes that all linked it firmly to the urban market economy.

VOLLEYBALL: NEW UNIFORMS AND ANCESTRAL FORCE

One of the larger public events that took place in the village in 1991 was a volleyball tournament, which everyone, from the youngest to the oldest, followed intensely every Sunday afternoon. Volleyball is a relatively new phenomenon, which has become common in most Mekeo villages. It is played at a rather high level and in strict accordance with the international rules of the game. Still, the game may be seen as yet another means to integrate modernity into the clan system and ancestral heritage.

The teams are organised according to clan membership, and the reputation of the whole clan is at stake during the tournaments. Each clan has a men's team consisting of bachelors and young married men, and a women's team for the young, unmarried girls. The players' outfits are locally referred to as 'uniforms' and consist of a singlet with the team name and player number, and matching shorts and socks. Depending on how far a team makes it in the tournament, the

---

6   A woman is only a temporary member of her husband's clan, as her corpse will be returned to her native clan for burial.

7   See Mosko 1999: 58–59 on beer as a men's symbol of modernity among the North Mekeo; and Mosko 2002: 102–05 on how North Mekeo women have recently started to incorporate beer and bachelor's clothing into their own practices.

players have new uniforms designed and printed two to three times during a six month playing season. The ever-new uniforms are a manifestation of the clan's common strength in terms of wealth and *stailo*. (See Figure 7.5 in the colour section.)

The success of a team further depends on their clan elders and ancestors. The elders supply the secret ancestral knowledge of powerful spells and substances that are necessary in order to make the adversaries weak and unfocused during the finals. The same spells and remedies were previously used by warriors preparing for war, and the players pay the seniors for their services by making a small feast for them. During the weeks before the finals, the men's teams each organise a training camp. Here they help to keep each other awake throughout the nights, as the soul of the sleeping person roams about and is exposed to nightly attacks from his enemies, who in this case are the other teams. What may appear as a simple import of a Western sport is thus organised according to very local principles. The volleyball matches are a test of clan strength, not only of the players, but also of their forefathers, both dead and alive. The training follows local ideals of making oneself strong – and keeping the image resplendent by continuing to wear new uniforms is a central part of this notion of strength. In these respects the volleyball games have much in common with the grand feast discussed below.

UNIFORMS AND FEATHER HEADDRESSES: MODERNISING CUSTOM

The most costly and significant event to take place in the village in 1991–92 was the big 'race' between the clans to build clubhouses (*ufu*) and install chiefs. At that time, the function of the clan chiefs had been reduced to mainly terminating mourning periods, whereas their wider political role of making regional alliances through exchange and large-scale feasts had long been losing importance. Now it was being re-enacted on a grander and costlier scale than ever before, fuelled by the increased cash inflow. Each step in the *ufu* construction process required feasting and formal food distribution to the other clans in the village. Endless food exchanges and feasts took place, as the demonstration of one clan's financial capacities challenged the other clans to follow suit. The atmosphere grew increasingly heated and antagonistic (Bergendorff 1996a).

One of the innovations to appear during the race were women's 'uniforms' (the local term) that became the standard outfit at feasts and food exchanges, making it easy for the anthropologists to see which clans were involved whenever a ceremony took place. The men of the Faingu clan were the first to order their wives and unmarried daughters to design and purchase a uniform. The women enthusiastically went to town and returned with one type of uniform for the married women and another for the young girls. Both types consisted of a plain skirt and a singlet with a printed clan slogan. The text on the girl's singlet read *F City*; the text on the woman's singlet read *Tsikuna ekailai*, meaning 'Noah's Ark will sail'. Together the two texts marked out the full circle of local history: according to a common myth, a great ark once brought 'all the races of people living in Papua New Guinea, the horses, the ships, the cows, the motorbikes, bicycles . . .' to the region; and the new name of the clan was Faingu City or simply F City. The new name expressed the recent prosperity and modern progress of the clan, manifested by a newly purchased generator that powered floodlights on the clubhouse and streetlights between the houses.[8]

Male Faingu *ipangava* workers were also told to wear uniforms when coming to assist during the feast preparations. But the wife-receivers found the demand excessive, as they had no wish to display their inferior status in their wives' native clan so conspicuously, and pay for the privilege too. Instead of ordering a uniform in town, they decided to wear identical red *laplaps* with any yellow T-shirt, thus keeping some of their integrity without directly challenging their superior in-laws.

Apart from these steps to modernise the appearance of the clan, the inauguration of the Faingu chief and clubhouse followed all customary prescriptions. The preparation took 10 months, during which time the partner clans from other villages were regularly offered large ceremonial gifts of food in order to persuade them to come to dance at the inauguration feast. Without the presence of the guests the inaugurations would have no formal validity. Also, according to custom, the guests 'played hard to get', delaying their arrival week after week, in order to extract even more gifts from the hosts. The long delay created serious problems for the hosts, as the pigs they had bought for the feast began to die and the food crops started to go rotten. When finally the dancers arrived, they came in splendour at the break of dawn. Numbering around 200 men and young girls, they continued dancing up and down the central village ground for two full days, taking turns to eat or rest, so that the dancing was not interrupted at any moment, day or night. All the young girls of one of the visiting clans had had their chests and stomachs tattooed for the feast, an old custom that was otherwise very rare among young people at that time.

The guests' official excuse for delaying their arrival was that their feather headdresses needed adjustment. The large headdresses worn by the front male dancers at the largest kind of feasts are the essential Mekeo emblem. The headdress is called *kangakanga*, a term designating tradition in general. It is a huge structure made from the feathers of birds of paradise, chickens, cockatoos and other birds. The feathers are arranged according to inherited family rights, and it may lead to fights and compensation claims if a person has attached a feather in a manner copyrighted by another family line. The male dancers' costumes further consists of long strips of bark cloth attached to the waist band; female dancers wear a 'grass skirt' made of yellow sago fibre and a small feather headdress. Both men and women are adorned with bride price valuables of dog's teeth necklaces, shell armlets, mother-of-pearl pendants and tortoiseshell ornaments. Their faces are partly or fully covered with intricate geometrical designs painted in yellow, black, red and white. The facial paint of the women is rather standardised, whereas men decorate their face with highly individual and often asymmetric designs. The dancer's appearance is meant to astonish and impress the spectators,

---

8   See Bergendorff 1996a: 230ff and 1996b; Wolff 2001.

as is also the case with the bachelor's *stailo* and the volleyball uniforms. Personal beauty, splendour and the ability to astonish make up a shiny surface that protects and shields the person against other people's direct attacks, as well as their indirect attacks of sorcery (Hau'ofa 1981: 95–96, 174–75ff, 301; Stephen 1995: 46–51).

The dancers' reference to their headdresses in the official excuse for their delay reflects the equation between beauty and power in the trial of strength between hosts and guests. The ambivalent relation of mutual friendship and dependency on

Figure 7.6: Dancers at the grand feast of Faingu Clan 1992. Photograph © Bente Wolff.

the one hand and competition and antagonism on the other became evident when the dancers arrived. They were met at the village entrance by the hosts who cheeringly welcomed them, but who also tried, not too seriously, to scorch the dancers' headdresses and skin with embers from big coconut leaf torches. The hosts' mock attack added to the dramatic effect of the dancers' arrival and accentuated the notion of beauty as a form of invulnerability, as the guests appeared completely unaffected while the embers rained down on them. During the two days of feasting the dancers kept their calm serenity, while the women of the hosting clan did not have a quiet moment, running to and fro with new food supplies and dirty dishes. The new uniforms made them easily distinguishable in the crowd, adding to the impression of the Faingus as being modern and professional feast organisers with a well drilled and diligent female workforce at their disposal.

The Faingu feast was said to be the largest in the village since the 1940s. A previous attempt in the 1970s to erect a new clubhouse had not been carried through, leaving the building incomplete and not formally opened. The clan's chiefly office had been vacant for decades, as the heir to the position had never been formally installed. He had spent most of his life in the district capital, while the secondary war chief performed the chief's formal duties in the village. People of means had gone to town for education and work, and although they kept their house and betel nut palms in the village, their status derived more from their urban position than from their engagement in customary affairs. With the increased incomes from betel nut, the number of young people seeking education dropped significantly, and customary projects became important. Together with a group of clan elders with customary offices, the men with good positions in town were the ones to take the initiative to stage the grand feast and thereby regenerate the glory of the clan and the ancestors. They brought the chiefly heir to the village, but without giving him much actual influence on the central part he was meant to play. He had little knowledge on custom and formal etiquette and was heavily prompted by the initiators throughout the ceremonies. In short, the grand feast did not simply represent an unbroken tradition carried on from the past. Both the customary aspects of the feast and the innovations of uniforms and floodlights were financed by the individual incomes from betel nut, and the whole project was orchestrated by people with strong ties to the urban sector.

The fact that money and imported goods derived from local inherited resources helped create all this renewed faith in ancestral knowledge as the original source of power and wealth. Moreover, in the micro-politics of the clan, the new wealth had threatened to further devalue the position of people with customary offices, as well as the status of those with urban positions. Most people had sizeable sums at their disposal and could challenge the existing social order by spending their money on individual projects. But with the cash inflow instead going into conspicuous clan projects of feasts, floodlights, uniforms, volleyball games and disco-*ipaipa*, the new wealth could support the existing order. In principle everybody could feel they gained from the common projects, as everybody shared the same clan ancestors. In fact, some had less interest in the events than others, and could be persuaded into participating only as long as the strategy seemed to work. After the Faingus had won the 'race' by successfully staging their grand feast, the other clans became less enthusiastic about completing *their* clubhouses, and the ceremonies gradually ceased. Shortly after, an economic crisis set in across Papua New Guinea, and betel nut prices dropped dramatically. Still the Mekeo were and are much wealthier than most groups in the country; but to many of the villagers it must have seemed that their sacrifices had been in vain. Despite all the work and money they had invested into revitalising tradition, the great times were not followed by even greater times, as they had expected, but rather the opposite.

AFTER THE PARTY: NO GRASS SKIRTS, NO DANCING

Ten years after the big feast, many of the villagers have lost their faith in the ancestors.[9] They have converted from Catholicism to either of two new Protestant congregations.[10] The members of the new churches deliberately abstain from many symbols of social interaction. They do not consume betel nut, beer or tobacco and they refuse to wear any of the traditional dancing costumes. They exchange washing bowls, pots, plates and other 'things that can be used right away' for bride price, rather than shell valuables, dog's teeth and plumes.[11] The vast quantities (truckloads) of these modern bride price valuables, however, indicate that even to the new Protestants, spiritual force manifests itself in impressive public displays of material wealth. Rather, the main difference between the Protestants and the modern 'traditionalists' lies in their relative positions in village politics. Among others, the new churches seem to attract successful businessmen (bus and shop owners) as well as less wealthy people without formal influence in their clan. The same two segments were being most reluctant to participate in the feasting of the early 1990s.

Despite the popularity of the new churches, the modern traditionalists have far from given up their attempts to keep the clan united. In 2002, the same men with urban employment who played key roles in organising the Faingu City feast raised around US$5,000 to stage a feast for the clan's married women. It was not a 'classic' *ipaipa* punishment, but a demonstration of wealth and beauty at which the other clans could watch their 'sisters' being presented as the public face of the Faingu clan. At the beginning of the feast all the women approached the clubhouse. Those at the front wore grass skirts and performed a traditional dance. Behind them followed the women of the new churches. They were dressed in ordinary clothes and walked instead of dancing, thereby participating in the feast without practising tradition. In the clubhouse, they were each presented with a new uniform and three items said to symbolise the male bachelor. First, a long strip of greasy pig's skin which was hung around their necks, symbolising the waist-belt of the bachelor of former times; secondly, a huge sausage said to

---

9   Data newer than 1992 derived from Steen Bergendorff who has made several field trips to the
    village since our joint field work in 1991–92. He did not, however, observe the clan feast in
    2002 directly, but only the video that was shot to document the feast by a Port Moresby
    photographer hired by the organisers.

10 The American Christian Outreach Church and the Australian Evangelical Bible Mission.

11 By far the largest share of the bride price consists in cash – this is true for the Protestants and
    others alike.

Figure 2.2: Woman modelling a new wedding dress, made by Agnes Kaltabang, Pango village, Efate, October 2002. Photograph © Lissant Bolton.

Figure 3.3: Women dressing the grave in Natewa, Vanua Levu 1996. Photograph © Chloe Colchester.

Figure 4.1: Jules Lejeune, *Les Deux Rois de L'Ile Borabora*, 1823. This watercolour, executed during the voyage of the French ship *La Coquille*, shows a Boraboran male and female titleholder closely related to the Pomare family. *Service historique de la Marine*, Vincennes (SH 356, 55).

Figure 5.1: Wahgi dancers (Omngar tribe) in full festive adornment, 1980. Some have added neck ties to their dress of aprons, bird of paradise plumes and body paint (Johnson's Baby Powder in place of paint in other cases). Photograph © Michael O'Hanlon.

Figure 5.2: Senior men, from groups which had long been formal enemies to each other, make peace through sharing pork in 1980. Many wear bandleaders' hats (some hats are also dressed with beads) along with shell ornaments. Photograph © Michael O'Hanlon.

Figure 5.3: Wulamb having her face painted and her headdress assembled before the presentation of her bridewealth. Her indigenous dress contrasts with the imported wear of her helpers (1990). Photograph © Michael O'Hanlon.

Figure 5.4: Contemporary Wahgi shield. The 'Cambridge Cup' referred to is a national rugby league competition around which Senglap Olkanem warriors co-ordinated their shield designs. Photograph of shield (No 1990 Oc 9.9) © Copyright The British Museum.

Figure 6.1: *In Maiden Meditation.*
From a series by Arthur Iles, circa 1900.

Figure. 6.2: *Kathleen, Maori Guide,
Rotorua, NZ,* her red headscarf forming
part of a Guide's dress. Gold Medal
series by Fergusson Ltd, circa 1908.

Figure 6.3: Te Arawa women holding *poi* with *piupiu* wrapped over European clothing, their heads adorned with feathers. Rauru House, Whakarewarewa, circa 1900.

Figure 7.1: Widowers attending a feast. Their clean and neat appearance shows that their bereavement is not very recent. One is wearing the traditional attire of perineal band and the waist belt of the fasting person; the others are dressed in a fashion that is far more common today. Photograph © Bente Wolff.

Figure 7.2: A bachelor dressed in the uniform of his clan's volleyball team. The facial band aid is part of his *stailo*. Photograph © Steen Bergendorff.

Figure 7.3: Married women disco dancing at the *ipaipa* mocking feast in 1991. Photograph © Steen Bergendorff.

Figure 7.4: 'Child women' of Eboa clan dressed up as men, bringing cash donations for the clan's new clubhouse. Photograph © Bente Wolff.

Figure 7.5: The winning girl's team at the 1991 volleyball tournament, displaying their trophy in all the Mekeo villages from a hired truck. Photograph © Steen Bergendorff.

Figure 9.1: Drag queen Buckwheat's performance, 'Heat'. Photograph © Lisa Taouma.

Figure 9.2: Shigeyuki Kihara's performance, 'Queens of the Pacific'. Photograph © Lisa Taouma.

Figure 11.3: Oronhyadekha wearing the outfit made for his presentation to the Prince of Wales in 1860. Photographed by Hill & Saunders, Oxford, 1862, private collection.

Figure 11.8: Coat belonging to Reverend Peter Jones, buckskin, cotton tape, quills and glass beads, 118 cm × 62 cm, Smithsonian Institution, NMNH 178 398.

represent the bachelor's tobacco stick; and thirdly, a tin of fish representing the bachelor's marihuana. The food gifts and the underlying sexual joke of giving bachelor's items to married women both had clear reference to *ipaipa* mockery. But the women were not expected to consume all the food and they only took a bite of each gift. Subsequently the women – who had all been drilled in advance by a military officer – marched to a military band, wearing their new uniforms.

The women's uniform has thus become an acceptable costume both for those who follow Christianity *instead* of the ancestors, as well as for those who ascribe the story of Noah's Ark and other biblical stories to their own ancestral past. Both groups cherish modern development, for example in the form of uniforms and marching, and both groups actively participate in ceremonial activities as long as these are not defined as custom. So, although they explicitly oppose ancestral custom, the Protestants have not (yet?) challenged a clan's right to decide the appearance of its inferior in-laws.

CONCLUSION

The dress codes of bachelors, mourners, brides and 'child women' are all examples of long-existing ways of marking different social positions. The more recently introduced modern types of clothing are additions to the existing dress

Figure 7.7: Aisa Olapu and Margaret Piauka presenting the new flag of Faingu clan in 2002. Margaret Piauka (right) wears the married women's clan uniform.

codes and they are locally regarded as complementary to ancestral heritage. The wives' uniforms and the child women's fashion clothes display the wealth and power of a clan towards other clans. Also, the volleyball games serve to maintain the formalised rivalry between clans, involving physical force, expensively maintained appearance (the uniforms) and powerful knowledge (secret ancestral formulae). The same may be said of the traditional feast, which is an even more costly and significant trial of strength between the clans.

From an outside perspective it is clear that the innovations are inseparable from long-existing local values and forms of social organisation (Bergendorff 1996a, 1996b; Mosko 2002). This does not mean, however, that the contemporary meaning of the Mekeo dress codes is identical to that of the past. Today's formal clothing does not differ from the customary attire by being imported. The bride price valuables used for personal adornment have always been obtained from neighbouring peoples, and thus imported wealth has always been necessary to maintain the fundamental social institutions of marriage and feasts. What has changed in the local consumption of garments, however, is that the modern clothes represent a great expense that is 'lost forever'. The customary valuables may be put back into circulation at any time, whereas the modern uniforms are designed and bought for the occasion without being re-circulated in any formal way. This points to an important function of the modern clothes, namely to channel the betel nut profits into projects that support clan unity and maintain the social order within the clan. Whereas the customary feasting costume displays wealth as an exchange potential to other clans and villages, the modern clothes display wealth as a process of 'killing' money in the constant renewal of appearance without any potential for creating external relations. By refraining from wearing or exchanging customary valuables, the adherents of the new churches have gone further in this direction than the traditionalists. Also, the anti-traditionalist Protestants, however, continue to celebrate the asymmetric relations between in-laws by marching dressed in uniforms and receiving 'waist-belts' of pig's skin, thereby constituting contemporary Mekeo modernity.

References

Bergendorff, S (1996a) *Faingu City: A Modern Mekeo Clan in Papua New Guinea*, Lund: Lund University Press

Bergendorff, S (1996b) 'Faingu City: a modern Mekeo clan' in Friedman, J and Carrier, J (eds), *Melanesian Modernities*, Lund: Lund University Press

Hau'ofa, E (1981) *Mekeo: Inequality and Ambivalence in a Village Society*, Canberra: Australian National University Press

Miller, D (1994) 'Style and ontology' in Friedman, J (ed), *Consumption and Identity*, Chur: Harwood Academic Publishers

Mosko, M (1985) *Quadripartite Structures: Categories, Relations, and Homologies in Bush Mekeo Culture*, Cambridge: Cambridge University Press

Mosko, M (1999) 'Magical money: commoditization and the linkage of *maketsi* ("market") and *kangakanga* ("custom") in contemporary North Mekeo' in Akin, D and Robbins, J (eds), *Money and Modernity: State and Local Currencies in Melanesia*, Pittsburgh: University of Pittsburgh Press

Mosko, M (2002) 'Totem and transaction: the objectification of "tradition" among North Mekeo' 73(2) Oceania 89–109

Stephen, M (1995) *A'aisa's Gifts: A Study of Magic and the Self*, Berkeley: University of California Press

Wolff, B (1995) 'Missing paradoxes and the evidential nature of things: material objects in a cross-cultural perspective' 2 Nordisk Museologi 107–22

Wolff, B (2001) 'Money is not for buying food, money is for buying things: modernity and consumption the Mekeo way' 43 Folk 9–39

CHAPTER 8

DRESSING AND UNDRESSING THE BRIDE AND GROOM AT A ROTUMAN WEDDING

Vilsoni Hereniko

I was puzzled by a number of traditional rituals and ceremonies that did not make sense to me when I was growing up on Rotuma, a remote island in the South Pacific. Part of the reason for my ignorance was that no one explained to me the reasons certain rituals had to be performed on special occasions, or why these rituals had to follow a prescribed order. Often, I did not feel it was appropriate to ask or probe into the reasons or meanings of these acts or actions. As a good Rotuman, my duty was to observe and listen. Sometimes I would hear complaints or criticisms levelled against individuals who did not follow the correct protocol because of ignorance or an inability to rise to the demands of the occasion. There would be tensions among community members until these 'sins of commission' or 'sins of omission' were forgiven by those who had been insulted: through apology via the performance of the appropriate rituals for forgiveness. Only then would harmony be restored.

One ritual performed at traditional Rotuman weddings that puzzled me then is called *fau ta* which translates as 'to cover'. Specifically, the bodies of the bride and groom are covered up or wrapped with fine mats, the most prestigious and valuable of Rotuman 'cloth'. Woven by the female relatives of the bride and groom, these fine mats that require tender loving care to produce are regarded as sacred by Rotumans. Unlike ordinary mats, they are never used as floor covering in the home. Instead, they are stored in secret places (such as under beds) until important rituals or ceremonies occur. Only then are they brought out and displayed publicly or used ritualistically. After their symbolic use, they become valuable items for the exchanges that consolidate relationships between families. These mats are then carefully folded and hidden again, until the next ritual or ceremony requires that they be brought out for public viewing and use one more time.

After the bride and groom have been wrapped in finely woven mats, they are lifted from the ground by male relatives (often the young, untitled men) of the bride and groom. Carrying the bride and groom on their shoulders, the young men transport the couple from the bride's side of the festivities to the groom's side. Supervising the activities is an old Rotuman woman dressed up like a ritual clown who entertains the wedding guests by hurling mock insults at the men carrying the couple or the chiefs seated nearby. Reaching the opposite side of the open arena, where the groom's relatives are seated, the young men lower the couple to the ground. Then the women, who had previously wrapped the mats and covered up the couple, undress them by unwrapping the mats. Having been clothed and unclothed symbolically, the bride and groom return to the special seat of mats that has been specially prepared for them to sit on. There they sit a little higher than everyone else and watch the wild or funny antics of the ritual clown.

Rotumans call the ritual clown, who is the supreme ruler of Rotuman weddings, the *han maneak su*. As the term suggests, one of the roles of the *han maneak su* is to 'spoil' the wedding. This she does by undermining the seriousness of the ritual of clothing the couple in fine mats. With her privileged licence to be disrespectful of everybody – particularly the male chiefs – she creates laughter by ordering the chiefs to do her bidding. On this particular occasion, this old funny woman can do whatever she wants and everyone else, according to custom, obeys her every whim. Sometimes she orders the chiefs to kneel in the hot sun, dance, fetch things for her, even climb a coconut tree: in short, anything that she thinks will entertain the assembled wedding guests. On this day, humour comes from overturning the power structure of society. The woman is now the chief, bossing the men around and telling them what to do as though they were little children.

No wonder, then, that as a boy I was puzzled by this custom that seems to operate on different and contradictory levels. There is the serious ritual of dressing and undressing the couple that entails a predetermined order – of who does what and when. Juxtaposed with this orderly act is the chaotic laughter instigated by the ritual clown. Her spontaneous and seemingly chaotic attempt to 'spoil' the importance of the occasion runs counter to the serious nature of arranged marriage.

On an island that is only nine miles by two, with only 2,500 people living on it, life for me was boring and often stifling. Pressures to conform to cultural demands and expectations meant little room for individuality or creative expression except through traditional forms such as dance or song. But it had its bright moments too, such as at weddings when the ritual clown performed, and temporarily provided relief from the mundane realities of a hierarchical society in which to be the youngest of eleven meant I was often at the lowest end of the pecking order. No small wonder that I identified with the ritual clown who had licence to 'destroy' this order and turn everything on its head, upside down.

It is significant that the ritual clown is always a woman and never a man. Unlike Samoa, where her counterpart is always male (usually young and untitled), this gender difference needs explanation. In my earlier research (Hereniko 1995, 1992), I suggested that the fact that the Rotuman ritual clown is always a woman fits in with the worldwide tendency for clown figures to be from the lowest rung of society. The common woman is among the most oppressed members of Rotuman society and is therefore the antithesis of the male chief. Although there is some truth in this, my recent research suggests that there might be another, more important reason.

According to Vafoou Jiare (personal communication), a well known historian living on the island, a woman was the first inhabitant of the island of Rotuma. This particular myth about the origin of the Rotuman people has never been published – nor did I hear about it during my early research. When I did finally hear Jiare's version of this story, I remembered that I had heard some of the names in this story when I was growing up. There is also a particular beach on the island where this first voyaging canoe had supposedly landed. The villagers who live around this area call this first woman *hanit te maus* or 'woman of the bush'. For them, she is their protector and guardian. They and other Rotumans as well, invoke her name and memory whenever they feel the need to appeal to a higher spiritual power, particularly in matters involving land disputes or boundaries. These specific details lend credibility to Jiare's story, which I retell below.

There was a canoe carrying seven brothers and their sister. Where the canoe originated from no one really knows, although it could have been a canoe from Samoa because another name for this woman is Salamasian, which means in Rotuman 'the light that lights my path'. During their long voyage at sea, Salamasian became pregnant. When the brothers knew of this, they were ashamed of what had happened. Thus, when they discovered the remote island of Rotuma, they abandoned her there and continued their journey to Fiji. Over time, this woman became known as *hanit te maus*, or the 'wild woman of the bush'. Her memory is immortalised in the Rotuman saying: '*Pear ta ma 'on maf, pear ta ma 'on 'al, ma 'incajema ne sei la noju.*' This literally translates as: 'The land has eyes, the land has teeth, and always knows the truth.'

Is it possible then that at Rotuman weddings, when the ritual clown overturns the political hierarchy, she is reminding the inhabitants of Rotuma that it is a woman who is the supreme ruler of the island? Does this also mean that at weddings she is reminding the islanders of the injustice that was done to her by her seven brothers? A number of cultural beliefs and practices support this interpretation.

First and foremost is that the practice of ritual clowning only takes place when the bride is believed by everyone to be a virgin. No virgin, no clown: as simple as that. Considering the violation of Salamasian on that voyaging canoe, is it conceivable that there is a link between this imposed virginity and what happened to that first woman inhabitant of the island? Is it possible that this prohibition is not only saying that sex between brothers and sisters is taboo but also that males should never force themselves upon females, their 'sisters' in other words? After all, on an island so small, every female is like a sister. There is a saying that 'all Rotumans are related', the implication being that we are all descendants of this first woman inhabitant of the island.

Rotumans believe the Rotuman ritual clown has *mana* that has to be obeyed. The belief is that she is a conduit for the *atua* or ghost and her criticism or mocking of the chiefs is therefore sanctioned. She is beyond reproach because it is the 'ghost' ('the wild woman of the bush' perhaps) within her that speaks, and not her as an individual. This belief allows her to be fearless in her mocking of the chiefs or those in authority. The chiefs, like everyone else, must succumb to the power of this 'wild woman'.

Another important reason why the ritual clown is always female is because the fine mats that are bound around the bodies of the bride and groom are always woven by women. It is these fine mats that are paraded around on this day for all to see. For women, there is no skill more respected than the ability to weave these fine mats that are essential for all traditional rituals or ceremonies. The women from the bride's relatives use the occasion as an opportunity to show off their wealth as well as their skills and talents. On the other hand, the groom's relatives show off their wealth in terms of the amount and size of their root crops and animals. These complementary displays of wealth and items for ceremonial exchange are part and parcel of the marriage ceremony, and are important because they demonstrate the likelihood of a future of plenty and therefore happiness for bride and groom as well as their extended families.

Since pre-Christian times, once a wedding date has been chosen, women (usually past childbearing age) choose to hold a *sa'a*, or gathering, to weave the fine mats needed for the occasion. During this period of mat weaving that could last for months, women behave in similar ways to that of the ritual clown at weddings. The belief is that this is a period when the *mana* of the dead ancestors is abundant, and women have licence to challenge the authority of the chiefs and other males. Like the *han maneak su* who is imbued with the *mana* of *hanit te maus*, the women weavers have been known to mock and ridicule males passing by on the road. Men avoid areas where the women weavers rule, and go to great lengths to keep their distance. In my earlier work (Hereniko 1995), I wrote that when the women wove these fine mats, they were symbolically weaving in the evil spirits of uncircumcised men that supposedly roamed the island. By capturing or snaring them in the weave of their mats, women transformed these malevolent spirits into positive ones. By the end of the weaving period, many fine mats imbued with the *mana* of the ancestors have been produced. From then onwards, these mats are sacred, and treated as if they are 'woven gods'. Thus they are always carried in a respectful manner (called *apeiak*) and presented ceremonially. To put them directly on the ground, for example, would be to make these mats profane, or to be disrespectful to these cultural 'gods'. It is these mats that are taken to the traditional wedding and used to clothe the bride and groom, albeit temporarily.

The use of fine mats as clothing has symbolic rather than practical significance. When Rotuman warriors went to battle, for example, some of them wore fine mats around their waists. By the same token, by clothing the married couple in fine mats, Rotumans symbolically surround the couple with the *mana* of ancestral spirits. The hope too is that the couple will lead productive lives in the community and be blessed with many children.

In order for the *fau ta* ritual to have efficacy, the process of covering the bride and groom with fine mats is accompanied by ritual clowning. In this instance, the laughter that the ritual clown instigates from the assembled community is in the service of harmony. My interpretation here comes from the second meaning of *han maneak su* which not only means the 'woman who spoils the wedding', but also the 'woman who plays the wedding'. Like playing the different strings of a guitar to produce a melodious tune, the ritual clown diffuses tension and deflects possible conflict among different strands of society (chiefs and commoners, men and women, relatives of the bride and groom for example) by making everyone laugh.

Because traditional marriages were arranged, and such alliances were not always evenly balanced in terms of looks or wealth, tensions and possible conflicts were a reality that ritual clowning helped deflect or diffuse and resolve through laughter. But not all ritual clowns are always well versed in the art of creating harmony, and more than one *han maneak su* has been known to have failed in mediating tensions. When this happens, she is not thanked at the end of her performance. No baskets of cooked *taro* or pork accompanied by chicken and several fine mats will appear at her doorstep. The disgraced clown will never be invited again to be the woman who 'spoils' the wedding and at the same time mediate conflicting forces in the natural and supernatural world in the hope of achieving harmony.

If harmony was difficult to achieve in pre-Christian times, it was even more difficult after the arrival of Christianity in 1839. For example, in pre-Christian Rotuma, the women were bare-breasted, and the men's private parts were barely covered. This makes sense in a climate that is hot and humid. The wrapping of fine mats around the bodies of bride and groom were therefore not meant to clothe them in the Western sense of covering up their shame, but rather to surround them with *mana*. But this changed when Christian missionaries linked lots of bare flesh with sex and imposed clothing on Rotumans, as they did elsewhere in the Pacific. The story of Adam and Eve in the Garden of Eden is a narrative that reinforces for Islanders the Christian requirement to cover up.

Today, there are few traditional weddings on Rotuma. There are a number of reasons, not least of which is the fact that marriages are no longer arranged. Instead, present-day Rotumans tend to marry someone they love and have known personally over a period of time. Virginity is no longer as prized as it was then, hence the reduced need for a ritual clown. In some people's eyes, this is probably a good thing, for it saves expense as well as the need to follow practices that have lost their meaning. Further, with the advent not just of Christianity but also of the money economy, individualism, Western materialism and capitalism (to name but a few), Rotuman culture is not as homogenous as it was when I was growing up. Ritual clowning, a social institution that was once central to Rotuman religious beliefs, is now almost extinct. Fine mats that were once the equivalent of 'woven gods' are now few in number, and those that do exist do not appear to have been woven under the same conditions of earlier times. In other words, these are mats or cloth without *mana*.

On Rotuma and Fiji today, the preference is for a Western style wedding, complete with a white wedding gown and veil for the bride and a suit and tie for the groom. Does it matter that young Rotuman men and women are getting married without being clothed ceremonially in fine mats? Do we lose something when what we wear is bought from a shop downtown rather than communally woven accompanied by ritual clowning? My answer to this is simply that I chose not to marry according to Rotuman custom, so I cannot talk from personal experience. However, I have personally experienced similar rituals performed in my honour in Rotuma and Fiji. The most compelling of these examples, because it closely mirrors the experience of a groom being honoured by strangers who are his bride's relatives, happened to me in May 2003.

During a visit to the University of Washington in Seattle, I became the undeserving recipient of Fijian mats, a beautifully designed *tapa* cloth, and a whale's tooth (the equivalent of the Rotuman fine mat). I had never met any of these Fijians before, but when they heard that a professor from Fiji was at the University, they insisted on performing in my honour a ceremony usually reserved for chiefs or visitors of high rank. As I watched the proceedings during the ceremony that followed, I must have felt the same way my father did when he married his wife, my mother. According to my father, his marriage was arranged and he did not set face upon my mother until the wedding. And yet, the young men on my mother's side of the family must have carried him on their shoulders after he had been wrapped in fine mats. They must have embraced and honoured him then as one of their own, just as the Fijians, on the occasion I am relating, honoured me according to custom.

A Fijian lady, whose name I learned later to be Buna, garlanded me with a *salusalu*, the equivalent of the Hawaiian *maile lei*, as *yaqona* or *kava* was ceremonially mixed, presented and drunk. Seated on mats, men and women clapped in unison at appropriate times during this ceremony. An elderly Fijian man orated eloquently in his native tongue, and my spokesman, allocated to me according to Fijian custom, responded in kind. At the very end, I improvised a speech of gratitude and heartfelt thanks. When the ceremony ended, I was told that the cultural treasures before me were all mine.

Needless to say, I was deeply moved by the performance of this ceremony in my honour, in perhaps much the same way a groom would feel during and after a *fau ta* ceremony. Most important of all, I felt a profound and deep sense of connection with the Fijian people who performed this ceremony. I felt I had become one of them, a stranger no longer, but one accepted into another community. I sensed they felt the same way too and this was proven by an invitation to one of their homes the following day (Sunday) for a lunch of fish in *lolo* (coconut cream) and *taro*. I accepted, and arrived for lunch to find *yaqona* and Fijian neighbours waiting for me. The host of the family kept telling me that I had come home, and to always remember to visit them should I ever return to Seattle. This then is the main value of communal interaction and collective experience: the feeling of oneness and acceptance by a new community.

After the bride and groom at a traditional Rotuman wedding have been wrapped in fine mats, the young men who are the relatives of the bride are the ones who customarily carry the groom, and vice versa. Symbolically, this says that the male relatives of the groom will uphold the honour of the new bride who has now entered their lives. Unlike the sister who was violated by their brothers, these men will respect and protect her. Similarly, the male relatives of the bride's side will support the new groom who has now come into their lives. To know this is to feel at home, in a deep and profound way. Likewise, to know that by being clothed in fine mats is to be protected by the *mana* of one's ancestors is to move into a new phase of life secure in the knowledge that one is not alone.

The profound sense of belonging I have just described is lost when what we wear ceremonially is not woven collectively with the blood, sweat and tears of our elders, but by cotton thread and needle pushed along by foreign machines.

References

Hereniko, V (1992) 'When she reigns supreme: clowning and culture in Rotuman weddings' in Hereniko, V (ed), *Clowning as Critical Practice: Performance Humor in the South Pacific*, Pittsburgh and London: University of Pittsburgh Press

Hereniko, V (1995) *Woven Gods: Female Clowns and Power in Rotuma*, Honolulu: University of Hawaii Press

Hocart, AM (1913) 'Field notes from Rotuma', manuscript in Turnbull Library, Wellington, New Zealand

Howard, A (1985) 'History, myth and Polynesian chieftainship: the case of Rotuman kings' 45 Transformations of Polynesian Culture 39–77

Howard, A (1986) 'Cannibal chiefs and the charter for rebellion in Rotuman myth' 10 Pacific Studies 1–27

Inia, EK (2001) *Kato'aga: Rotuman Ceremonies*, Suva: Institute of Pacific Studies

CHAPTER 9

'DOUBLENESS OF MEANING': PASIFIKA CLOTHING, CAMP AND COUTURE

Lisa Taouma

Oscar Wilde once famously said that 'it is not life that art imitates, but the viewer' – a turn of phrase that succinctly sums up many of the ways in which Pacific peoples have been imagined by Western audiences. Today, issues of viewing – who is telling the story and who is the audience – are at the forefront of arguments about Pacific image-making.

UNDER WESTERN EYES

Some of the freshest and most dynamic works within this discourse are those literally made to be worn. Body adornments – from T-shirt slogans to the subversive works of *fa'afafine*[1] pageantry – are making waves in the realm of how Pacific people intend themselves to be seen. As many Polynesian strategies of resistant representation rely on satire and parody, there is a heavy reliance on the world of popular culture as a site for challenge and change. Images of *palagi* (foreign) men and women may have differed radically in popular culture over the centuries, and Polynesia may have become heavily Westernised; but most images we see of Pacific people are still caught up in fantasies of an ancient, untouched world full of semi-naked natives – a world that has remained largely unchanged since the 18th and 19th centuries.

These stereotypical representations have produced a specific set of knowledge about Pacific people. Although this has been well documented and is not particularly new, it is worth noting the impact that these images have had on our history – which must itself be considered when attempting to understand what is happening in the present.

Much of the visual anthropology of the Pacific has glimpsed us as representative of unchanging cultures. Early paintings, photographs, postcards and film have positioned Pacific people into 'prototypes', in order for us to be understood by the consumer more readily. Many of these 'types' have come from previously established clichés from other cultures. Due to the later exploration of the Pacific region, the perceptions of the Polynesian body were shaped by a

---

1 Samoan *fa'afafine* are boys who are raised as girls, who fulfil a traditional role in Samoan culture. In the past they have shared women's traditional work but today are becoming more Westernised and look more like drag queens.

European political and representational system heavily involved in concepts of the African 'black' or the 'Oriental' body. Prototypes like the 'mammy figure', the brute nigger and the exotic Odalisque are all latent signifiers with corresponding Polynesian images, such as the Polynesian mama, the heathen savage and the dusky maiden.

As we have shared a common visual history with other 'ethnic' peoples within the colonial schema, it is clear that we need to point to the nature of these images as constructs. The role that many travelling artists played in their visits to the exotic regions opened up by colonial expansion has historically served a multitude of purposes – largely in providing material for the benefit of Western viewers 'back home'. The use of the 'dusky maiden' image is, I argue, one of the main signifiers used in this manner of *surrogate possession*. In order that the changing contexts of these images can be reinterpreted, it is necessary to first examine the social, political and economic motivations behind their production.

Even in recent accounts of Polynesian culture that talk about the 'fatal impact' of colonialism and the corrosive effects of civilization, the imagery remains the same. Polynesian women are portrayed as shy, alluring creatures – sexually knowledgeable but fundamentally naïve – while the men are prone to acts of savagery but can also be dignified, noble and wise (Moorehead 1966; Stanley 1998). I want to suggest that there is no point in judging these images as right or wrong. Rather, these images are produced by a complex interweaving of many factors, mostly governed by the realities of the capitalist world of consumption.

No one expects advertisers to be leaders in social reform: you are going to see Polynesian Islanders smiling away as if their lives depended on it in advertisements for everything from lottery tickets to anti-smoking, simply because a client wants to pitch a product at a consumer. But the popular ideology behind the appeal of these stereotypes – as much as the stereotypes themselves – is significant because it affects the way that our identities are formed; it shapes how people interact with us on a day-to-day basis. Once formed, cultural stereotypes are almost impossible to shake off.

Of the vast spectrum of images of Pacific Islanders that have been made for a Western market from the early 1900s up until the 1980s, none have been created by a Polynesian artist and very few have been produced primarily for Polynesian consumption. It was not until the recognition of Pacific visual artists like Fatu Feuu and John Pule in the 1980s that our own representations of ourselves were put onto the same marketing platform. So what we have had is a very one-sided representational view of the Pacific that has relied on pre-coded stereotypes to convey certain information about Pacific people and about Pacific islands.

It is useful to examine the kinds of images of the Pacific that have interested a Western audience, as well as the means by which they were manufactured, transported and consumed. What is really important is to recognise what lies behind the image-making process, what the voice and audience of an image are – in other words, who is speaking in the image and who are they speaking to?

Of the many images of Pacific people in popular culture, the most popular ones have been of women, and a certain image of Pacific women has been the aforementioned 'dusky maiden', the Pacific belle, the hula girl, the velvet vixen. 'Dusky maiden' was a term that was coined in the kitsch era of the 1950s when it was popular to do prints and velvet paintings of naked breasted Polynesian women who looked like the tanned *palagi* (foreign women). The concept of the dusky maiden illustrates two things: 'dusky' meaning almost white but 'not quite'; 'maiden' suggesting the notion of a Polynesia that is eternally in a pure, unspoilt, static, childlike state.

The image of the dusky maiden in early explorers' images of the Pacific was synonymous with Polynesia and the bounty of the land itself: naive, untouched and passively inviting of Western penetration. In the 1920s, Margaret Mead's book *Coming of Age in Samoa* (Mead 1930) launched her to international stardom. She went on to become *The Times* Woman of the Year – purely on the basis of her theory that adolescents in Samoa were untainted by the stresses of the modern world and were allowed to be sexually free and promiscuous in their island paradise. Although she has since proved to have been misled by her Samoan subjects in what is known as *taufaase'e* or the Samoan practice of trickery, her book and the images of Pacific Islanders that it perpetuates are still hugely popular today.

When images of the Pacific were first presented to the Western world, they were often presented as an aspect of the neo-classical tradition of the late 18th century. In this fashionable art genre of the period, Polynesia was crafted into an idyll of lost, ancient lands – with parallels to the pure, golden era of the 'classical' Greeks (Thomas 1999). This is something that seems to have lasted into the 20th century, as there are many more recent depictions of Polynesia as an elegiac, untouched civilization that is somehow suspended in time.

In the same vein, many images for the tourist market and images on film and television use this 'lost in time' device to show Pacific Islanders in native dress or semi-naked, conveniently escaping any reference to modern life and the often extreme socio-economic problems of the Pacific. These are the real conditions that are being usurped and exploited by the ideologies and images of today's Pacific image-makers.

MAKING A DIFFERENCE IN 'PARADISE'

As the notion of a homogenous modernist culture is questioned and rewritten, many Pacific artists are denying the authority of the 'universal communicable'– the Western assumption that a centred position or narrative can speak for all aesthetic and human experience. There has been, in recent years, a reverse imaging of the clichés of Polynesia, which enables us to negotiate a space for our own visual representations, either through the making of an 'oppositional gaze' or the reworking of an old representation. In subverting the naturalisation of these age-old images by pointing to the artifice of their construction, the arbitrary nature of their meaning and the fact that their parameters can be shifted becomes apparent.

Manthia Diawara emphasises the agency of the spectator in this context: 'Every narration places the spectator in a position of agency; and race, class and sexual relations influence the way a subjecthood is filled by the spectator' (Diawara 1992: 117). Motifs that have commonly been employed to depict this region as paradise have been turned inside out and upside down by artists reinventing these images on their own terms. Rather then working against the images of the 'dusky maiden' or the 'jolly-polys', these images are presented in different contexts to point to the very nature of their construction.

Visual and moving-image artists in Polynesia have incited these stereotypes of 'paradise' in order to destabilise their inherent meanings. Here the language of camp is often deliberately used to invoke contexts where everything is seen in quotation marks and nothing is what it seems. *'Muu'muu'* Mamas and dancing duskies have been given a new signification for the Pacific spectator, through the reuse of the old signs of Polynesia after a transformation of the terms of their usage. By employing a new landscape of Pacific iconography, these artists are engaging with the politics of who is speaking and who is being spoken to.

The velvet Jesus, the corned beef can, the coconut-frond broom have all become proud Pacific symbols in the reinvention of our own popular culture. This new Pacific iconography speaks to the viewer who is 'in the know' in the same coded language that European art images speak to their select audience. The corned beef can is a signifier to those who are acclimatised to its signification in a specific context, but remains nonsensical to those outside of it.

The biographical background of the makers of 'anti-colonial' images that work though re-appropriating contexts has an important bearing on their meaning. These works appear to reproduce the collusive relationship between colonial image-maker and consumer: there is a distinct reference to a particular spectatorship, a specific 'gaze' is sought. However, the clichéd 'signs' of the Pacific, created for a Western market by the media, are replaced by specifically modern day Polynesian 'signs'. These signs can be read as constituting a form of anti-colonial refusal: they signify, yes, but not for the mainstream White gaze.

As a sense of irony is usually inherent in these new Pacific images, they are more playful parodies than sites of 'resistance'. One of the most important areas of this new iconography is to be found in the work of a vocal group of artists working in the competitive world of T-shirt production. T-shirts, with their lowbrow 'street cred' borrowed from the fashion realm, have become the new Pacific canvases, a site for satire based on the 'double entendre' (*faleaitu*), an essential part of the Pacific tradition of trickery which can also be found in the Samoan practice of comedy (Hereniko 1995; Colchester 2003).

This 'doubleness of meaning' is being seen more and more in T-shirt and fabric production. The slogans 'FOB' and 'FRESH' are emblazoned along with Pacific Nike symbols, coconut cream cans, corned beef and tinned fish cans, sitting proudly on the front of T-shirts, making Pacific household staples into 'art icons'. 'Boogie Nights' becomes 'Bunga Nights', 'Coca-Samoa' replaces 'Coca-Cola', the Pepsi label reads Pisupo (a brand of corned beef) instead. These are just some of the lingua franca of T-shirt slang.

DRAG QUEENS: GLAMOUR AND PARODY

The liveable, wearable nature of these new 'canvases' means they contain a world of pop culture connotation in themselves. Historically used as a site for souvenir logos and consumer brand labels, T-shirts also engage with the world of street fashion, where the label creates the 'cred' of the wearer. This T-shirt art is best seen in parallel with another area of Pasifika clothing that I want to explore: the glamour and innovation inherent in the costume and adornment work of *fa'afafine* beauty pageants.

Representations of drag queens in popular culture present a myriad of different messages and meanings: from flagrantly subversive gender blending to parodies of the feminine and counter-culture spectacles. In the Pacific, the image of the *fa'afafine* is more complex. In Samoa, where there is a proportionately high incidence of *fa'afafine* in comparison to the rest of the Pacific, the role has been historically and culturally determined.

It is not my interest to argue about the origins and role of the *fa'afafine* and the reasons why they emerged. I want to focus on the presentation of the popular iconography of *fa'afafine* in performance and body adornment – which seems to me to reference and effectively destabilise the 'dusky maiden' tradition of female representation in the Pacific. I want to look at ways of understanding this costuming and performance as parody and reappropriation of the stereotype of the Pacific belle image.

In deliberately employing the power of spectacle and by blurring the boundaries of gender stereotypes, the contemporary image of the *fa'afafine* in Pacific cultures, particularly in Samoa and Tahiti, is open to several readings within the framework of post-structuralism and post modern irony. The image and reading I want to concentrate on is that of a very aggressive *fa'afafine* who thrives on artifice in his/her presentation of the image of a long-haired, dusky maiden.

Arguably, the Pacific take on transvestism is worlds apart from the Western drag queen's often misogynist renditions of female caricature. In Pacific cultures, the image and public performances of *fa'afafine* produce a different response: they are considered 'as women' and have historically had an active role as women in society. The photographic images of *fa'afafine* produced in Samoa, and the marketing of the island's popular *fa'afafine* revue, are all administered by Samoa's most notorious *fa'afafine* – Cindy[2] – whose image and on-stage parodies are all based around the western perception of the classic 'dusky maiden'.

Cindy's performances are explicitly produced for the tourist market. The *fa'afafine* who consider themselves 'women' rather then female impersonators play to the tourist notion of the sexually available Pacific belle. The parody lies in the fact that they are biologically men and aggressive rather than passive in their presentation. The apparent coyness of the performer is a device deployed to lure the Western male 'gazer' into believing this parody.

---

2   A *fa'afafine* in Western Samoa whose show is a feature at Magrita's, a popular bar in town.

Ngahuia Te Awekotuku has made the case that many of Gauguin's images may have been of *mahu* (the Tahitian term for *fa'afafine*) instead of the South Seas belle of popular imagination, pointing to the inherent androgyny of many of his figures (Te Awekotuku nd). Did these *mahu* have the last laugh or were Gauguin's images deliberately laden with this subversion of the dusky maiden image?

One can look in a similar vein at the debate between Margaret Mead and Derek Freeman on the sexual promiscuity of Samoan women (Orans 1988). In Heimans's documentary, the original 'subject cases' of Mead's study came out and said that they 'made it all up' for a joke and 'told her what she wanted to believe' (Heimans 1988). In a lecture by Freeman at Victoria University in February 1998, he was asked by the audience why the Samoan people themselves didn't refute Mead's arguments; to which Samoan journalist Tino Pereira replied: 'Because we were too busy laughing at the naivety of Western anthropology' (Pereira unpublished).

This sense of 'telling them what they want to believe' is a notion that can also be seen in the popular images and cabaret shows of *fa'afafine* aimed at a predominantly tourist audience. The careful styling of many *fa'afafine* into the 'dusky maiden' stereotype employs all the coy sexual references and 'accommodating' attitudes that the image has historically signified. In the same ways that Mead's adolescent subjects used the Samoan practice of parody (*taufaase'e*) to lead her on an elaborate hoax, the *taufaase'e* used by *fa'afafine* in their iconography is a knowing device that subverts an image that is overused in the selling of 'paradise'.

The popular image of *fa'afafine* is currently exemplified by the *fa'afafine* icons known as Bertha and Buckwheat, who were featured on TVNZ's *Tagata Pasifika* in a five minute weekly show called 'Eaten Alive' from February to March 1998. The style of these two *fa'afafine* is a double parody in itself, being a parody of a parody with their 'larger than life' take on the Polynesian belle. In an interview with Harold Samu, who plays Bertha (and is in real life the Pacific Island Education Officer for the NZ AIDS Foundation), he talks about the ways in which his alter ego, Bertha, can be seen as a parody of the so called traditional roles of Polynesian men and women. He says:

> The *fa'afafine* is an aggressive and dominant role in contemporary culture – we present ourselves as Pacific Island women styled in that classic vein of the sexual belle. Recently I organised a photo shoot for AFA – our Polynesian gay awareness group – where we had a number of *fa'afafine* styled as mermaids, lying on rocks, luring in the sailors. Now the message here was 'safe sex' – the mermaids all had condoms – but there's a deeper signification here. We are trying to take the piss out of all the tired tourist images of Polynesia with semi-clad, lightly tanned brown women lying around the place. As a sexual health administrator for the NZ AIDS foundation I also think that the image of the sexualised Pacific woman can be a dangerous one because it works directly hand in hand with things like Mead's myth of sexual promiscuity in the islands. It encourages a certain tourist attitude towards Polynesian people as being freely sexually available, and as the AIDS statistics in the island continue to grow that can be a very worrying attitude to cultivate. (Samu 1998)

Here *fa'afafine* are referenced in relation to the common Samoan practice of *faleaitu* which is particular to Pacific Island audiences. The nuances of language and gesture that are employed make it one of the biggest sites of anti-colonial sentiment that uses comedy.

Representations of 'otherness' for Western sensory gratification have been refined in today's media culture – and continue to play a significant role in maintaining social inequality. Some of the most effective resistance to this has been in the form of anti-colonial parody where the practice of reinvention is paramount. Beauty pageants in the Pacific are huge and have become the stage for *fa'afafine*. These pageants on 'the other side of town' are generally for a local audience rather then for tourist consumption. The most risqué and raucous of performances are also showcases for some of the most innovative and resourceful design works in the vast spectrum of Pasifika.

The notion of 'glamour' has a long and entrenched history in Polynesia. From the days of Cook's arrival, ornate Pacific body adornments and hair designs have been assiduously recorded. When the missionaries and early sailors, whalers and traders made their impact, new forms of clothing and adornment were enthusiastically adapted. The use of Victoriana alongside Pacific forms of dress was a common feature of 20th century Pacific fashion. Observers at the time considered this to be colonial mimicry and evidence of the 'buffoonery' of the natives; it certainly constituted a merging of European style into our own, age old form of glamour.

Fa'afafine pageantry involves stunning pieces of couture, with dresses made out of recycled straws or plastic forks bound together with sinnet. These pieces celebrate our age-old ideas of glamour and adornment in contexts that are not 'traditional' in the flax-weaving, bark-beating sense, but are ideologically and thematically historical, social and political.

THE PERFORMANCE OF OTHERNESS

One group of Samoan *fa'afafine*, called the Pasifika Divas, work extensively in this type of Pacific body adornment. Their performance pieces are politically motivated and incorporate elaborate costuming and adornments. The Divas' show on the opening night of the Asia Pacific Triennial at the Queensland Art Gallery in 2002, consisted of five items evoking different Pacific themes.

The first one, titled 'Heat', featured the drag queen Buckwheat. Her performance and song, while dressed in a three-dimensional version of the colonial two-piece *puletasi* outfit, ostensibly celebrated big Pacific mamas in church. The *puletasi* was in itself a larger-than-life parody of this popularised piece of clothing – introduced by missionaries to increase island modesty. Here, big glow-in-the-dark plastic flowers make up the whole outfit, crowned by a huge white 'church hat' made of ostrich feathers. (See Figure 9.1 in the colour section.)

This mockery of 'church-going taste' is deliberately employed to highlight the raunchy nature of 'Heat' – a spoken word piece about the underlying bitchy nature of big, brown women in church. Appearances belie the reality, stressing again the typical theme of *faleaitu*-type performances.

The second act was called 'Queens of the Pacific' and was performed by artist Shigeyuki Kihara. In this piece, she merges the ideas of Victorian royalty, that bestowed itself in the islands, with Samoan royalty. Wearing a full-length black Victorian dress replete with bustle, Kihara was adorned in a floor-length necklace and armlets made of red lopa seeds that emulate Victorian pearls. (All these accoutrements were made by the artist Sofia Tekela-Smith.) Projected behind her were huge images of Pacific Island women from the mid-19th century – all similarly attired in this eclectic mix of clothing from both Samoa and Europe. Shigeyuki presents herself as a Pacific 'Queen' who is trapped in the 'ethnographic mode' of the 19th century photographs behind her.

At the end of the performance, the photos are projected directly onto her body, timed to fit the moment where she breaks out of the image of a submissive Samoan woman and transforms into the violent movements of a Samoan warrior. Her costume, a picture of European elegance, comes to life in a swinging motion as she laments, 'I cry for the lost royalty of Samoa's past'. (See Figure 9.2 in the colour section.)

Here the concept of colonial 'mimicry' is invoked in reappropriating the material culture of the colonial era and also reasserting the regal stance of Pacific women whose power was subverted in this period. Shigeyuki finally plays with the fact that she is not a real Pacific princess at all – though by all accounts a 'queen'. This brings the gender issue into play in more complex ways, perhaps, than is considered by Homi Bhabha in his use of the term 'colonial mimicry' (Bhabha 1994b). Bhabha bypasses gender and refers only to race, reinscribing mimicry as a male strategy without acknowledging its gendered specificity.

If Pacific images have long been colonised by male desire, with the 'sign' of the coloured woman being used in widely varied agendas, these *fa'afafine* artists 'stage' their own versions of the 'dusky maiden' image, to point to the nature of its construction. In this way the 'dusky maiden' is re-created by the *fa'afafine* in performance pieces that point to the very concept of the image as a lie or construction. These are not the passive sexual belles languidly inviting the white man, they are the 'third sex' – presenting an often aggressive and in many cases ironic performance. In these cases, the image-making of Pacific artists deliberately uses the images that have been constructed of the Pacific in order to convert a form of subordination into a mode of affirmation. The destabilising of images of the colonial past involves the decoding of stereotypes and shifting the position of 'normality', turning what have become standardised images into transgressive ones. This is fundamentally about displacing the authority of an established stereotype in questioning its universal 'truth', and about historical agency – making the 'ambivalence' (Bhabha's term for the quality of colonial subjectivity and deliberate mimicry) inherently subversive.

In some cases, works that negotiate new meanings for old colonial images can be seen as a form of anti-colonial refusal. Mimicry in this sense 'marks those moments of civil disobedience within the discipline of civility; signs of spectacular resistance' (Bhabha 1994a).

In this way, many images created by Polynesian peoples of themselves are working against the grain – reclaiming that which has been denied, made invisible and forced to the margin as much as being distorted and misrepresented. The politics of 'looking' and being 'looked upon' have in this way been counteracted. The Pacific subject is looking back and speaking to this specifically Pacific audience.

CONCLUSION

Pasifika pageantry is an 'underground' arena of performance and adornment little seen outside the bingo halls or nightclubs of the 'queen scene' in the islands and in our adopted home in Aotearoa (New Zealand). By recognising the intrinsic value of these performances – with their fantastical array of costuming – as 'art pieces', we can promote further displays and celebrate the talent that creates them. In areas as obscure as the *fa'afafine* nightclubs of Apia, the *faleaitu* dance performances and the wearable art pieces of the Pacific Sisters, the illusion of the 'dusky maiden' as passive, accommodating and submissive is shown to be a thinly shrouded fantasy of the past. Instead, in the words of the famous Cindy of Samoa as she dances on the laps of unsuspecting tourists: *'Pule Lava Oe'*, which might be translated as 'Girl Power Pacific style is here to stay'.

References

Bhabha, HK (1994a) 'Of mimicry and man' in *The Location of Culture*, London: Routledge

Bhabha, HK (1994b) 'Signs taken for wonders' in McClintock, A (ed), *Imperial Leather: Race, Gender and Sexuality in the Colonial Contest*, London: Routledge

Colchester, C (2003) 'T-shirts, translation and humour: on the nature of wearer-perceiver relationships in South Auckland' in Colchester, C (ed), *Clothing the Pacific*, Oxford: Berg

Diawara, M (1992) in Hooks, B (ed), *Black Looks: Race and Representation*, Boston: South End Press

Heimans, F (1988) *Margaret Mead and Samoa*, documentary film, New York: Wombat Film and Video, Brighton Video

Hereniko, V (1995) *Woven Gods: Female Clowns and Power in Rotuma*, Honolulu: University of Hawaii Press

Mead, M (1930) *Coming of Age in Samoa: A Psychological Study of Primitive Youth for Western Civilisation*, New York: Morrow

Moorehead, A (1966) *Fatal Impact: Account of the Invasion of the South Pacific, 1767–1840*, London: Hugo Hamilton

Orans, M (1988) *Not Even Wrong: Margaret Mead, Derek Freeman and the Samoans*, Chandler and Sharp Publishers

Pereira, J (1998) Victoria University, Freeman Lecture

Samu, H aka 'Bertha', Interview, March 1998, NZ Aids Foundation

Stanley, N (1998) *Being Ourselves for You: The Global Display of Cultures*, London: Middlesex University Press

Te Awekotuku, N (1996) Auckland University, Women's Studies Lecture
Thomas, N (1999) *Possessions: Indigenous Art/Colonial Culture*, London: Thames & Hudson

PART III: FASHIONING MODERNITIES

"Kathleen", Maori Guide, Rotorua. N. Z.

CHAPTER 10

TRANSLATIONS: TEXTS AND TEXTILES IN PAPUA NEW GUINEA

Paul Sharrad

My personal engagement with translations of textiles began in the context of the gradual decolonisation of Papua New Guinea in the 1960s. This has led me, as a teacher of literature, into an inspection of textual translations of textile history and given rise to some small thoughts on the shifts in cultural meanings that took place as tradition was translated into modernity. I leave it to anthropologists and people with a more intimate and contemporary connection to Papua New Guinea to develop these in ways I myself cannot.

In my time as a high school student in Port Moresby, I remember cutting stencils from heavy cardboard and inking – in an appallingly amateur manner – some bright, lime green cotton cloth lengths on the dining room table. Black enamel house paint was, I think, the colourfast washable medium applied, and the design was the predictable frieze of coconut palms.

In those days, amateur enthusiasm was almost the norm for colonials in what was known as 'the Territory'. With the arrogance and opportunity of privilege, many people carved out careers that elsewhere and nowadays you would need certificates and years of experience to begin. But even in such a context, it taxed my brain to figure how a schoolboy could get roped into the first Western style fashion parade in Papua and why items were being created by whites for young Papuan women to wear. After interrogation of my mother, who 'volunteered' me for the experiment, I discovered that the mother of one of my schoolmates was the wife of the then Director of Education. Mrs Johnson had the idea that the young women of Port Moresby needed to find ways of supporting themselves and of localising fashion design in a society where modernity had meant mission paternalism and white man's culture. The fashion parade (which mercifully involved many other would-be designers!) was one attempt to kick-start a national clothing design industry, or at least a series of cottage productions.

In the 1960s, modernisation was gathering momentum as part of a general push towards equipping the local populace for self-governance. Histories about the period talk mostly of government policy, trade training, education for a professional elite, co-operative societies and agricultural innovations. What they often fail to indicate is how such change was predominantly aimed at men. Literature dealing with this period indicates how colonialism utilised the largely patriarchal traditions of Papua New Guinea to redeploy male energies into plantation labour, policing and low level trades and professional support roles. The first autobiographies from Melanesia covering the transition from colonial rule to decolonisation are all by men (Kiki 1968; Matane 1972; Somare 1975). Women are generally mentioned only as wives, even though they continued to support the subsistence economy of the country by gardening and pig raising in the villages.

One of the common factors linking male and female in the transition to modernity was a change of clothing. As the illustrations from newspaper advertisements, school magazines and literary gatherings show, Western dress from manufactured cloth became the outward show of 'progress', or, from a local point of view, access to the 'cargo' and power of modern life. Sir Paulias Matane's inspirational story for school children, *My Childhood in New Guinea* (Matane 1972), tellingly sandwiches its text between two photos. One photograph is of a village 'medicine man' or sorcerer, emphasising skin and traditional power; the other photograph is of Matane as a public servant in shirt and tie. As his desk, pen and glasses demonstrate, the further link between writing and clothing was also a close and consistently represented one. Writing itself can be seen as part of the 'costume' of the modern person, and, as I have argued elsewhere (Sharrad 2000), performs its particular uneasy translation of identity from oral tradition to modern print culture by 'signing' its regional belonging and national construction through references to dress and traditional material culture.

Attention to women's issues began to form around the problem generated by creating a professional class of native men. Urbanised, Westernised men with continued links to traditional family and clan systems obtained wives from their home villages. These women would be brought into multi-lingual communities operating mostly on a cash economy and relying on modern forms of communication and socialisation. For the upwardly mobile, proto-national male, an illiterate, shy wife could be an embarrassment; for a woman suddenly moved into an alien world, 'advancement' could be a terrifying and lonely experience. The common trope of change was the perceived impossibility of the 'new woman' continuing to wear no more than a grass skirt.

Papua New Guinean women were taught to sew for Christian modesty's sake and as a way of helping them enter the modern world. They could use this as a substitute for the hours spent gardening in the village; clothe themselves with a modern skill that would confer self-respect; and get their children into school by providing them with the necessary uniforms. Sewing classes were also a useful means of socialising amongst women in new cross-tribal groups. This was the case in the Pacific Islands Regiment, where some of the white officers' wives worked with the wives of native troops to bring them together socially and promote informal education in modern domestic culture. They did this through exchange of recipes, sewing patterns and also some English-language training. This was a secular version of the many women's clubs organised by missions at the time.

For example, Mrs Gray, a London Missionary Society (LMS) worker at Veiru, a pastor training station in the Gulf District of Papua, sought to provide wives of mission workers with skills appropriate to their social position. She drew the tattoos on their skins onto paper that was then used as an embroidery pattern to produce table napkins and other domestic items. These could become part of the embroiderer's own store of cultural credit or could be a means of moving into the cash economy. The effect of this translation of inalienable body art tradition into tradable commodities is something worth considering, though I have no immediate or simple conclusions.

The colonial management of Papua New Guinea was certainly the usual affair of spatial control and large-scale systems: exploration, patrols, movements of labour, punitive expeditions, 'opening up' new administrative districts. But this rested upon the smaller-scale regulation of the body, a regulation measured in terms of clothing across several discourses – health, racial difference, spiritual worth, cultural progressiveness, criminality and law. The dominant discourse of colonial times, of course, was the familiar binary of 'benighted savagery' and 'enlightened progress' wherein the criteria were all derived from Western, Christian (and largely Victorian British) culture. This narrative suggests that there are no 'translations' that do not comply with the general framework of 'conversion', the total shift from tradition to modernity. Between these polarities, however, much translation went on: between white and black, skin and cloth, textile and text, male and female traditions, to cite only those shifts this chapter works with.

The Church of England, unlike later fundamentalist missions in Papua New Guinea, preserved traditional symbols and translated them into a Christian context. Thus, sorcery stones were placed beneath the feet of Christ and a stone relating to a myth of bringing fire to the region became a symbol for the Gospel bringing light to the benighted (Henslowe 1957: 22). Similarly, local *tapa* cloth was incorporated into the regalia of the Archbishop (Henslowe 1957: 38). This syncretism is firmly explained by Dorothea Henslowe as a triumphalist assimilation of the old to the new when she writes up her tour of the missions for home consumption amongst the faithful of Tasmania. However, the devout Miss Henslowe reveals that certain unsettling effects accompanied the attempt to blend Western and Papua New Guinean dress codes:

> At Wedau, while we were waiting for the boat we saw a man wearing a cotton singlet and on his nether limbs nothing but a G string; the G string alone looks all right, but when topped with our style garments, looks strangely nude! (Henslowe 1957: 69)

Paulias Matane has a similar story of the incongruous translation of fashions. His traditional childhood in New Britain was disrupted by the arrival of a pastor who built a school and forced the boys to attend. He inducts them into football as a substitute for fighting and commands them to shed their 'string aprons' in favour of shorts, which he provides and then hands out 'work to do in payment' (Matane 1972: 68–69). Stripped of their spears, clubs and clothing, the boys chew magic roots, dance and 'paint up' with oil and ochre: 'on top of this we drew snakes and the faces of our dead grandfathers.' The teacher is finally obliged to let them combine the old ways of performative body rituals with the new ways of clothing and games.

There are many photos and touristic observations of the incongruities of tradition meeting modernity in the Pacific: Highlanders with Biros through their noses, keys hanging from shell breastplates, surgical bandages streaming as *bilas*

for a 'sing sing' (Henslowe 1957: 104–05). These are not translations as such –
merely additions and substitutions within the same cultural code. More
significant are those alterations that change both tradition and what is added to it.

Vincent Eri's pioneering novel *The Crocodile* (Eri 1970) is based mostly on his
father's stories of childhood and being pressed into service as a bearer in the
Second World War, but also carries elements of Eri's own growing up in
Moveave in the Papuan Gulf. The book gives us a translated account of colonial
policies in practice. It charts the uncertain entry of a Papuan villager into direct
contact with colonialism and then with the full-frontal modernity of the Second
World War.

Hoiri Sevese is sent to live with his aunt after his mother dies. She obliges
him to attend the local Catholic school instead of the LMS one by refusing to
give him a *rami* (sarong-like wrap, otherwise known as *laplap*) otherwise (Eri
1970: 6). It is not clear why he should feel ashamed to be seen without one in
front of the girls, since non-local clothing is evidently only just making its
appearance: the village constable, for instance, is referred to as 'the cloth man'
(Eri 1970: 16). Colonial police are called 'black dogs' because of their black serge
rami and sweatshirt uniforms (Eri 1970: 21) but Hoiri envies them and others
who can talk to the white man and get access to colonial power and the goods
that go with it. These goods include cloth, since, as we see when Hoiri
accompanies his father on a trading voyage to Port Moresby, natives are not
allowed to wear shorts (Eri 1970: 42). The *rami* is the closest thing available, and
in many cases – ostensibly for health reasons, but clearly also as a marker of the
race-power colonial divide – Papuan natives were not permitted to wear shirts
or blouses without permits until 1941 (Wolfers 1975: 46–48).

Albert Maori Kiki alludes to this in his autobiography (Kiki 1968). His father
had gone to work near Moresby:

> The workers were supplied with a weekly ration of bully beef and rice and were
> issued *laplaps* to tie round their waists. In those days native workers were expected
> to go bare chested. My father thought that the white man believed that the 'natives'
> were incapable of keeping a shirt of singlet clean, so they were discouraged from
> using them. The remnants of this curious colonial attitude can still be seen in the
> large hotels in Port Moresby and Boroko today, where the waiters still wear only
> *laplaps*. (Kiki 1968: 8)

Maori Kiki himself is 'kidnapped' into attending an LMS school. At first boys
went along naked and girls wore grass skirts, but gradually bits of clothes are
acquired from relatives in the city and those without become envious. Maori
Kiki's first items of clothing are make-do 'translations': a sugar bag with holes cut
in and then a *laplap* made from the covering of an umbrella, so that he gets the
nickname 'flying fox' (Kiki 1968: 58–59).

To return to Eri's novel, after Hoiri's father completes his trading in Moresby,
the boy trades bows and arrows for *rami* lengths and buys a skirt, brassiere and
panties to give to his girlfriend Mitoro back home (Eri 1970: 45). Her response is
interesting in so far as it shows the complexity of translation occurring in the
modernisation of local fashion. Hoiri's gift is a kind of traditional 'bride-price'
exchange for his seduction of her, but it is also a modernising sign which

transforms their perfunctory coupling into an uneasy romance that demands a Western sign of approval such as a church wedding (Eri 1970: 62–64). At the same time, Mitoro's pleasure in the gift is both pragmatic (the brassiere stops her breasts bouncing about when she moves) and traditional: 'She was no longer afraid of going to bed as she was when wearing only a skirt. The wandering spirit men, who went about at night peering at naked women in their sleep, would not be able to worry her' (Eri 1970: 58). This translation of the meaning of items of clothing for the people adopting them is reflected in the later use of the brassiere as an acceptable mode of dress among older Papuan women, an alternative to both the mission-style '*meri* blouse' or 'Mother Hubbard' and to 'bush-kanaka' nakedness.

Tradition and modernity do not always come into alignment so harmoniously as in Mitoro's wearing of trade-store clothing. Under the pressure of the Second World War, the culture clash becomes confusing and violent as it begins to create the conditions for pan-regional consciousness and decolonisation. In Eri's novel, the protagonist is left stranded, hoping that his small gains might give his son the means of coping better with white ways. He does, however, have the traditional satisfaction of revenge, courtesy of the war. The man alleged to have caused Mitoro's death by crocodile sorcery is shot while absconding from carrier duty. Even this arch-traditional figure has taken on the new signs of power: he is wearing a white shirt and so presents an easy target in the dark (Eri 1970: 163).

The work of Russell Soaba takes up the story of decolonisation in the generation extending beyond the close of *The Crocodile*. His 1977 novel *Wanpis* depicts a '*lusman*' university dropout who begins what promises to be a brilliant career as prefect in the All Saints Anglican boarding school, which has been set up – like some real schools – on donations by a soldier grateful for native help during the Second World War. The head boys debate their own and their country's future. One option is to return to village life. In the words of the would-be creative writer of the group:

> But I shall return to tradition
> when I have died me that alien death;
> and for our reunion I'll bark you
> a *laplap* of *tapa* cloth designs and cry:
> ORO DA! (Soaba 1977: 30)

Another response is to be groomed for leadership of the soon-to-be independent country. Playing it cool, the narrator and his friend drift amongst the keener university students 'in colourful floral or posh western dress' toned down in 'faded blue jeans or inferior looking grey shorts and random or All Saints T-shirts' (Soaba 1977: 45). Town life shows up the contradictions of the times and the self-serving ambitions of the trainee elite. The narrator's outgoing friend takes on student politics, and assumes the costume of globalising Third World solidarity 'in his newly adopted Afro-Asian cloak . . . The cloak was too loose, oversized – it must have been one of the Political Science tutor's – like a woman's nightgown' in anticipation of his trips around the world (Soaba 1977: 86). Others of the younger set take up evangelical Christianity, party in hot-pants or settle into bureaucratic jobs, get pregnant and start wearing *meri* blouses (Soaba 1977: 106, 110). Our narrator takes a third option and mixes with the masses: the drunks, beggars and street girls 'washed from their villages to the city like drifting seaside coconuts . . . wearing what should have been once bright floral dresses, [that] now appeared as loose calico heavily greyed by the seasons of urban blind conformity' (Soaba 1977: 82). The narrator sees himself separated from the materialist dreams of the urban masses by his existential nihilism. Disillusionment is expressed in the lyrics of a mock pop song in which contact with tradition has been lost and the ancestral spirit masks are exposed as half-dressed with modernity:

> My hero he turned away in outspoken anger;
> he cursed; he wept perplexing tears
> that fogged his vision of internal consolation:
> and to the stubborn wind that hissed by
> he cried: 'Ah *Mama*! I have seen the *duk duk*
> tonight in commercial underwear!
> But where is the beautiful *tubuan*?' only to
> hear his own echoes: *Na tubuan we?*
> *Mama! Tubuan we?* (Soaba 1977: 150)

The same kind of discomforting loss can be found in the central character of Albert Toro's feature film, *Tukana*. Itself a translation between dramatic fiction and social documentary, this film is set in Bougainville, and tells the story of Tukana, a student who has dropped out of university and returns to his village, drifting aimlessly until his family arrange a marriage and tragedy forces him to take stock of his life. The film charts the incommensurable gaps between modern city and subsistence village, but also allows for some translation across the two. Given its literal meaning of 'changing place', the term 'translation' is appropriate for this picaresque story, since in it people are constantly moving around by foot, bicycle, boat, motorbike, truck and plane. The overall movement is into modernity: to town for a good time; off island to get higher education; to Panguna to get money in the copper mine; to government training in cacao farming.

Everything is measured, however, against tradition, and this is often seen through the coding of dress. Tukana returns from Moresby in 'slick threads and shades', but gradually adopts village everyday wear of shorts and T-shirt. He arrives during the opening of a local government co-operative – the Western-clad dignitaries are surrounded by 'sing sing' warriors in a mixture of paint, leaves, axes, bows and arrows and trousers, as well as a bunch of school children in traditional headdress. Later, Tukana goes to earn some money in the copper mine and changes into work boots and company overalls – with 'Aussie Rules' togs and 'Country and Western' jeans and check shirts from the town store for the weekend. In the end, his generation's power is shown as resting on an inauthentic veneer of Western 'cargo' – which in the village becomes a frozen affectation expressed as a kind of puzzled adolescent rage. This Western veneer is challenged by a sorcerer performing traditional spells, and the film finally seems to promote a conservative ideal of settling down in the village, of working on the land and bettering oneself through modern farming or teaching, albeit in service to the collective, and in harmony with others.

We are left in doubt, however, about the tidiness of all this. It is unclear whether the denouement is caused by sorcery or a truck accident; all men – old and young – are seen to be engaged in internecine power struggles that corrupt and lead to violence; and cash and alcohol permeate all levels of society, from the Beatles-strumming dance hall players to the sorcerer himself. It is the women who deal in plain talking and who work the land and sea while men debate the benefits of returning to traditional ways. Apart from the Councillor's daughter, Lucy, who plays temptress in tight, store bought dresses and ends up disgraced as an abandoned, unmarried mother; women maintain the hybrid traditional wear of the '*meri* blouse' and cotton skirt. Male picaresque slides into female romance as Tukana's waywardness is tamed and he resolves to take over his dead wife's job of village teacher. Women appear at the end of the film as traditional mourners, bare-breasted and painted, but are, as in the opening, seen as elements of a translation of tradition that includes shorts and skirts. The women are juxtaposed with the male translation of fight culture into shows of prowess and aggression in beer hall dancing. The conclusion of the film asks, in the same open-ended manner as *The Crocodile*, which way Papua New Guinean society will go.

Cowboy and Maria in Town, a documentary film about life on the immigrant fringes of Port Moresby, suggests, at a quick viewing, the total failure of experiments in modernising local fashion and localising global consumerism. This is especially the case with the men of the urban settlements, who mostly appear in pants, T-shirts and tractor caps, usually advertising some Western product. Town life appears to offer them no alternative to Western culture. The women, left to scrabble a subsistence living from Moresby hillsides, seem to manage a wider range of cultural expression. At the beginning, Maria appears topping her full facial scarification with a variant of traditional headdress, apparently made from cassowary feathers. Later we see her in a T-shirt, but throughout the documentary she and most of the other women wear versions of the '*meri* blouse' that has obviously become, for an older generation at least, a translation from mission-imposed modesty and civility into workaday localised fashion.

For the men, there are also moments where small translations can be seen, suggesting all is not complete capitulation to globalised Western commodity fashion. The occasional knitted hat flits by, pointing to the adoption of forms of the Jamaican 'tea cosy'. This can be seen in part as a reggae-based political expression of alignment with a non-specific, Third World subjectivity; and partly as a translation of the traditional male hair net of some Highland tribes. Occasionally we also see berets worn; a result of cast-offs from the military but also, like the 'tea cosy', a way of translating into modern urban style the warrior traditions and 'radical' politics of conflictual, postcolonial society.

There is a lot in all of this of the *bricolage* and subversive play that de Certeau speaks of: fashion tactics within the strategies of nationhood and globalisation (de Certeau 1984). But, alongside this, there is also the translation that occurs through decontextualised emulation. For instance, a '*raskol*' youth tries to make good by becoming a busker. He adopts the persona and costume of a 'cowboy', but in doing so makes himself something that is neither a cowboy nor the movie image that inspired him and gave him his hold on an audience. We see Cowboy in clothes that directly reference Elvis, but we find him sitting on a wooden bench in an urban slum, cringing as his colourful father harangues him for never coming to visit and for wandering around singing 'rubbish' songs. When we see Cowboy performing, he looks awkward and stiff and he chants his topical narratives in a creolised English that is itself a translation of a kind between Toaripi, Motu and Pidgin. This is neither Elvis nor an imitation of him, but something uncannily new. Many things are both lost and gained in the translation.

Cowboy is a useful figure, since his people come from the same place as Vincent Eri's. In Cowboy's life we see a possible sequel to *The Crocodile*. Hoiri, at the end of that novel, hopes that his son, Sevese, will gain the wisdom to make sense of the postcolonial flux. But the boy is already hooked on sugar and sweet biscuits and headed for more schooling and separation from village life. Perhaps we can see, in the figure of Cowboy, how this would all have ended. There is a scene in *Cowboy and Maria in Town* in which Cowboy, stripped for a moment of his performance finery, watches his father and some old men enacting the traditional ceremony for initiating boys into the first stage of manhood. It is a scene of pathos and loss: one old man has lost the skill to blow the conch shell; the father is semi-clowning; the *kovave* mask is cobbled together for the occasion (Kiki 1968: 42; Beier 1970). Cowboy looks on, completely alienated, embarrassed both for the old men and by his own lack of initiation – or perhaps he is just indifferent to something that has no relevance to his modern urban life.

I have been suggesting that the translations of clothing culture are gender specific. Decolonisation brought immediate benefits to a generation of young men, some of whom, like Soaba's characters, anguished over cultural alienation while taking on, *holus-bolus*, the paraphernalia of modern governance and trade. In most literary texts, the woman is identified with nation and tradition, and similarly satirised by male writers for departing from village habits and traditional dress. Dus Mapun's pidgin poem *O Meri Wantok* laments:

> Oh, woman of my people
> Before your lips were brown
> Now your lips are red
> Before your hair grew high and free
> Now it's all crimped down
> Before your breasts hung soft and loose
> Now they stand out tight and hard
> You look into the mirror and you say
> 'The price is twenty dollars a go!'
> Oh, woman of my people, I am sad for you.
>   (Mapun 1980)

Baluwe Umetrifo similarly accuses his country's women of trying to outdo the Queen herself with their English names and their 'high heel shoes and stinky perfumes'. He exhorts them to change 'quick smart': '*Yupela meri i senis hariap pinis.*'

In a 'big man' culture where any kind of power is feared, admired and coveted, rituals and knowledge that will bring more 'cargo' and thereby enhanced social standing are to be taken on, irrespective of the old ways. Males get the chance to tap into Western culture, to work for the colonial government, and later to return cash and goods to their family and clan, and they adopt the outward shows of modernity as comprehensively as they can. Even if they use them to establish themselves as leaders in village society and perpetuate traditional relationships, there is little subtlety in the syncretic flaunting of new style. It is the marginal figures such as artists and women who seem to make more of hybridity; and occasion unsettling disruptions of old and new in their encounter between the two.

Literary texts and some textile practices chart historical movements in terms of a shift from tattoos and grass skirts to modern clothing. There is something in this suggesting the alienation of identity as body signs are externalised and commodified; but there is also a trade-off in finding new ways to perpetuate traditional symbols. Mark Mosko has studied the Mekeo, showing how modern changes in managing the skin/clothes boundary or interface are a continuation of traditional mappings of highly sensitive personal and social space (Mosko, unpublished). The modern, naked body is translated by the donning of the painted T-shirt; the painting is translated from body art to fabric design; the T-shirt is moved from its usual social space of generic design and casual modernity into a specific, owned tradition – as is demonstrated by the adoption of slogans on shirts by the Mekeo, which translates a commercial practice into a display of social power. Something of the same two way translation occurs beneath the apparently one way appropriation of *tapa* cloth into the robes of the Anglican Archbishop of Dogura and the adoption of 'cowboy' or Elvis rig by a Moresby street entertainer.

We can argue about how significant these shifts of register in fashion actually are, but they all share to some degree in the uncanny gain-loss interzone of linguistic and literary translations. Homi Bhabha, in speaking of postcolonial, diasporic identities and their literary expressions, describes this kind of ambiguous dynamic of difference in which 'the people are the articulation of a doubling of the national address, an ambivalent *movement* between the discourses of pedagogy and the performative', working in and through the gaps and contradictions of binary structures that would seek a totalised uniform whole (Bhabha 1990: 299–300). Another useful way of thinking about the relationships between textile and text, between the various languages of tradition and modernity, and between translations of body and cloth, is perhaps Jacques Derrida's idea of the *supplement*: one thing operates as a substitute for the other while simultaneously signifying it – thus never fully replacing it (Derrida 1976: 144–45). Bhabha describes this supplemental logic as: 'where adding-*to* does not add-*up* but serves to disturb the calculation of power and knowledge' (Bhabha 1990: 312). We can think of this as a mutual relationship between different 'registers' or 'languages' and then see a similarity to Dipesh Chakrabarty's notion of translating subaltern and minority differences. All these approaches suggest that we need to find ways of accounting for translations from one term to another without assimilating either to some universalist medium of meta-language, whether it be scientific discourse, liberal humanism or capitalist globalisation (Chakrabarty 2000: 83; Bhabha 1990: 314).

Following the experiments in handcraft production that I outlined earlier in this paper, a co-operative was established in Port Moresby. It sold through the YWCA and became an important outlet for items that were translations across tradition and modernity, across skin and cloth. Along with woven baskets and fans and *tapa* items from outer regions, women from the Papuan coast appliquéd masks onto aprons and oven mitts. This was perhaps an early manifestation of the tourist trade – since I don't imagine local women paid money for things they made themselves to earn cash – and is a good example of how the Pacific exotic has been a production at the margins of local society, a production stimulated by expatriates for consumption by outsiders. But it also traces an interesting and complex path by which locality, women and tradition are inserted into the circulations of global modernity with and against its tendencies to externalise and de-personalise identity.

What clearly occurs in the material translation of design and technique is a further translation in which women in the act of modernising become the transmitters of tradition. Masks in the Gulf (as seen in the brief mask dance by Cowboy's father) were almost exclusively the property of the men's house and its rituals (Williams 1940: 25–26). Now, they continue to signify identity and tradition, but in a different context. What seems clear from the iconography of art, literature and film, is that the localisation of fashion as a 'translation' – in other words, as a continuous movement to and fro between tradition and modernity, between the local and the global – has been predominantly represented as a simple binary opposition, an 'either/or' centring on the body of the woman. The poems already cited are examples of a fairly common postcolonial Papuan iconography of split or dual subjectivity. More visual examples include Gigs Wena's painting in which a woman is vertically divided between jeans and grass skirt, entitled *Bipo na Nau* (*Before and Now*); and illustrations for Umetrifo's poetry, including the one previously cited and another, *Moden Girl*, which is a lament for the loss of female Pacific identity.

In and around this dual or split construction, subtle 'inter-languages' have occurred, however. James Porter's novel *Hapkas Girl* (Porter 1980) tells the story of a young Highlands woman – with a village mother and a white, patrol officer father – who is given work and educated in town to develop her talents as an artist. As she oscillates between town and village, she changes into Western dress and then back again into string *pulpul* – in a kind of dance across two worlds. This is not just a steady progress into modernity (Porter 1980: 12, 31, 52–53, 61). Some things bridge the gap undramatically: her *bilum* (string bag) goes with her everywhere, holding garden produce and books alike. The only difference is in wearing it on one's head or following the 'educated girls' in town and slinging it over the shoulder (Porter 1980: 52, 90).

This seemingly innocent fashion shift has important real-life implications that the novel only hints at. Christopher Tilley uses MacKenzie's work on Highlands' culture to show that traditionally, when men wear the *bilum* on their shoulder, an item usually associated with the fertile womb is appropriated and used by men. This appropriation is validated using the symbolism of the male cassowary nursing eggs (Tilley 1999). What is important to note is that the *bilum* swings ambiguously across genders while retaining its meanings of nurture and clan identity (Tilley 1999: 62–68). What becomes of these meanings when the *bilum* is translated into a 'shoulder bag' and produced as a commercial item (Cochrane

2001: 91–97, 100)? This is open to question, but the *bilum*'s traditional function in negotiating 'inconsistencies of sexual autonomy/opposition and sexual co-operation/integration' (MacKenzie 1991: 206 cited in Tilley 1999: 68) is definitely translated into the cultural negotiations taking place in modern Papua New Guinea. Such translations will continue to emerge as national identity, everyday life and global markets continue to modify each other.

References

Apuatimi, JB (2002) 'Body Pattern' silkscreen on cotton, Tiwi Designs, collection of Diana Wood-Conroy

Beier, U (1970) 'Explanatory note' 1(1) Kovave 1

Bhabha, HK (1990) 'Dissemi-nation: time, narrative and the margins of the modern nation' in Bhabha, HK (ed), *Nation and Narration*, London: Routledge

de Certeau, Michel (1984) *The Practice of Everyday Life*, Randall, S, (trans), Berkeley: University of California Press

Chakrabarty, D (2000) 'Translating life-worlds into labor and history' in *Provincializing Europe: Postcolonial Thought and Historical Difference*, Princeton, Oxford: Princeton University Press

Christen, K (unpublished) 'Out bush: negotiating difference in a global modernity', paper presented in the 'Gender and Identity' panel of the Pacific History Association Conference, Australian National University, Canberra, June 2000

Cochrane, S (2001) *Bérétara: Contemporary Pacific Art*, Nouméa and Sydney: Centre Culturel Tjibao & Halstead Press

Derrida, J (1976) *Of Grammatology*, Chakravorty Spivak, G (trans), Baltimore: Johns Hopkins University Press

Eri, V (1970) *The Crocodile*, Brisbane: Jacaranda Press

Faitali, A (2001) 'Beyond the waves' 4(1) Savannah Flames 24

Henslowe, DI (1957) *Papua Calls*, Hobart: self-published

Kiki, AM (1968) *Kiki: Ten Thousand Years in a Lifetime*, Melbourne: FW Cheshire

MacKenzie, MA (1991) *Androgynous Objects: String Bags and Gender in Central New Guinea*, Chur: Harwood Academic Publishers

Dus Mapun, B (1980) 'O Meri Wantok' in *Lali: A Pacific Anthology*, Auckland: Longman Paul

Matane, P (1972) *My Childhood in New Guinea*, Melbourne: Oxford University Press

Mosko, MS (unpublished) 'Melanesian mod: the agency of traditional and contemporary dress among North Mekeo', paper presented at 'Body Arts and Modernity' colloquium, Pitt Rivers Museum and Institute of Social and Cultural Anthropology, Oxford, June 2002

Owen, C, McLaren, L and Stiven, A (1991) *Cowboy and Maria in Town*, Institute of Papua New Guinea Studies and Australian Film Commission

Panga, S (1990) 'Moden Girl' 10 Ondobondo 14

Porter, J (1980) *Hapkas Girl*, Stanmore, NSW: Cassell

Sharrad, P (2000) 'Trading and trade-offs: textiles and texts in the Pacific' 36 New Literatures Review 46–63

Soaba, R (1977) *Wanpis*, Port Moresby: Institute of Papua New Guinea Studies

Somare, M (1975) *Sana: An Autobiography of Michael Somare*, Port Moresby: Niugini Press

Tilley, C (1999) *Metaphor and Material Culture*, Oxford: Blackwell

Toro, A and Owen, C (1984) *Tukana*, Papua New Guinea: Institute of Papua New Guinea Studies

Umetrifo, B (1987) '*Yupela meri i senis hariap pinis*' in Powell, G (ed), *Through Melanesian Eyes*, South Melbourne: Macmillan

Vagi, N (1980) 'Which way big man?' in Beier, U (ed), *Voices of Independence*, St Lucia: University of Queensland

Wena, G (1999) '*Bipo na nau* (half/half woman)', acrylic on canvas, in Cochrane (2001), *Bérétara: Contemporary Pacific Art*, Novméa and Sydney: Centre Culturel Tjibao & Halstead Press

Williams, FE (1940) *Drama of Orokolo*, Oxford: Clarendon Press

Wolfers, EP (1975) *Race Relations and Colonial Rule in Papua New Guinea*, Sydney: Australia & New Zealand Publishing Company

DRESS AND ADDRESS: FIRST NATIONS SELF-FASHIONING AND THE 1860 ROYAL TOUR OF CANADA

Ruth B Phillips

Western colonialism, in its global engagements with indigenous forms of visual representation, was possessed both of a monolithic sameness and an infinite variety of local resonances. The missionaries, traders, government agents, soldiers, travellers and settlers who worked to impose a new order were universalists whose agendas for and responses to indigenous peoples were remarkably homogeneous, despite the variety of climates and cultures in which they intervened. This book focuses on local processes of negotiation and response to the new materials, styles and norms of dress introduced to indigenous peoples in the Pacific. The topic is equally central and important for students of colonialism and indigenous art in North America, where dress has been a key site for the visual expression of individual and collective identities since pre-contact times. I offer this case study of the role of dress in the Great Lakes region as a way of revealing both the commonalities that underlay colonial processes during the 19th century and the specificities that mark local engagements.

I define dress as an assemblage of clothing, body decoration and held objects; and I take it as a given that in modernity the creation of such assemblages is a key act of self-fashioning, one that shapes relationships both to human and non-human others. Discursively, the standard hierarchies of fine and applied arts have worked to devalue dress as a site of aesthetic and cultural expression, just as the standard typological and functional categories of anthropological material-culture study have inhibited the holistic appreciation of its expressive value. In both disciplines, too, essentialist constructs of authenticity have caused outsiders to bracket or silence precisely those mixtures, fusions, and inventions that are most characteristic of the dress produced in colonial encounters, whether they involve the combination of elements deriving from different material traditions or the invention of new techniques and forms.

We lack, as yet, refined tools with which to evaluate the resonance and variety of mixed dress as it arises in different historical moments and geographic locations, and as it occurs in the dress of both the colonised and the colonisers. Rather, such assemblages are most often lumped together under the totalising and unhelpful rubric of the 'hybrid'. I count myself among those who have ignored, puzzled over, and lumped together. It has, for example, taken me nearly 20 years after my first reading of the 1861 *History of the Ojebway Indians* by the Ojibwa missionary, Peter Jones (Kahkewakwonaby) (Jones 1861), to return to the plates

THE RIPPLING STREAM.
(OMUDDWAJECOONOQUA.)

Figure 11.1: Omuddwajecoonoqua, a female chief, from Peter Jones' *History of the Ojebway Indians*, 1861, p 56.

Figure 11.2: Nahtawash, from Peter Jones'
History of the Ojebway Indians, 1861, p 24.

portraying prominent 19th century Ojibwa chiefs in formal dress. The images of
Omuddwajecoonoqua in her beaver hat embellished with trade-silver ornaments
and feathers, or Nahtawash, the Miscocomon chief, with his frock coat, leggings
and bow, long seemed to me eccentric and impenetrable.

I will argue here, first of all, for the need to regard such dress assemblages as
historically situated in highly specific ways. Secondly, I will urge that such dress
should, whenever possible, be considered not only as a set of discrete items that
can be analysed on their own, but as an assemblage reflecting its wearer's
intentionality – that is, as a *composition* whose individual components must be
understood relationally. The diverse modalities of juxtaposition and integration
that colonial dress assemblages display were sensitive to shifts in taste, ideology
and power. Viewed as compositions and understood relationally, dress
assemblages become useful barometers of such changes, helping us to locate
individual examples along the continuum defined by the poles of attraction and
estrangement, desire and repulsion, appropriation and repression that most
characterise the colonial milieu.

Before launching into the specific examples with which I will illustrate these
points, I want to flag several technical and conceptual problems that arise from the
approach I am recommending. First of all, to recover the sense of dress as

assemblage we must perform acts of historical reconstruction that are often hindered by the prior acts of disarticulation that occurred when collections were processed through the standard taxonomic and classificatory structures of museums and archives: textiles in one room, photographs in another; all belts together, all hats together. Secondly, to reveal the aesthetic negotiations, technical inventions and histories of use whose traces are discoverable in the materiality of objects, we need to call upon old-fashioned skills of connoisseurship and technical analysis. These skills are becoming increasingly rare among scholars – an unintended casualty, in my view, of the recent and important re-theorisations of material-culture study. On a discursive level I also want to problematise the marked tendency of the recent literature to construct histories of colonial dress and expressive culture in terms of celebratory narratives of resistance, continuity and creative hybridity that are framed within a dialectic of 'tradition versus innovation and difference' versus dialogic negotiation. While seemingly inescapable – and certainly present in this paper – these dialectics pose problems of their own. I hope the larger project of which this paper is a part will ultimately be able to address these problems by developing more historically nuanced understandings of the operation of visual culture in the Great Lakes; especially how it has operated in relation to shifts in power and to changes in paradigms of visuality and materiality across the four centuries of European contact and colonisation.

The negotiation of tradition and modernity through the expressive medium of dress was highly active in the Great Lakes during the 19th century, as indigenous peoples were forced to come to terms with the extent and irreversibility of Euro-North American settlement and political domination. These dynamics became particularly visible during the summer of 1860, when Queen Victoria's eldest son, Prince Albert Edward, made the first royal tour of the Canadian colonies. The Prince's tour electrified all Canadians, and he was greeted everywhere with elaborate pageantry, ceremonial arches, night time illuminations, and grand receptions and balls. Officially, the Prince had come to represent the Queen at the inauguration of the new Victoria Railway Bridge at Montreal, one of the engineering marvels of the age. Unofficially, the tour carried deeper undertones, providing a ritual and performative space for the expression of old loyalties and new tensions as the Canadian colonies prepared for confederation and greater political separation from Britain. For the First Nations,[1] the visit offered an occasion to reaffirm their long-standing allegiance to the British crown and to represent to the Prince and the high-ranking colonial officials in his party their urgent grievances, especially over illegal land appropriations. The Royal Proclamation of 1763 had established a formal treaty with the Crown as the only legal basis for the alienation of Indian land, and the Canadian First Nations had continued to regard the British monarch as the ultimate protector of their rights. Their speeches, presentations of gifts, and modes of self-display were thus intensely meaningful and highly ritualised, forming part of a long sequence of such exchanges stretching back to the 17th century.

---

1   I use the terms 'First Nations', 'Native', 'Aboriginal' and, in historical contexts, 'Indian'
     interchangeably in line with current usages in Canada.

Like all travellers to North America, the Prince and his party had a particular interest in seeing indigenous people. As Ian Radforth has shown (Radforth 2003), the presence of Indians was also viewed by the Canadian organisers as integral to the projection of the prospective dominion's unique identity, and they went to considerable lengths to ensure that formal greetings and performances by Native representatives would punctuate the Prince's itinerary. I will focus here on two presentations that made particularly strong impressions on the foreign visitors: one by Anishnabe[2] chiefs at Sarnia, on the shores of Lake Huron at the western frontier of the Canadian colonies; and the other by the Six Nations Iroquois at Brantford, near Niagara Falls. These meetings have also left behind the richest deposits of material evidence and visual documentation.

The gaze of the British visitors is represented here by the sketches and letters of one of the members of the Prince's party, Dr Henry Wentworth Acland.[3] In general terms, Acland's sketches emanate from an upper class milieu of private viewing and amateur aesthetics, taste and social responsibility. They also reflect the progressive, scientific world of which Acland was a part (Atlay 1903). Acland was Oxford's first Regius Professor of Medicine, a founder of the Oxford Museum and a close friend of John Ruskin. His portrayals are closely observed, exhibiting the scientific eye of an anthropologist *avant la lettre*. Individuals' names are carefully noted, and several letters record his discussions with his subjects about the 'condition of Indians'. It is tempting to see in the immediacy and directness of his drawings a response to the goals defined for the amateur artist in Ruskin's *Elements of Drawing*, published only three years earlier, to 'set down clearly, and usefully, records of such things as cannot be described in words ... and to preserve something like a true image of beautiful things that pass away' (quoted in Bermingham 2000: 243).

Acland's drawings are both more intimate and less reliant on stereotypes than the generic and picturesque images published by professional journalists and artists in newspapers and the new illustrated weeklies. In such popular media, Indians appear as marginal figures, alternately romantic, tragically doomed or laughably gauche. In contrast to the rich array of texts and images of the royal tour created by non-Native observers we have, however, only the most meagre documentary record of indigenous voices. The object archives of the museum can, I suggest, supply historical evidence that cannot be found in the written archive, although articulated in material and visual forms that are *sui generis*. The dress Native people wore for their presentations to the Prince offers direct and often unique evidence of their active self-positioning at this critical historical moment.

One of the most important surviving dress assemblages from the summer of 1860 is the suit of clothes that was worn by Oronhyadekha, or 'Burning Cloud',

---

2   'Anishnabe' refers to neighbouring Ojibwa (Chippewa), Odawa (Ottawa) and Potawatomi peoples who share a common sense of nationhood grounded in language, historical alliances and shared lifestyle.

3   The Acland collections related to the 1860 royal visit in the National Archives of Canada (NAC): MG 40 Q40 (journal); and Accession No 1986.7.1–302 (sketchbooks).

the young 18 year old who was chosen to deliver the address of welcome to the Prince on behalf of the Six Nations Iroquois.[4] (See Figure 11.3 in the colour section.)

The relative obscurity in which this dress assemblage has lain since the early 20th century amongst the collections of the Los Angeles County Museum of Natural History illustrates key conceptual issues at the heart of this discussion. As I have discussed in more detail elsewhere (Phillips 1998), during the latter decades of the 19th century, as notions of authenticity derived from cultural evolutionism became established, most of the art produced by eastern and Great Lakes Native North Americans came to be regarded as too 'acculturated' and commercialised to be of value to anthropological study. This was because of the prominence of trade materials and motifs of European origin, and because much was made for the souvenir and curio trades. This devaluation radically reversed the views of mid-Victorians, ranging from intellectuals like Lewis Henry Morgan to middle class consumers, who tended to regard those same features as virtues (for example, Morgan 1852: 111). At the time of the Prince's visit, Native-made textiles ornamented with floral bead work similar to that of Oronhyadekha's clothing were, for example, being sold in great numbers to appreciative tourists visiting Niagara Falls – and were also being imitated by non-Native needlewomen (Phillips 1998: 218–23).

Yet, even within the loose category of the 'hybrid', Oronhyadekha's presentation outfit stands out because of its unusual number of unique features. In ethnographic collections – unlike fine art collections – the typological tradition has remained so strong that unique objects have tended to be ignored, misidentified, or valued only for their antiquarian interest rather than being seen as original, innovative or experimental. It is thus not surprising that museum curators doubted the authenticity of Oronhyadekha's clothing until recently, despite the existence of documentation clearly tying it to the 1860 royal visit.[5] If I had not happened to have recently seen the newly acquired Acland sketchbooks at the National Archives of Canada together with an early photograph, I too would no doubt have dismissed them as anomalous. Scholarly and curatorial practices of attribution that are still current have been profoundly informed by the taxonomic approach derived from evolutionist theory, and by the taste reforms introduced by the Arts and Crafts movement, two key movements that combined to bring an end to the transcultural fashion for Iroquois beadwork. It thus required a special effort to recognise that the stylistic features of Oronhyadekha's clothing are artefacts of the preceding period of relatively fluid and open exchange between Aboriginal people and Euro-North Americans; and to understand his clothing as a negotiation of Iroquois identity within norms of taste and decorum specific to that period.

---

4   The dress ensemble consists of a shirt, leggings, armbands, leg bands, bandolier sash and two bags (Los Angeles County Museum of Natural History, anthropology collection accession file A1572.26.1–5).

5   The garments were donated in 1926 by Gordon C Day of Inglewood, California, who stated that they had been made by his grandmother and other Mohawk, and worn by a chief, whose name was transcribed as 'Ronnatucka' to welcome the Prince of Wales.

CLOTHING, CULTURE AND INDIAN IDENTITIES IN 1860

How, then, might Oronhyadekha's garments have been 'read' by viewers in 1860? And how might we understand details of design, media and style as the result of the particular rationality of the makers? In order to answer these questions it is necessary to sketch briefly both a diachronic and a synchronic context. Pre-contact Great Lakes clothing was made of finely tanned deer and moose hide and decorated with paint and porcupine quill embroidery. Tattooing, body painting and ornaments displayed personal histories of achievement and the empowering gifts conferred in dreams and visions by spirit guardians (Phillips 1987; Penney 1992). After contact, indigenous people began, highly selectively, to incorporate trade goods, such as woollen cloth, calico, vermilion, glass beads and silk ribbon, as well as finished garments such as shirts, coats and hats. As Richard White (White 1991) has pointed out, for members of 18th century Native communities, the wearing of laced hats and European coats by a chief signalled his ability to look after his people through the successful negotiation of annual gift distributions from French and British allies and trading partners. To most European observers, however, such mixed styles of clothing seemed bizarre reversals of familiar dress conventions. The Anglo-Irish officer, Jasper Grant, for example, wrote in 1807 of the warriors who frequented Fort Malden on Lake Huron that, 'with Cloaths of white People, their heads ornamented with feathers, faces tattooed and painted with vermillion, Indian leggings and shoes, tomahawks, pipes with stems a yard long, tobacco pouches … they cut a most curious figure'. To his eye, the woman's calico blouse ornamented with trade silver brooches resembled a 'bedgown' turned into a 'Coat of Mail'.[6]

The War of 1812, though a standoff from the American and British points of view, was a final defeat for the Indians of the Great Lakes, opening up previously protected lands to rapid settlement. Within a few decades, sources of traditional materials for clothing vanished along with hunting preserves. Native people came under pressure to become farmers and Christians, and a new wave of missionisation brought injunctions against 'pagan' styles of dress and body decoration, as well as lessons in sewing and tailoring. By 1860, as Acland's sketches show, the daily dress of Iroquois and southern Ojibwa often differed little from that of the settlers amongst whom they lived.[7] Dress worn on formal occasions, however, remained an important medium for the expression of distinctive identity and connection with past traditions; although it continued to evolve through incorporations of new settler styles. As the Reverend Peter Jones noted: 'At present, those Indians who have the means of obtaining clothing of European manufacture have adopted the same, but the style of wearing it is somewhat after the fashion of their ancient dress' (Jones 1861: 75).

---

6 Letter to Rev Alexander Grant headed Amherstberg (Ontario) 20 January 1807, published in Phillips 1984: 33.

7 The English settler Catherine Parr Trail wrote of the Mississauga Ojibwa living near Rice Lake in the 1830s, eg: 'These Indians appear less addicted to gay and tinselly adornments than formerly, and rather affect a European style in their dress … The squaws, too, prefer cotton or stuff gowns, aprons and handkerchiefs … to any sort of finery' (Trail 1997: 209).

Foreign visitors' expectations of what Indians should look like were formed, in contrast, by images and examples that had been circulating in Europe for centuries – and by the visits of Indian delegations and troupes of performers who had travelled to Europe more recently. In the mid-1840s, for example, a cousin of Peter Jones named Maungwudaus, or George Henry, left his work as a Methodist missionary to form a travelling troupe of performers (Smith 1976). During their visit to Europe in 1843, they were entertained by prominent people, performed dances and gave exhibitions of scalping and shooting with bow and arrow. As shown in contemporary photographs and in sketches made by the American painter George Catlin, with whom they teamed up in Paris, the troupe dressed either in European garments embellished 'after the fashion of their ancient dress' or – for the war dances performed by men – in body paint, breechclouts and leggings.[8]

Elements of performance dress were in evidence at the gathering organised at Sarnia on September 13, 1860, which is generally agreed to be the most impressive and satisfying Indian spectacle of the Prince's tour. He was welcomed there by several hundred Ojibwa, Odawa and Potawatomi chiefs and warriors from the major Anishnabe reserves at Manitoulin Island and Walpole Island (the home reserves of Maungwudaus and his troupe). Radforth has shown that this colourful spectacle had been actively encouraged and subsidised by officials of the Indian department and that it had a specifically historicist intent. 'Our great object', wrote one official, 'is to show the Prince of Wales how the Indians dressed in their aboriginal state ... We want if possible to have a very grand affair' (quoted in Radforth 2003: 14). This active encouragement of displays of traditional Indian dress is startling in the context of the Prince's visit, because it reversed, if only temporarily, the official civilization policy that had been in place for several decades and that was increasingly being formalised and codified in law. Government policy discouraged the cultural forms and observances associated with the 'pagan' usages and beliefs that traditional dress forms referenced. The effort of colonial officers to show the Prince Indians in 'authentic dress' – stimulated, as we have seen, both by the Canadian desire to show off distinctive identity and by the sense of loss of traditional forms that marks modern Western culture more generally – thus exemplifies the kinds of contradictions produced by the non-Native desire for spectacles of 'Indian-ness'.

Journalists duly stressed in their reports that the Indians at Sarnia were (at last) the 'genuine Indians', in contrast to those in the east whose more obviously hybrid styles of dress had evoked much caustic commentary. At Sarnia, as one reporter wrote, 'the red men in question had all the characteristics of their nature apparently unaltered by intercourse with their civilised brethren' (Cornwallis 1860: 139). One of the fullest descriptions was in the *Hamilton Spectator*:

Some of them had headdresses made of hawk's feathers, others of embroidered birch bark, set off with woodpecker's tails; some had buffalo horns on their crowns, others again long squirrel or fox tails hanging beside their ears. Some were clad in wolf or coon skins, other in well tanned moose hide; some had tom toms, some

8   Catlin's sketch of Ojibwa performing for Queen Victoria is reproduced in Mulvey 2002: 72.

conch shells, some hollow gourds, half filled with lumps of stone which they rattled as they walked. All had weapons of some kind, whether tomahawks, bows and arrows or war clubs. And all were horribly beautified with paint. Blue, white, red, yellow and black were all used in profusion. (Quoted in Radforth 2003: 25)

These written texts evoke Catlin's romantic portraits of the 1830s and 1840s, and the ornaments and headdresses described can easily be identified with 18th and early 19th century objects in museums. Yet the depictions of the delegates assembled at Sarnia that were published in the *New York Illustrated News* on 28 September 1860 give a very different picture.

They show the members of the Indian delegation dressed in the semi-tailored, fringed coats and trouser-like leggings worn by the travelling troupes of performers. The body decoration worn at Sarnia, which was also documented by Acland's quick sketches, thus seems to have drawn on styles developed in the mid-19th century for public performance before non-Native audiences – and these acquired official sanction at Sarnia as revivals of authentically traditional usages.

It must have been evident to Acland and many of the other spectators that the Sarnia dress assemblages were not 'unaltered by contact'. How then do we account for the emphasis on a primordial authenticity in their written reports? On one level, this episode evidences the power of the Western desire for the authenticity of the primitive; an authenticity that enables this desire to create its own reality through the invention of traditions. This has been well documented in other 19th century

INDIANS OF THE OJIBBEWAY TRIBE FROM THE MANITOULIN ISLANDS PRESENTING AN ADDRESS TO THE PRINCE OF WALES, AT SARNIA.

Figure 11.4: Anishnabe delegates at Sarnia to greet the Prince of Wales. Taken from *New York Illustrated News*, 28 September 1860.

contexts (Hobsbawm and Ranger 1983). In 1860, as after, this desire converged and colluded with a Native desire to defend tradition. A second and less widely understood explanation can, however, be found in the structural contrast with the dress worn by the Christian converts who also attended the Prince at Sarnia. One of these was the venerable Odawa chief Assiginack – 92 years old, a veteran of the War of 1812, a Catholic missionary, trusted government interpreter, and the leader who had brought his people to Manitoulin Island from north western Michigan in the 1830s (King 1994). The *Sarnia Observer* reported that Assiginack was among the 'Christian Indians who in a great measure had laid aside their native costume and habits' and 'appeared clothed as nearly as possible after the style of the white brethren' (quoted in King 1994: 47). A portrait of Assiginack from the early 1850s painted by Father Nicholas Point shows him wearing the sober black coat favoured by Native missionaries and gives an indication of the appearance of these men at the Sarnia meeting. In comparison with the unrelieved blackness and European cut of their coats, the 'traditional' clothing worn by the other chiefs, however modified, signified clearly distinctive identities; although the specific elements of these

Figure 11.5: *Portrait of Jean-Baptiste Assiginack*. From Father Nicolas Point's drawing book, *Souvenirs et mémoires illustrés Mission de Sainte-Croix Grande Manitouline Wikwemikong*, circa 1840. Drawing, 11.1 cm × 8.2 cm, Archives de la Compagnie de Jésus, St-Jérôme, Cote #1604.

distinctions had constantly to be revised in relation both to evolving fashions and to the shifting spectrum of differences.

This clothing also referenced a particular politics of resistance. Walpole Island, Manitoulin Island, and neighbouring First Nations of the region had up to this time resisted many aspects of the government's civilization program, and in 1860 the questions of further land cessions and conversion to Christianity still remained unresolved (Chute 1998). Although Catholic missionaries had been active on Manitoulin since the early 1840s, encouraging a settled agricultural lifestyle, the Native population remained relatively isolated and still lived primarily by hunting and fishing. On Walpole Island, most Ojibwa had become farmers, but as late as 1858 about two-thirds of the community was still considered to be 'pagan' (Nin Da Waab Jig 1987). Refusal to convert could have a heavy cost. As one Indian agent reported in the 1840s, for example, membership in a Christian church was a great advantage in fighting the illegal encroachments of the squatters who constantly threatened the viability of Native communities. 'They find,' he wrote, 'the great disadvantages under which they labour from being heathens, not being heard in a Court of Justice, and often wrongfully despoiled [by squatters] in consequence' (quoted in Nin Da Waab Jig 1987: 40). In this milieu, then, choices of clothing style could carry risks, and the clothes worn for different kinds of occasions are indicators of individual and strategic decisions. With historical hindsight we can recognise the specific political significations of Assiginack's wearing of Western dress at the Sarnia reception. Two years later he would be the only one of the Manitoulin chiefs to agree to the government's plan to open most of Manitoulin Island to white settlement (Shanahan 1994).

The situated and strategic nature of the decisions Native leaders made about the styles of clothing they wore during the mid-19th century is further illustrated by the case of Peter Jones, the Ojibwa Methodist missionary whose name has already come up several times and who had died four years before the royal tour. Jones used dress to express his strong sense of Indian identity throughout his life, but he carefully calibrated the mix of European and Indian in relation to the specific occasion. His preferred mode of self-presentation is established by two portraits commissioned by his English fiancée during his first trip to England in 1832. In these he wears European dress with the significant additions of a distinctively Native finger-woven sash (interestingly, this is itself a 'hybrid' textile form with both French and Native origins) and a chief's medal (both were official presents from British officials). A chief always wore his medals on public occasions, as Jones wrote, 'as a mark of recognition of his office' (Jones 1861: 108). On another trip to England, in 1840, Jones was granted an audience with the Queen in order to present a petition for confirmation of his community's land claim. Victoria wrote with apparent approval in her journal that on that occasion Jones wore 'his National dress, which is entirely of leather, leather leggings, etc' (quoted in Smith 1987: xiii). Key components of this dress assemblage survive, and the coat is well known as a particularly fine example of mid-19th century clothing.[9] Its lapels display images of the eagle – Jones's clan *dodem* – as well as

---

9   The United States National Museum of Natural History, Smithsonian Institution, acquired
    them from Jones's son. The coat is accession number 178,398.

Figure 11.6: *Chief Peter Jones (Kahkewaquonaby).* Matilda Jones, 1832, oil, 8.2 cm × 10.9 cm, Victoria University Library, Toronto. Peter Jones Fonds, Box 6.

other images associated with traditional Ojibwa cosmology. During a visit to Edinburgh in 1843, the Scottish photographers Hill and Adamson invited Jones to sit for a series of calotypes. Of the eight images they made, three show Jones wearing his Indian outfit, apparently at the photographers' express request (Smith 1987: 150).[10]

---

10   For the Hill and Adamson portraits, see Stevenson 1981 and Bruce 1973.

Figure 11.7: *The Waving Plume (Peter 'Kahkewaquonaby' Jones).* David Octavius Hill and Robert Adamson, 1845, calotype, 19.6 cm × 14.3 cm, National Portrait Gallery, London, NPG P6(145).

On the surface of it, the wearing of such clothing by a Methodist minister is unexpected. We know that Jones disapproved of the exhibitions of Indian-ness being put on by travelling dance troupes, to which displays of similar fringed clothing and pagan imagery were central. He expressed his disapproval of his cousin Maungwudaus' activities, for example, when he wrote to a friend: 'In my opinion such exhibitions before the British people by men who have professed Christianity and civilisation are well calculated to injure and impede the benevolent intentions of our good government and the missionary societies for the amelioration of the Indian tribes' (quoted in Smith 1976: 6). Jones's biographer, Donald Smith, has cited another letter in which Jones explicitly states his own dislike for the necessity of appearing in public in what he termed his 'odious Indian costume'. As Smith observes, however, Jones was a pragmatist who knew that the 'winning formula' for attracting crowds was a combination of 'the Indian talk, the Indian costume, the specimens of "heathen gods" and the Indian curios'

(Smith 1987: 204).[11] Throughout his life, Jones also affirmed his Indian identity by his consistent use of both his English and Ojibwa names. Kahkewakwonaby, 'Sacred Feathers', is a name that is associated with Jones's clan *dodem*, the eagle. From the evidence, we might speculate that he chose to highlight the thunderbird image on his coat both because it was emblematic of his personal identity; and in order to assimilate the coat's complex cosmological iconography and references to traditional spiritual beliefs to a more general notion of 'national' identity. (See Figure 11.8 in the colour section.)

Against the background of these examples of mid-19th century negotiations of Great Lakes clothing traditions, the meaning of the clothing worn by Oronhyadekha for his presentation to the Prince on the day following the Sarnia meeting begins to come into focus. Like the fringed garments of the Sarnia chiefs, Oronhyadekha's clothes completely covered his body, a clear outward signifier of 'civilization'. Yet beyond this basic similarity his garments unite two different impulses. On the one hand, the garment types – leggings, tunic, armbands, garters, moccasins, bandolier bag – are Iroquois in concept and design. Except for the headdress, all these components translate into a new idiom the basic style of dress worn by the great Iroquois leader Joseph Brant in William Berczy's 1802 portrait.

Although more tailored, the blowsy fullness and length of Oronhyadekha's tunic recall the long muslin and calico shirts worn during the second half of the 18th century over a breechclout and leggings. The omissions of key elements of dress that were identified with the image of the noble savage – the blanket cloak, the shaved head and the roach headdress – are equally significant. Interestingly, too, Oronhyadekha did not wear the traditional Iroquois *gustoweh* headdress given such prominence in Lewis Henry Morgan's reports on Iroquois material culture (Morgan 1852), but rather the Plains feather bonnet already identified by non-Natives with authentic Indian-ness.

For viewers today, the manufactured materials of which the outfit is made defamiliarise its traditionalism. In 1860, however, the floral designs and beadwork that decorate all but the leggings would have been recognisably linked to the much admired beadwork that Iroquois women were selling at Niagara Falls and other tourist resorts; and that non-Native women were making themselves. Oronhyadekha's leggings, in contrast, display much older geometric designs that have cosmological references. The symbolic and expressive qualities of the materials used are as meaningful as those of the overall design and motifs. George Hammel has persuasively argued that the Iroquois use of glass beads – particularly the translucent and white beads used in much mid-19th century beadwork – is continuous with ancient usages of light reflective materials such as

---

11 Lilly Koltun has cogently argued that these images must also be read in the context of a Scottish tradition of heroic and nationalist portrait painting, 'which mixed a distinctive, exotic culture with a tragic subjection, now assimilated and diluted, to a conquering English civilisation. In this context Kahkewaquonaby's portrait was not ethnographic record, nor antiquarianism; it was inheritor and promulgator of this fanciful contemplative and picturesque tradition where, like the heroes of Scott's novels, he represented the glory of the noble primitive, but as a ruin from a greater national past' (Koltun 1998: 11).

Figure 11.9: *Thayendanegea (Joseph Brant)*. William Berczy, circa 1807, oil on canvas, 61.8 cm × 46.1 cm, National Gallery of Canada, 5777.

white shell wampum beads, copper, and quartz crystals (Hammel 1983). These indigenous materials are traditionally associated with cultural values of spiritual enlightenment, wisdom, and the good; they express a moral aesthetic central to the Iroquoian worldview. Beads, then, seemed to serve as 'analogues' for indigenous materials, just as, throughout the fur trade era, red woollen cloth was preferred because of its analogic relationship to red ochre and indigenous scarlet dyes. I suggest that a similar argument can be made with regard to the deep brown velvet chosen for Oronhyadekha's clothing, which recalls the texture and colour of native tanned and smoked deerskin.

Like the clothing of the Sarnia chiefs, then, Oronhyadekha's outfit expresses the postures of difference and accommodation that he would adopt throughout his life. Educated by Methodist missionaries at Six Nations and at Kenyon College in Ohio, Oronhyadekha took advantage of his meeting with Dr Acland to go on to study at Oxford and the University of Toronto. After practising medicine briefly, he joined the International Order of Foresters and was largely responsible for building it into one of the most important insurance companies of its day (Nicks 1996; Jameson 2000). Oronhyadekha was not a hereditary chief and was in many ways out of sympathy with traditionalist factions in his community. Yet at the mansion he built near the Mohawk reserve at Tyendinaga, he insisted that Mohawk be spoken exclusively; and he remained committed to the preservation of distinctive Aboriginal identity in the face of the increasing repressiveness of official Indian policy. The survival of some of the outfits worn by Anishnabe leaders to greet the Prince in 1860 is due to his sense of their historical importance (Silverstein-Wilmott 2003).

Acland's travel diary records his conversation with Oronhyadekha while he sketched, and reveals the latter's perception of the role played by dress as an outer sign of resistance to assimilation. When asked why he wore a ring through his nose, Oronhyadekha answered: 'I told you I take delight in all that concerns my people – this ring is part of the old Indian dress.' Acland replied, 'Well, but it is not a pleasant custom', to which Oronhyadekha responded, 'It is the custom – that is enough'.[12] During a subsequent conversation, Acland debated with him 'against his too great confidence in the wisdom of preserving his nationality', and also tried to persuade him that the petition of the Six Nations chiefs for the continuation of British Indian gifts and nation-to-nation alliances was a vain effort. 'On the white man will go,' said Acland, 'and ... your people must be as them, seizing their merit without their vice, or fade away – You must settle and till, and be educated, and be trusted as merchants, as clerks, as farmers, as servants, and come in to the stream of modern life, or be swept before it.' Oronhyadekha replied: 'I know all these things ... I can write only what the greater number of the chiefs in council agree – and the greater number will not see.'[13] Although Oronhyadekha would 'come in to the stream of modern life' with a vengeance, he would resist the loss of identity that even relatively open minded liberals like Acland thought of as inevitable.

The women who made Oronhyadekha's ceremonial clothing in 1860 were negotiating the same issues of modernity and tradition; not in words, but through

---

12 Letter from Dr Acland to Mrs Acland headed London, Upper Canada, 12 September 1860, NAC MG40 Q40, p 113.
13 Letter from Dr Acland to Mrs Acland headed Detroit, Michigan, 21 Sept 1860, NAC MG40 Q40, p 123.

the media of cloth, thread and beads. The unique features of this clothing are artefacts of the experimentation and unsettlement of these people. If we seek insight into the lived experience of First Nations people forced to adjust to the expanding settler world of the mid-19th century Great Lakes region, it is to such apparently anomalous objects, and to their nuanced mediations of settler and Native visual conventions, that we should especially attend.

CONCLUSION

Looking back, the summer of 1860 appears as a pause before events that would prove cataclysmic for nations and for individuals. The Victoria Bridge, whose opening had occasioned the royal tour, was emblematic of the dynamic energies of industrialisation that were transforming the material conditions of life: conjuring farms out of forests and cities out of farms; filling houses with machine made goods; hurtling bodies across the landscape in railway cars; and proliferating visual images through new technologies of mechanical reproduction. In the year after the tour, Prince Albert's premature death would throw the Queen into permanent mourning, and civil war would break out in the United States. In the years that followed, slaves would be freed and indigenous spiritual practices would be outlawed in Canada. In 1860, however, the most repressive elements of assimilationist policies had not yet been formulated or imposed. When we read the sources for the middle decades of the century, we find evidence of greater proximities and exchanges between Natives and settlers than would later be possible. These interactions both contributed to the destabilisation of traditional Aboriginal lifestyles and created a climate in which innovation could flourish. Although Native people could not prevent the loss of their lands and subsistence patterns, they continued to hold to many aspects of their traditional expressive culture. In this they were aided by the desires of settlers and visitors to see, experience and consume indigenous cultures as spectacle and commodity – desires born of the sense of loss produced by immigration and the effects of 'progress' and industrialisation. The extraordinary nature of the Prince of Wales's visit heightened the importance of material, performative and spectacular modes of expression; allowing us to see both the contradictions in which Indians and settlers were caught and the instrumentality of visual and material expression in their mediation.

The alternative to the stasis of typological understandings of dress is not a generalised invocation of hybridity. Rather, we need to think of dress as historically situated, individually nuanced and motivated by a desire to maintain boundaries and identities. Notions of agency, strategy and resistance are, of course, central to postcolonial considerations of hybridity. But what we have been looking at is not the subversive, ironic and self-conscious hybridity theorised by Homi Bhabha (Bhabha 1994) as a form of mimicry. Rather, I find more useful Nicholas Thomas's notion (Thomas 2000) that we should not think of objects or identities as hybrid, but rather of the use of hybrid forms as 'technologies'. These technologies are 'conservative, in the sense that they attempted to preserve a prior order rather than create a novel one … [their] value inhered in their doubleness'.

As Thomas writes, the dress of Omuddwajecoonoqua, Nahtawash, Peter Jones and Oronhyadekha 'mobilised certain precedents, on the one hand, but possessed novelty and distinctiveness on the other' (Thomas 2000: 209). When we succeed in seeing Great Lakes dress assemblages, not in terms of stable cultural 'types', but as products of individual negotiation and manoeuvre, then the anomalous rather than the typical is introduced into the history of colonialism, destabilising this tradition that is in varying degrees a definition of the modern condition. Thus considered, the mixture itself – continuously shifting and in process of reconfiguration – is normative. It is not the hybrid that is anomalous, but rather the occasional moments of apparent fusion and homogeneity that have in the past been constructed as essential expressions of 'Kultur' and 'culture'.

References

Atlay JB (1903) *Henry Acland: A Memoir*, London: Smith, Elder & Co

Bermingham, A (2000) *Learning to Draw: Studies in the Cultural History of a Polite and Useful Art*, New Haven: Yale University Press

Bhabha, HK (1994) 'Of mimicry and man: the ambivalence of colonial discourse' in *The Location of Culture*, New York: Routledge

Bruce, D (1973) *Sun Pictures: The Hill-Adamson Calotypes*, Greenwich, Connecticut: New York Graphic Society Ltd

Chute, JE (1998) *The Legacy of Shingwaukonse: A Century of Native Leadership*, Toronto: University of Toronto Press

Cornwallis, K (1860) *Royalty in the New World: Or, the Prince of Wales in America*, London: Arthur Hall, Virtue & Co

Hammell, G (1983) 'Trading in metaphors: the magic of beads' in Hayes III, CF (ed), *Proceedings of the 1982 Glass Trade Bead Conference*, Research Records 19, Rochester, New York: Rochester Museum and Science Centre

Hobsbawm, E and Ranger, T (eds) (1984) *The Invention of Tradition*, Cambridge: Cambridge University Press

Jameson, K (2000) 'The invincible Oronhyatekha' 33(1) Rotunda 33–37

Jones, P (1861) *History of the Ojebway Indians; With Especial Reference to Their Conversion to Christianity*, London: AW Bennett

King, C (1994) 'Assiginack: arbiter of two worlds' 53(1) Ontario History 33–51

Koltun, L (1998) *Regalia of Conversion: The Hill and Adamson Portraits of the Reverend Peter Jones, or Kahkewaquonaby*, Studies in Photography Annual, Edinburgh: The Scottish Society for the History of Photography

Morgan, LH (1852) 'Report on the fabrics, inventions, implements, and utensils of the Iroquois' in *New York State Cabinet of Antiquities Annual Report*, 5: 66–117, Albany: Printer for the Legislature

Mulvey, C (2002) 'George Catlin in Europe' in Gurney, G and Heyman TT (eds), *George Catlin and His Indian Gallery*, New York: WW Norton and Smithsonian American Art Museum

Nicks, T (1996) 'Dr Oronhyadekha's history lessons: reading museum collections as texts' in Brown, JHS and Vibert, E (eds), *Reading Beyond Words: Contexts for Native History*, Peterborough, Ontario: Broadview Press

Nin Da Waab Jig [Jacobs, DM] (1987) *Walpole Island: The Soul of Indian Territory*, Walpole Island, Ontario: privately printed

Penney, DW (1992) 'Expressions of ethnicity: nineteenth-century dress' in *Art of the American Indian Frontier*, Seattle: University of Washington Press

Phillips, RB (1984) *Patterns of Power: The Jasper Grant Collection and Great Lakes Indian Art of the Early Nineteenth Century*, Kleinburg, Ontario: The McMichael Canadian Collection

Phillips, RB (1987) 'Like a star I shine: northern woodlands artistic traditions' in *The Spirit Sings: Artistic Traditions of Canada's First Peoples*, Calgary, Alberta: Glenbow Museum

Phillips, RB (1998) *Trading Identities: The Souvenir in Native North American Art from the Northeast, 1700–1900*, Seattle: University of Washington Press

Radforth, I (2003) 'Performance, politics, and representation: aboriginal people and the 1860 Royal Tour of Canada' 84(1) Canadian Historical Review 1–32

Shanahan, D (1994) 'The Manitoulin Treaties, 1836 and 1862: the Indian Department and Indian destiny' 53(1) Ontario History 13–31

Silverstein-Wilmott, C (2003) 'Object lessons: an Ojibway artifact unravelled – the case of the bag with the snakeskin strap' 34(1) Textile History 74–81

Smith, DB (1976) 'Maungwudaus goes abroad' The Beaver, Autumn Issue

Smith, DB (1987) *Sacred Feathers: The Reverend Peter Jones (Kahkewaquonaby) and the Mississauga Indians*, Toronto: University of Toronto Press

Stevenson, S (1981) *David Octavius Hill and Robert Adamson, Catalogue of their Calotypes Taken Between 1843 and 1847 in the Collection of the Scottish National Portrait Gallery*, Edinburgh: National Galleries of Scotland

Thomas, N (2000) 'Technologies of Conversion: cloth and Christianity in Polynesia' in Brah, A and Coombes, AE (eds), *Hybridity and its Discontents: Politics, Science, Culture*, New York: Routledge

Trail, CP (1997) [1836] *The Backwoods of Canada*, Peterman, MA (ed), Ottawa: Carleton University Press

White, R (1991) *The Middle Ground: Indians, Empires, and Republics in the Great Lakes Region, 1650–1815*, Cambridge: Cambridge University Press

EPILOGUE

"Kathleen", Maori Guide, Rotorua. N. Z.

EMBLEMS, ORNAMENTS AND
INVERSIONS OF VALUE[1]

Marilyn Strathern

My underlying question is: what motivates the anthropologist to turn something into an ethnographic object? Or rather, how can one surrender to capture? When we make ethnographic objects – objects of study – we do not just produce them: we have to have already capitulated to their fascination.

THE BASEBALL CAP

Listen to this story from Suau (Leileiyafa village, Milne Bay Province, November 1999). It is not mine but Melissa Demian's.[2]

When it comes to fundraising for the church (the United Church), ways of drumming up 'community' support have momentarily settled into a regular pattern.[3] With plans to construct a new permanent materials church, Suau people have turned to the competitive Motuan *boubou* system[4] that was imported to western Suau in the early 1990s. Leileiyafa itself held its first festival in 1997 and they are getting ever more frequent and elaborate. Groups compete to raise the most money and to make the best presentation of it, often with decorations and ceremony – innovation and idiosyncrasy are appreciated. Rather than decorating their donation with banners and song, one group tucked it away inside a crab

1   This is the text, more or less as spoken, of a paper delivered to a conference organised by Susanne Küchler and Graeme Were as part of the ESRC funded project on 'Clothing the Pacific: A Study of the Nature of Innovation' (Lissant Bolton, Chloe Colchester, Susanne Küchler, Nicholas Thomas, Graeme Were). I am most grateful to the organisers for the invitation, and for spurring me to write this account. The title does not really reflect the theme of the paper which eventually took over.

2   Melissa Demian is a member of the PTC research project ('Property, Transactions and Creations: New Economic Relations in the Pacific', organised by Eric Hirsch and Marilyn Strathern over the period 1999–2002; ESRC Award No R000237838). See Hirsch and Strathern (eds), forthcoming.

3   In addition to the annual tithe of K20. K20 is also the order of fine which the Village Court may impose (in addition to compensation, in one adultery case this being set by the Court at K500 and 5 pigs worth K100 each). My source for this information is a personal communication from Demian.

4   Documented in Gregory 1980.

shell, in reference to them having made their money by selling mangrove crabs at an urban market.[5]

The innovation with the crab, regarded as idiosyncrasy or 'style' in the vernacular, may or may not have inspired the ethnographer Melissa Demian.[6] She wanted to offer K100 (the range turned out to be K11–K400) but was embarrassed to give that sum from one person, so she pretended to find the money under her baseball cap. Afterwards the Suau pastor said he had a question for her: 'Is that the way you do things in your place (*kastom*) or did you make it up (your style)?'

The baseball cap, like the crab shell, offered a cavity in which the money could be hid. The crab shell also referred to a value beyond itself – the crab shell was made present in lieu of the money inducing crabs. So where was the analogy with the cap after all? I doubt if anyone thought of the crowds that baseball games draw in the USA, Demian's country of origin. But I suspect that because it was *an article of clothing*, she was able to deploy the immediacy of the association with her person – and therefore with any success she as a person had in gathering money – and that this contributed to the fascination that the baseball cap now had as an object of enquiry. In true ethnographic fashion, the pastor wanted to know if this was traditional practice or something she herself had made up. The latter of course would carry all the resonances of innovation that the crab shell did. (Or perhaps he was hoping that it was a Western tradition and that the Suau people had stumbled on Western money making practices.)

A final issue that might have been at the back of his mind was recognising that Melissa's baseball cap – like the discarded carapace – was in one sense a bit of 'rubbish'. In this case a cheap and insignificant eyeshade. But I am extrapolating.

THE *MERI* DRESS

So look at me instead. Here I am in one of my mother's favourite dresses. It is a slightly longer version of, but equally as shapeless as, ones I used to wear in Port Moresby when I was undertaking a study of rural migrants in the city in early 1970s.[7] She would not have bought it like this, but as a piece of cloth which she then had made up. It looks like a sort of derivative from the Mother Hubbard

---

5   A flagpole was constructed near the church and the flag was 'won' by those contributing the most money, a total of K1300 from some eight different named entities. These were: four deacon's groups from small clusters of contiguous hamlets; three 'families' or representatives of in-married lineages from other villages which gave on a separate basis; and the Local, the smallest organisational unit of the United Church.

6   'Style' is used to refer to the distinctive characteristics or flourishes that mark one individual out from another – the individual may be a kin group whose members claim ownership of that 'mark' and the flourishes as a sign of power. It may be possible to purchase a style, or demand payment for unauthorised imitation.

7   As a fellow of the New Guinea Research Unit, ANU, 1970–72. I was a resident in Port Moresby between 1973 and 1976. The study was published in Strathern 1975.

style, known in Papua New Guinea as *'meri* [women's] dresses', but altered to expatriate taste.[8]

This dress of my mother's (Joyce Evans) is not only shapeless, it is also botched and mended – signs of care, of course – and I have left the all too visible marks of mending as an *index of circumstance* – of the fact that this is now rubbish of a kind. She left the dress behind when she went into a nursing home and it was destined for the black bin bag. So I have not borrowed it, I have rescued it. A discarded shell.

Wearing other people's rubbish has something of a history in the Papua New Guinean Highlands of course. Any of you who have seen the film *First Contact* (Connolly and Anderson 1987) will recall the scene of a present-day Highlander – he was from Mount Hagen – mimicking the cunning with which a man managed to secure a discarded lid from a tin can to wear as an ornament. The thief's fascination with the lid is evident as he sidles up to the shining object, hoping to snatch it with no one looking. The point is how hilarious people nowadays find the episode. In fact, people from Mount Hagen very quickly cottoned on to the fact that when they exchanged vegetable food for the shells that the Australians used for trade, the new settlers were giving them something they themselves (the Australians) did not value. This was reciprocated: Hagen people did not rank vegetable food the equal of shell valuables and were more than happy for the newcomers to get *their* 'rubbish' vegetables in return.[9]

Of course, the dress has only become rubbish over time because it wore out, and because my mother – who had been so fond of it – no longer had use of it.[10] It was too idiosyncratic to give to anyone else. However, that does not render it without interest. I have every intention of turning it – literally – into an ethnographic object, since the plan is that the CUMAA should take some examples of this cloth. Why on earth should the Museum be interested? Because, I hope, of the fascination in the circumstances of its production.[11]

HARA HARA ENTERPRISES[12]

Now, in Port Moresby I was not concerned with any old set of migrants but specifically with people – the vast majority young men, uneducated, 'unskilled' –

---

8   Truth to tell, I do not recollect now whether, on her visit to Port Moresby in 1973, Joyce Evans bought the material or I did. I do know that she had the dress made up in England (Bickley, Kent).

9   On inversion – what is rubbish and what is of value – see Strathern 1999, Chapter 6.

10 For an opposite case I recollect Ru Kundil, on a visit to the UK in 1999, seeking out items he had sold us (Andrew and Marilyn Strathern) in 1964–65, long lodged in the Cambridge University Museum of Archaeology and Anthropology (CUMAA). Looking at the feathers and ornaments lifted out of their storage containers, he was delighted to find that they were still fresh – that they hadn't turned into rubbish.

11 After Gell 1982. I told my mother, Joyce Evans, that I was going to wear it and turn it into an artefact with her permission.

12 This section is based on (a) Beier 1974, 2001; (b) lectures given in an MPhil course by Helena Regius, 'National and local imagery in Papua New Guinea', at Cambridge University in 1999, including material I had relayed to her; (c) my imperfect recollections – field notes not being available for checking.

who had come to the capital city from the Mount Hagen area. They included Tipuka and Kawelka people from the place where I had lived in Mount Hagen. A man called Tipuka Papuga (Georgina Beier's spelling) made the print I am wearing. He was a partner in an enterprise that went under the name Hara Hara Prints, a workshop with a commercial frontage.[13] While the clientele would have included tourists, the cloth was made for a largely local market. There are a couple of photographs of Hara Hara shirts worn by fellow Hagen migrants in Strathern 1975 (plates 20, 27), but the most secure market consisted of resident expatriates like myself. In fact the idea had come from an English woman newly arrived in Port Moresby who could find no substitute for the Yoruba indigo batiks from which she had been used to making clothes for her and her family. She started printing her own and Papuga, who was then working in her house and garden, learnt from her how to do the printing.

The English woman was Georgina Beier, an artist and a teacher and patron of artists, who had formerly lived in Nigeria.[14] She inspired a number of Papua New Guineans to work in a variety of media: drawing, painting (oils, acrylics), metalwork and silk-screen printing.[15] As far I can tell, the designs were all Georgina's: while they have the boldness and look of some of the Nigerian cloth with which she was familiar from Yoruba (Oshogbo), the design elements come from Papua New Guinean motifs. Regius (unpublished) identifies possible sources of inspiration: faces of ancestral spirits from Wosera (Abelam and Sepik) used on the facade of men's houses; Gopi boards from the Gulf region (the Papuan coast); painted bark cloth from Oro or Northern Province.[16] One pattern was synthesised from the drawings of Akis, a Highlander from Simbai and the first Papua New Guinean whom Beier encouraged to work as an artist.[17] But inspiration aside, in effect these were 'new types of images in new types of media' (Regius unpublished: 5). I found the designs and colours quite mesmerising and bought far too much.

---

13 Papuga, from the Western Highlands, was in charge of production; the business manager, Henry Vileka, was from the Eastern Highlands. They were initially (1971) unable to register the business in their own names (Beier 2001: 24). I am amazed in retrospect that their business figured so little in Strathern 1975.

14 Georgina and Ulli Beier came from Nigeria (Oshogbo) in 1967, and stayed in Moresby until 1971, before returning to Nigeria (Ife). Ulli Beier was subsequently invited back to Papua New Guinea to establish the new Institute of Papua New Guinea Studies (IPNGS), at the time of prospective Independence in 1975. They stayed from 1974 to 1978. Georgina held an appointment with the University of Papua New Guinea's Centre for Creative Arts, under Tom Craig, for which she herself had laid the foundations in 1970–71. The Hara Hara business continued as a going concern in the interlude, despite Beier's (1974) doubts.

15 Ulli Beier helped produced poetry, prose literature, plays – a veritable creation of textual arts. It was perhaps inevitable that her activity was later seen as establishing a new orthodoxy of 'contemporary PNG style' – one that could be found in magazines, on the covers of government reports, etc. At the time it was a joyful explosion of new forms.

16 Bark cloth production, often decorated in bold designs which offer the nearest local analogue to Beier's, is restricted to certain areas in Papua New Guinea.

17 Who in turn inspired Kauage, the most well known of her protégées.

WHY THE OBJECT HAS TO CAPTURE

I said that I was going to make the dress into an ethnographic object by depositing it, along with unused cloth, in CUMAA. However, perhaps this paper turns the dress into two other kinds of ethnographic objects as well.

First, because of the Museum's own intentions: curator Amiria Henare has embarked on an intriguing programme called *Artefacts in Theory*. It is almost as though she had taken Webb Keane's admonitions on board and wished to translate them into institutional form (see Chapter 1).

A key premise of this initiative is that our understandings are constrained less by a failure to take account of 'materials aspects of life', than by the very act of maintaining a position from which materiality can only be a grounding corrective to a discursively oriented discipline (Henare 2003: 55).[18]

Henare first points out the extent to which anthropological understanding – conceived as refinements of discourse, and as abstract modellings of social life – continues to reproduce 'material culture' as a resource which lies beyond the field worker's notebook. Then she draws the rug from under the feet of that argument by observing all the ways in which practising anthropologists have in fact enjoyed 'multiple forms of engagements' with things, including that apparently most mundane of activities, making museum collections. The problem is (as so often) in the account we give of ourselves; in the fact that so 'little emphasis is placed on the way in which [anthropologists'] work has been informed through their engagement with things' (Henare 2003: 60).

What is the institutional form here? Perhaps I can extrapolate. Partly the way we make anthropology accountable, that is, the accounts we give of it. Partly the kind of house we turn museums into, where cataloguing is more than the documentation of artefacts, more than words attached to things, but signs of capture, indices of circumstance. What circumstance? One strong candidate would be the 'ethnographic moment' itself.[19] And that is as much to do with how the ethnographer summons the energy to respond to, to be captivated by, what is staring him or her in the face as it is to do with finding the words to describe it. The ethnographer needs to create an ethnographic object in order thereby to become an index of his or her own agency.[20]

---

18 See Keane (p 3 of this book): 'As this tradition dematerialises signs, it privileges meaning over actions, consequences and possibilities. Yet we must be wary of merely reversing this privilege and thereby inadvertently reproducing the same dichotomy.'

19 Elsewhere I have recorded the dazzle of mounted pearl shells which drew me into the description of Hagen life (Strathern 1999: 8–9); although critic Krause (2003: 15–16) criticises my formulation as too detached, she in effect recapitulates the connotation I had hoped 'dazzle' would carry – the abduction of the observer's agency.

20 Some of the fascination of deploying IT, Powerpoint and AV aids as energising adjuncts to lecturing might be germane here. I myself find I cannot keep away from some engagement with Hagen materiality. I have been giving a short series of lectures on Melanesian visual theory for years, for the sheer pleasure of re-visiting the slides of 'artefacts' from Papua New Guinea.

I suggested that this paper turns the dress into two kinds of ethnographic objects beyond its location in Port Moresby. In the second instance, we come to the origin of my question: 'what motivates the anthropologist to *turn* something into such an object? Or rather, how can one surrender to capture?' There is something of an answer here.

Because I have to confess to you that I had to *search* for motivation to write this paper. For a long time I couldn't: the fact that this is not my field was not enough! Nor that I am thus an interloper into the conference; I knew I was delighted to be invited, just as I was uncertain as to what I could contribute. It was the idea of talking about clothes, cloth, clothing that stumped me. I knew of some fascinating work on *meri* dresses (Regius, see Acknowledgments below), but had next to nothing to add of my own. There was no 'sign of recognition' (Keane 1997: 14–15).

Of course it would have been easy enough to subordinate the topic to some other set of interests – exactly the point that Keane and Henare have made – including perhaps issues in intellectual and cultural property (the 'emblem' in my title is a residue of the fact that I had thought this is what I would do). But the truth was that *I was being tugged by the objects I was thinking about*. They had captured me in a particular way. I needed to *do* something with these artefacts in my mind. So I have put on this dress.

The start of it, then, was the fact that, coming from the Papua New Guinea Highlands, I had no theoretical framework with which to think about clothing.[21] But more than that – the release lay in keeping it that way, and thus allowing the fact that I had no theoretical frame to take its course. One might think of this as the 'entry' into the field: the moment when one (momentarily) abandons theoretical frames is the moment at which one allows oneself to be captured by this thing 'the field'. At any rate, that opened up an option. I have, after all, made something of a *paper*, and I hope I have made it work, by adding artefacts to the words.

But of course the conjunction won't last: papers are made to endure and occasions aren't. I can't go on walking around in this outfit simply to accompany the written words. The obvious institutional solution is to deposit the dress in the long-suffering CUMAA – alongside the other examples of Hara Hara prints – like putting a paper in a file. But that very indulgent solution in turn has opened up its converse. I also have to make those *artefacts* work – and one way of doing so is by adding words to them.

Putting on a material exemplar, an instance of what some of the cloth was made into, has worked (for me) as a concrete mode of submitting to the Hara Hara prints. (Of course it is only one among many possible modes.) But it is as though this submission has created a counter-need to find a rationale for talking about the prints. It was as though in inverse proportion to the materialisation of the cloth I needed to recover a mode of dematerialisation. For searching for motivation to

---

21 I refer to Mount Hagen, an area of the Highlands where little use is made of bark cloth. Before colonisation, there were no mats apart from *pandanus* leaf raincapes and almost no metaphorical use of 'wrapping' imagery. Net bags turned imagery in the direction of what is contained, hidden or taken outside and revealed.

write the paper drove me to think of something else I had singularly failed to find motivation for. That donation to the Museum has been hanging about for four or five years now. For ages the cloths have been in a heap under my dressing table – along with a number of Highlands net bags I have also wanted to donate. I simply couldn't find the motivation to produce the short paper that would document them and make them interesting. Now I am able to use *this* occasion to get them into the Museum.

What had been holding me up? After all, nothing more was required than a few ethnographic notes. But the notebook was precisely the problem. The notebook is an index of a particular kind of agency, in the field and in the Museum. There was never any problem writing notes about 'artefacts' that had come freshly from 'the field' (Henare 2003: 60), that were recently gathered, smelled, handled, bundled up. But now, years later, everything was stale, I was lacking the immediacy of presence; I found myself having to *create* a material connection with what I was writing about. Translated, that means that wearing this dress energises me to write out the Museum notes, and to contribute some words to this book.

A final note. Elsewhere I have offered a relational view of materiality.[22] What is missing from this account is anything about the energy that comes from others that one captures for oneself.[23] I wouldn't have put on this item of clothing if I weren't going to be talking to people.

Acknowledgments

My special gratitude extends to Papuga Nugint (Papekla Nykint) and his eye-diverting displays; to Puklum El (John Kenny) for all his help at that time; to Ann Chowning for her companionship in Port Moresby. Georgina Beier remains a generous friend. Hélena Regius collected unique and intriguing material on *meri* dresses; I thank her for the inspiration behind this account, as I do Lissant Bolton at the British Museum. Alfred Gell's influence will be evident.

References

Beier, G (1974) 'Hara Hara prints' in *Modern Images from Nuigini*, Special Issue, *Kovave, a Journal of New Guinea literature illustrated by New Guinea Artists*, Milton, Queensland and Port Moresby, Papua New Guinea: Jacaranda Press
Beier, G (2001) *Georgina Beier*, 'Verlag fur Moderne Künst Nürberg' (Accounts of GB's work from fellow artists and performers, art critics and pupils)
Connolly, B and Anderson, R (1987) *First Contact*, in association with the Institute of Papua New Guinea Studies, Arundel Productions

---

22 Items are made material through the relations that elicit them (Strathern 1999: 54), which comes from an argument about substance (Strathern 2001). I warmly acknowledge but do not reference here Susanne Küchler's arresting work on this theme.
23 Depositing the cloth in the museum works as a potential solution in so far as it will enrol the energies of curators and spectators.

Gell, A (1982) 'The technology of enchantment and the enchantment of technology' in Coote, J and Shelton, A (eds), *Anthropology, Art and Aesthetics*, Oxford: Clarendon

Gregory, C (1980) 'Gifts to men and gifts to God: gift exchange and capital accumulation in contemporary Papua' 15 Man (ns) 626–52

Henare, A (2003) 'Artefacts in theory: anthropology and material culture' 23 Cambridge Anthropology 54–66

Hirsch, E and Strathern, M (eds) (forthcoming) *Transactions and Creations: Property Debates and the Stimulus of Melanesia*, Oxford: Berghahn

Keane, W (1997) *Signs of Recognition: Powers and Hazards of Representation in an Indonesian Society*, Berkeley and Los Angeles: University of California Press

Krause, IB (2003) 'Learning how to ask in ethnography and psychotherapy' 10 Anthropology and Medicine 3–21

Regius, H (unpublished) 'National and local imagery in Papua New Guinea', lectures given in MPhil course (Part 1: The National Arts School), Cambridge, March 1999

Strathern, M (2001) 'Same-sex and cross-sex relations: some internal comparisons' in Gregor, T and Tuzin D (eds), *Gender in Amazonia and Melanesia: An Exploration of the Comparative Method*, Berkeley and Los Angeles: University of California Press

Strathern, M (1999) *Property, Substance and Effect: Anthropological Essays on Persons and Things*, London: Athlone

Strathern, M (1975) 'No money on our skin: Hagen migrants in Port Moresby' New Guinea Research Bulletin No 61

Index